Wendy R. Williams, Berea College, United States
Sabrina Zirkel, Mills College, United States

Past JSI Editors
Robert Chin (1960–1965)
Joshua A. Fishman (1966–1969)
Jacqueline D. Goodchilds (1974–1978)
Rick H. Hoyle (2006–2009)
Irene Hanson Frieze (2001–2005)
John Harding (1956–1959)
Phyllis Katz (1997–2000)
Harold H. Kelley (1949)
George Levinger (1984–1987)
Sher R. Levy (2010–2013)
Ronald Lippitt (1944–1950)
Joseph E. McGrath (1979–1983)
Stuart Oskamp (1988–1992)
Daniel Perlman (1993–1996)
Bertram H. Raven (1970–1973)
Leonard Solomon (1963)
M. Brewster Smith (1951–1955)

Journal of Social Issues, Vol. 72, No. 1, 2016, pp. 5–25
doi: 10.1111/josi.12153

Progress on Understanding Ageism

Sheri R. Levy* **and Jamie L. Macdonald**
Stony Brook University

Almost 50 years ago, ageism (negative attitudes toward older adults) was introduced as a significant social issue. Since then, the worldwide population of adults ages 60 and over has rapidly become the fastest growing age group, making the study of ageism an even more pressing social issue. This review outlines three broad and intertwined themes as the field continues to develop a fuller understanding of ageism: studying both positive and negative aspects of ageism, taking a lifespan focus, and integrating the study of ageism with the study of aging. The review also focuses on several timely subthemes such as the need and benefits of expanding measures of ageism and intervening variables, expanding the diversity of study samples, expanding the research methodologies, and expanding the contexts under study toward greater cross-cultural and within-culture investigations. This review and the international, interdisciplinary research showcased in this special issue are intended to set the stage for the next wave of international research on ageism across the lifecycle and of effective interventions and public policies supporting older adults and positive intergenerational relations.

Almost 50 years ago, "ageism" was introduced as a "serious national problem" in a landmark article in 1969 by Robert N. Butler, who later became the first Director of the National Institute on Aging in the United States. Butler described ageism as "a form of bigotry we now tend to overlook: age discrimination or ageism, prejudice by one age group toward other age groups" and as "a deep seated uneasiness on the part of the young and the middle-aged – a personal revulsion to and distaste for growing old, disease, disability; and fear of powerlessness, 'uselessness,' and death" (p. 243). Since then, more and more scholars around the world have documented forms of ageism in their respective countries. Also, the worldwide population 60 years and older has been growing rapidly, doubling from 1980, and representing the fastest growing age group, which has been projected

---

*Correspondence concerning this article should be addressed to Sheri R. Levy, Department of Psychology, Stony Brook University, Stony Brook, New York, NY 11794–2500. Tel: 1-631-632-4355; [e-mail: sheri.levy@stonybrook.edu].

5

to reach 22% of the worldwide population in 2050 (WHO, 2015). Thus, understanding ageism has become an even more pressing social issue than it was nearly 50 years ago.

In 1980, Butler assembled a special issue of *Journal of Social Issues*, placing a much needed spotlight on ageism and urging the field toward greater study of ageism. Similarly, in 2005, Todd Nelson assembled scholars for an issue of *Journal of Social Issues* and called upon the field to make more progress on understanding ageism. Now, in 2015, we see that the calls are increasingly being answered, and the literature on ageism is continuing to expand. There is not sufficient space in this article to take stock of all the exciting developments and trends in the field of ageism. In this review of the literature on understanding ageism, we outline three broad and intertwined themes that we see as particularly pressing as the field continues to develop a fuller understanding of ageism: studying both positive and negative aspects of ageism, taking a lifespan focus, and integrating the study of ageism with the study of aging. We also focus on several subthemes that grow out of these broad themes such as the need for and benefits of expansions in terms of measures of ageism and intervening variables, of the diversity of study samples, of the research methodologies, and of the contexts toward greater cross-cultural and within-culture investigations. The set of international, interdisciplinary scholars whose work is showcased in this special issue in *Journal of Social Issues* help illustrate these important developments and trends as will be outlined below. This special issue is intended to help set the stage for the next wave of international research on ageism across the lifecycle and for making greater progress on designing and implementing effective interventions and public policies supporting older adults and positive intergenerational relations.

Broad Themes in the Expansion of Understanding Ageism

From a Negative Focus to Integrating a Positive Focus

The literature on ageism began with a focus on the problem of negative ageism and has slowly integrated a more positive focus, although we suggest more is needed to achieve a more balanced and thus fuller study of ageism. Before Butler (1969) coined the term "ageism" with a focus on negative attitudes toward older adults, the imbalanced focus on negative perceptions of aging had begun in the literature such as with the first measures of attitudes about older adults in the United States (Tuckman & Lorge, 1953). Tuckman and Lorge (1953) described "the problem" as "In our culture with its emphasis on youth and speed, old people are expected to play a decreasingly active role in our social and industrial life. These cultural expectations encourage the formation of misconceptions and stereotypes about old age" (p. 249). Only 11 of the 137 survey items were positive items. Books directed at summarizing the ageism literature also focused on negative ageism (see Palmore, 1999). As Editor of a special issue of *Journal of Social Issues* in 1980, Butler expanded on a negative ageism definition noting that "there are three distinguishable yet interrelated aspects to the problem of ageism: 1) Prejudicial attitudes toward the aged, toward old age, and toward the aging process, including attitudes held by the elderly themselves; 2) discriminatory practices against the elderly, particularly in employment, but in other social roles as well; and 3) institutional practices and policies which, often without malice, perpetuate stereotypic beliefs about the elderly, reduce their opportunities for a satisfactory life and undermine their personal dignity" (p. 8). Butler (1980), then, distinguished between two negative forms of ageism: benign ageism "as discomfort, anxiety, or fear of aging" and malignant ageism as a "more damaging form of stereotyping in which older people are characterized as being worthless" (p. 9). Perhaps due to some acceptance or validation of the negative basis of physical aging in early writings (e.g., Tuckman & Lorge, 1953) or lack of documentation of positive aspects of aging (e.g., see Palmore, 1979), denouncing negative ageism lags behind other important areas of attitudes toward groups based on race or gender. For example, the American Psychological Association's (APA) resolution that APA is against ageism in all its forms, did not occur until 2002 (APA, 2002). According to WHO (2015), "ageism may now be more pervasive than sexism or racism." In 2005, Todd Nelson as Editor of a special issue of *Journal of Social Issues* suggested that the lagging focus on ageism has to do with the institutionalism of ageism such as in the negative portrayal of older adults in the mass media as well as in the general beliefs that aging and getting older are inherently negative.

Scholars have continued to document negative ageism such as characterizing older persons as burdensome, forgetful, ill, incompetent, and unattractive (e.g., Cuddy, Norton, & Fiske, 2005; Kite, Stockdale, Whitley, & Johnson, 2005). Negative behavior toward older persons has also been well-documented, including disrespectful, avoidant, and patronizing behavior as well as unwarranted simplified and slow communication, physical and financial neglect and abuse, and unwanted segregated housing (e.g., Hummert, & Shaner, 1994; Kite et al., 2005; Palmore, 2004). Ageism in the workplace, for example, continues to be a common occurrence including negative treatment in the general work environment, less access to salary increases and promotions, forced early retirement, and discriminatory practices in hiring (e.g., Carrns, 2013; Duncan & Loretto, 2004; Gee, Pavalko, & Long, 2007; North & Fiske, 2012; Rampell, 2010, 2011). Moreover, ageism and age discrimination continue to be documented in health contexts including in terms of the health care of older individuals; problems that could be treated with medication are instead considered a natural part of the aging process or ignored as reflecting the stereotype that older adults complain more as they age; there is also elder abuse by caregivers (e.g., Coudin & Alexopoulos, 2010; Dong, 2014; Nussbaum, Pitts, Huber, Krieger, & Ohs, 2005; Rabin, 2011). Furthermore, researchers have pinpointed the negative effects of ageism across contexts on people's cognitive, mental, and physical health (e.g., Abrams, Eller, & Bryant, 2006; Hausdorff, Levy, & Wei, 1999; Hess, Auman, Colcombe, & Rahhal, 2003; Levy, 2009; Levy, Slade, & Gill, 2006; Swift, Abrams, & Marques, 2013). Positive ageism also exists, but positive outlooks of aging and older persons have been studied much less so (e.g., Cuddy et al., 2005; Hummert, Garstka, Shaner, & Strahm, 1994; Kite et al., 2005; Levy, Slade, Kunkel, & Kasl, 2002; Palmore, 1990; Swift et al., 2013). In Tuckman and Lorge's (1953) measure of attitudes, noted earlier, while only 11 (or 8%) of the 137 survey items were positive, some of the positive items were endorsed by a majority of participants and at a comparable degree to the negative items. As examples, 93% of participants reported that older people were proud of their children; 83% reported that older people are good to children; 64% of participants reported that older people are kind; 81% of participants reported that old people love life. Measurement tools that emphasize negative assessments of old age have persisted in the literature (as elaborated on in the section on Expansion of the Range of Measures of Ageism).

Erdman Palmore (1990, 1999, also see 1979) was one of the early pioneers who wrote about positive ageism and noted positive views. Palmore (1990) in his drive to highlight positive forms defined ageism as "any prejudice or discrimination against or in favor of an age group" (p. 4). Positive views of aging and older adults include characterizations of older adults as calm, cheerful, helpful, intelligent, kindly, neat, and stable as well as more reliable and careful workers, engaging in less criminal activity, participating more in voluntary organizations, and as having higher social status in terms of wealth and holding positions of power in companies and government (e.g., Brewer, Dull, & Lui, 1981; Cuddy et al., 2005; Hummert, 1990; Palmore, 1979; Patterson, Forbes, & Peace, 2009). Additionally, older adults may receive unique positive treatment such as discounts, low-rent housing, pensions, special health care, and tax exemptions (e.g., Palmore, 1979, 1990).

General calls by leaders in the field, such as Erdman Palmore (e.g., 1979, 1990, 1999), to address the positive side of aging and ageism have not gone unheard by the field, but more progress is needed. An emphasis on negative views of aging and older persons may be intentional in the sense of bringing to light that ageism and negative views of aging are nontrivial problems in numerous countries warranting study and action (e.g., Butler, 1969). Nonetheless, an unintentional underemphasis on the study of positive views of aging and older persons is still problematic, resulting in an insufficient understanding of the actual range of views of aging and older persons including the psychological, social, and political consequences of such views as well as an insufficient understanding of how to improve the lives of older persons and improve cross-age relations (see also Palmore, 1990, 1999; Levy, under review). As will be seen in subsequent sections on subthemes related to this broad theme (such as Expansion of the Range of Measures of Ageism and

Expansion of the Cross-Cultural Study of Ageism), there are numerous concrete ways to engender a more balanced study of positive and negative ageism.

Taking a Lifespan Focus

Although Butler's (1969) definition of ageism suggested that middle-age adults in addition to young adults are negative toward older adults, research on ageism has historically been narrow in scope, examining attitudes toward older adults (adults 65 and older) among one age group of participants (e.g., young adults). Scholars have called for the study of ageism to go beyond these traditional assessments by taking a more lifespan approach (e.g., Giles & Reid, 2005). Several articles in this special issue represent this trend toward considering a wider age range of participants. It remains timely to make progress in the study of ageism as a lifespan issue since there is not agreement on what constitutes old age, people are living longer which influences conceptions of old age, and aging is a lifelong issue influencing people along the age continuum (WHO, 2015).

To begin, there is a lack of agreement in what constitutes old age, with old age seemingly representing a potentially wide and ever changing age range. Accordingly, Giles and Reid (2005) emphasize that age is a "social construction." People have different notions of old age depending on where they are on the age continuum, and as individuals age, their perceptions of what constitutes "old" or even "middle-aged" or "young" changes. For example, in a study by Davidovic, Djordjevic, Erceg, Despotovic, and Milosevic (2007) in response to the question, "how old is an old man?" U.S. children (ages 10 to 16, mean age = 13) reported between the ages of 35 to 80 years (mean 63), nurses (ages 20 to 47, mean age = 34) reported between the ages of 50 to 75 years (mean 60), and older adults (ages 65 to 85, mean age = 75) reported between the ages of 45 to 80 years (mean age = 67). As pointed out by Chrisler, Barney, & Palatino (2016), old age is defined differently as applied to oneself versus others and along gender lines as exemplified by the first author's 90-year-old mother who "regularly refers to an acquaintance of her same age, as "the old man," whereas she does not think of herself as an "old woman." (pp. 84–85).

Even though people have different constructions of age depending on their vantage point, conceptions of age can take on new meanings as people are living longer. In the mass media and on television, there is a shifting of views of old age with popular sayings such as "65 is the new 50" (Rose, 2010). Thus, some of the cut-offs for different age groups may be seen as arbitrary as pointed out by Kooij and Zacher (2016). At the same time, the youth-centered focus of numerous modern societies suggests that a wide age range of adults are considered old and/or approaching old age as antiaging campaigns address increasingly younger age groups as opposed to older age groups (e.g., see popular antiaging skin care regimen recommendations for women in their 20s and 30s in magazines such as Allure; http://www.allure.com/skin-care/anti-aging-skin/).

Thinking about age as more fluid impacts study designs and analytic strategies in studies of aging and ageism. One way to approach age as a lifespan issue is to investigate age as a continuous variable in study designs, which is the strategy used by Kooij and Zacher (2016), Macdonald and Levy (2016), and Ramírez and Palacios-Espinosa (2016). Kooij and Zacher (2016) suggest using "old" and "young" as descriptive labels and note how using age as a discrete variable "has negative consequences, such as loss of information on individual differences and associated reduction of statistical power" (p. 145). The study of a broad age range is, for instance, increasingly important in studies of age discrimination at work as age discrimination seems to be not a concern just among older adults but also among middle-aged and young adults (e.g., Duncan & Loretto, 2004; Gee et al., 2007).

As we consider age as a more fluid and potentially shifting social construction, it is imperative to consider people's perceptions of their age and how that influences judgments of aging and behaviors. Consistent with this, Macdonald and Levy (2016) suggest greater focus on identity issues such as the degree to which people identify with their age group across the age continuum (also see Sneed & Whitbourne, 2005). Previous research has focused on people's identification with old age (specifically as an older worker), with the assumption that identification has negative consequences in the workplace. However, Macdonald and Levy (2016) found that age identity was related to increased job satisfaction, commitment, and engagement. This highlights the potential positive influence of age identity, and the need for further exploration.

Thus, taking a lifespan approach suggests re-evaluating traditional conceptions of age. As elaborated in the sections on the "Expansion of Diverse Study Samples" and the "Expansion of Research Methodologies," a lifespan approach suggests considering a wider age range of study participants who are evaluating a wide age range of older adults (and are told specifically which age range or age to think of) and if possible, including longitudinal assessments.

Integrating the Study of Ageism with the Study of Aging

As the literature continues to move toward integrating greater study of positive ageism and expanding to take on a lifespan approach, our understanding of ageism would also benefit from greater movement toward embracing relevant literatures. Despite the tremendous strides that have been made in the ageism literature over the past 50 years, it is still somewhat not well integrated with relevant literatures such as the aging literature (and as later discussed, the ageism literature would also benefit from greater links to the literatures on racism and sexism, see section on "Expansion of Diverse Study Samples"). Leading scholars have continued to note the need for a more complete and integrative approach. Robert Kastenbaum in the Encyclopedia of Ageism (Kastenbaum, 2005) noted that while there is research on aging among individuals and on ageist attitudes and behaviors, "ageism and theories of aging tend to bypass each other. Furthermore, none of the major theories of aging were designed to explain ageism, nor has much effort been made to discover possible links" (pp. 318–319).

The aging and ageism literature have sometimes been on parallel paths, and greater integration would expand the ageism literature in productive and important ways. The literatures on aging and ageism each began with a negative focus; however, the literature on aging has evolved with a more balanced focus. Early research on aging focused on pinpointing and understanding age-related declines relative to declines related to disease. Eventually, the literature on aging turned toward examining "normal" or nondiseased aging in greater detail with a focus on usual development along with "successful" aging resulting in theorizing, research, and interventions focusing on optimal or successful aging, such as being free of diseases and being cognitively and physically engaged and fit throughout the lifespan (e.g., Nesteruk & Price, 2011; Rowe & Kahn, 1987; Schulz & Heckhausen, 1996; Wolff, Warner, Ziegelmann, & Wurm, 2014). The large literature on aging continues to focus on understanding both deficits or diseases with age and high functioning aging, but generally is not well-linked to ageism research (e.g., see Kastenbaum, 2005).

The time seems ripe to move toward greater integration with the aging literature as the literature hopefully continues to move toward a lifespan approach and expands the study of the positive side of ageism. The lifespan approach moves the study of ageism away from a narrow span of old age (however old age is defined) and more along a continuum of aging from birth to death, which places the study of ageism on a complimentary parallel course with the aging literature.

The ageism literature could become more integrated with the aging literature in numerous ways. For one, the ageism literature could incorporate greater study of the positive views of physically and cognitively fit older adults. These additions could be applied to measurement tools as elaborated in a later section on a wider range of ageism measures. The ageism literature could address these positive successful aging characterizations along with the traditional characterizations of older adults as calm, cheerful, helpful, intelligent, kindly, neat, and stable (e.g., Brewer et al., 1981; Cuddy et al., 2005; Hummert, 1990; Palmore, 1999; Patterson et al., 2009).

Expanding measurement tools toward greater positive assessment of aging also promotes an expansion of the study of ageism in particular contexts. For example, most research on workplace contexts focuses on negative views of aging employees, consistent with concerns about age discrimination. With expanded measures, researchers could be better poised to study older workers who defy the negative stereotypes including older employees and older employers who are well-respected leaders and resources in their companies. Similarly, where much of the focus in health contexts has been on negative views of aging patients due to concerns about neglect and abuse of older adults, there can also be a focus on aging patients who are physically or cognitively fit. This also could include a greater focus on views of older doctors, practitioners, and nurses who challenge the stereotype of older adults as poorly functioning in a domain. Focusing on the study of positive views of successful aging is timely as more adults may stay or need to stay in the workforce longer. Individuals that do not embody successful aging may be evaluated more negatively, which is something to be considered and studied.

Beyond advancing the ageism literature with insights from the aging literature, a greater consideration of the interface between aging and ageism within theorizing, research, and practice would yield fruitful insights. Considering the role of aging would help to expand the study of ageism and move beyond the traditional type of studies which focus on judgments of aging and less so on participants' perceived and actual aging. Studying both perceptions of aging along with participants' perceptions of their own physical and mental health with age provides a fuller understanding of the experiences of ageism, the interconnections with health, and can help pinpoint avenues for intervention (e.g., Abrams et al., 2006; Lamont, Swift, & Abrams, 2015; Levy, 2009; Levy et al., 2006; Swift et al., 2013). As an example, Becca Levy's stereotype embodiment theory (2009) focuses on individuals who may embody the stereotypes of aging in self-fulfilling ways that influence their health. In a 23-year longitudinal study of U.S. adults ages 50 and over, Ng, Monin, Allore, and Levy (2016) found those in agreement with positive stereotypes about physical health during retirement lived 4.5 years longer and those with positive stereotypes about mental health during retirement lived 2.5 years longer. Several other articles in this issue collectively focus on the interface between aging and ageism across several distinct cultures. Bai, Lai, and Guo (2016), in a study of adults 60 years and older in China showed that older adults who see themselves as a burden on their families and society report heightened depression, even when controlling for current physical and functional health and quality of family relations. Similarly, Ramírez and Palacios-Espinosa (2016) in a study of adults ages 44 to 89 in Colombia showed that endorsement of negative stereotypes of older adults is related to negative views of one's own physical health.

A greater connection between the aging literature and the ageism literature can be an interdisciplinary effort, as illustrated by contributors to this special issue. Ageism and aging are studied and addressed by scholars in numerous fields including communications, gerontology, medicine, psychology, public health, social work, and sociology (e.g., Abrams et al., 2006; Garstka, Hummert, & Branscombe, 2005; Levy, 2009; Nelson, 2009; Palmore, 2004).

Subthemes in the Expansion of the Understanding of Ageism

In the previous sections, we reviewed three broad and intertwined themes in the expansion of the ageism literature toward a fuller understanding of ageism in contemporary times. In the next sections, we consider several themes that grow out of these trends and that can further advance the ageism literature.

Expansion of the Range of Measures of Ageism

One subtheme growing out of the three broad themes is the need to expand measures of ageism including both positive and negative ageism across the life-cycle. This necessitates casting a wider net in assessing ageism. As noted earlier, Butler (1969) originally defined ageism as including prejudice and discrimination and in 1980 he expanded his original definition of ageism to include institutional practices and policies. Nonetheless, measures have been limited in scope, with many focusing on stereotyping and negative stereotyping in particular. To aid in the expansion of research in this area, we suggest studying ageism as a tripartite attitude (e.g., see Kite et al., 2005) including a positive and negative focus, with a stereotyping or cognitive component (e.g., associating positive and negative attributes), a prejudice or affective component (e.g., liking or disliking, valuing or devaluing), and a discrimination or behavioral component (e.g., behaving positively or negatively, approaching or avoiding group members, voting for or against policies or practices that hurt or aid the group).

In terms of stereotyping measures, the image of aging scale (Levy, Kasl, & Gill, 2004) is one of the only evenly balanced measures with one negative item and one positive item in each of nine domains: "activity (walks slowly, active), appearance (wrinkled, well-groomed), cognition (senile, wise), death (dying, full of life), dependence (helpless, capable), personality (grumpy, positive outlook), physical health (sick, healthy), relationships (lonely, family-orientated), and will to live (will to live, given up)" (p. 209). Using this measure allows participants to rate both positive and negative perceptions separately for each domain, which is different from the more commonly used semantic differential where participants are forced to choose a response on a continuum of positive to negative. Allowing participants to rate positive and negative aspects of one particular domain separately is potentially more informative. Indeed, Levy et al. (2004) lamented that "an age-stereotype scale for systemically assessing both the positive and negative perceptions that individuals hold of old people is absent from the literature" (p. 208).

Following on this, Ramírez and Palacios-Espinosa (2016) in creating the first measure of stereotyping to be used in Colombia built upon Levy et al.'s (2004) measure to study the effects of positive and negative stereotyping on aging anxiety and the physical and mental health of a community sample of Colombians. In addition to general measures of positive and negative stereotyping about aging, scholars have begun to create stereotyping measures that are contextualized, thereby allowing a more fine-grained analysis of the context under study. Ng et al. (2016) examine older adults' (50 years and older) positive and negative stereotypes of retirement (a transition they are approaching) to help predict longevity.

Similar to research on stereotyping of older adults, research on discrimination tends to focus on negative discrimination such as in the workplace (Bevitt, Horne, & Waldmann, 2006; see also Carrns, 2013). Consistent with integrating a positive focus into the study of ageism, Macdonald and Levy (2016) focus on individuals' perceptions of negative discrimination as well as social support in the workplace.

Studies that focus on all aspects of positive and negative ageism attitudes (stereotyping, prejudice, and discrimination) can offer a more comprehensive understanding of the nature of ageism. In addition, expanding the study of ageism includes an expansion of related or intervening variables such as aging anxiety. Aging anxiety has not been a central variable in studies of ageism. Most research has focused on what Butler (1980) referred to as "malignant ageism" and relatively less research has focused on what he defined as benign ageism "as discomfort, anxiety, or fear of aging" (p. 9). Applying their Terror Management Theory to ageism, Martens, Goldenberg, and Greenberg (2005) highlighted the potentially central role that aging anxiety might play in negative ageism. Ramírez and Palacios-Espinosa (2016) in a community sample of Colombia adults ages 44 to 89 years old found that less agreement with negative stereotypes about older adults, greater perceptions of social support, positive perceptions of mental and physical health predicted less aging anxiety, and additionally, greater aging anxiety was related to expecting worst physical health in the future. Macdonald and Levy (2016) examined aging anxiety in U.S. adults ages 18 to 80 years old, in relation to workplace outcomes, finding that aging anxiety is negatively related to job satisfaction, commitment, and engagement.

Shifts in the growing aging population along with a youth-centered focus in many cultures point to the need to focus not just on ageist attitudes, but also on intergenerational relations. North and Fiske (2013b, 2016) have developed an individual differences measure, Prescriptive Intergenerational–Tension Ageism Scale, to help disentangle the nature and scope of intergeneration relations, and its three subscales (Succession, Identity, and Consumption) allowing for a fine-grained analysis of such relations. In their study of 18- to 75-year-old participants, North and Fiske (2016), showed that younger participants in their study who agreed more with the succession subscale (that older workers should turn over resources to younger workers) reported wanting to invest less in older worker training.

Abrams, Swift, and Drury (2016) also make a unique contribution to this line of inquiry by examining characteristics that are associated with younger versus older workers. In pilot work, they determined characteristics associated with younger workers (e.g., learning new skills, being creative) and older workers (e.g., dealing with people politely, carefulness). Then, across three studies, Abrams et al. (2016) show that profiles of job candidates possessing these traits influenced willingness to hire them. Specifically, they found that job candidates with characteristics of younger workers were more likely to be chosen to be hired than job candidates with characteristics of older workers

The theme of expanding the study of ageism to encompass a lifespan approach also suggests changes to the instructions or age specificity given in measures. As noted earlier, age has different definitions along the age continuum. Thus, in measures of ageist attitudes, it is important for the instructions to specify what is meant by "older adult" to increase predictive validity. For example, Ramírez and Palacios-Espinosa (2016) specify the age of the target group (65 years old) in the instructions for their new stereotyping measure, which allow for firmer conclusions to be drawn from their study. The gender of older adults that participants have in mind while they evaluate measures of ageist attitudes might also be considered as there are differences in attitudes toward older women and men (see Chrisler et al., 2016, also see Kite et al., 2005).

Expansion of Diverse Study Samples

Related to expanding the measures of ageism and with consideration of participants' definitions of "older adults," there is a need to expand the sample of study participants to be more diverse in order to more fully address positive and negative ageism across the lifespan. The history of ageism research includes a limited range of study participants, lacking representative samples of people along the age continuum, and it seems that some of the typical study participants are skewed toward those with a negative outlook of older persons (such as younger adults).

In 1982, Palmore (1982) noted that "Most of the research has been on small groups of college students" (p. 342). Other unrepresentative samples of participants include health care providers such as medical students, nursing students, and social workers who are targeted because of a concern over their potentially negative attitudes and behaviors toward older persons including elder abuse (see Palmore, 1999; Wang & Chonody, 2013). Kite et al.'s (2005) meta-analysis of ageist attitudes highlighted the paucity of research on middle-age adults, while Kwong See and Heller (2005) noted that there is little research with children.

Such limited samples constrain the generalizability and conclusions that can be drawn from the findings and is another way that our understanding of ageism is lacking. It is not clear how perceptions of older adults and aging change over time, as individuals and close others age. Using more diverse populations, in terms of age, gender, and race/ethnicity, for example, will allow researchers to gain a greater understanding of ageism (see Chrisler et al., 2016).

Contributors to this special issue are part of the trend toward investigating age-diverse samples of participants. Several contributors recruited community samples across a relatively wide age range such as Bai et al.'s (2016) study of adults ages 60 to over 80 years of age, Kooij and Zacher's (2016) study of adults ages 18 to 69 years old, Macdonald and Levy's (2016) study of adults ages 18 to 80 years old, Ng et al. (2016) study of adults ages 50 to 94 years old, North and Fiske's (2016, Study 2) study of adults ages 18 to 75 years old, and Ramírez and Palacios-Espinosa's (2016) study of adults ages 44 to 89 years old.

Although age-diverse samples can allow for greater understanding of ageism across the lifespan, it is important that these types of samples are not treated as homogenous, thereby limiting the potential for uncovering differences within age ranges. For example, there is a history of treating a wide age range of older adults as one age category. Neugarten (1974) originally proposed using age distinctions such as "young-old" (55–75) and "old-old" (75+). Defining age groups across a 20-year span limits nuanced understandings of the issues faced by different age groups (e.g., North & Fiske, 2013a). Adults in the young-old category, for instance, may face different kinds of age discrimination compared to adults in the old-old category (North & Fiske, 2013a) and in order to effectively inform efforts to reduce ageism and change policies, it is important to investigate these differences. Sometimes, age categorization is also contextualized (Giles & Reid, 2005) such as in health care contexts where health benefits are realized at certain ages or in the workplace where retirement ages may vary by occupation.

Expansion of Research Methodologies

In moving toward a comprehensive approach to the study of ageism across the lifespan, researchers are moving toward expanded methodologies and study designs. Research on ageism has generally tended toward one-time survey studies using correlational designs.

Experimental designs expand our understanding of the causes and consequences of ageism. Abrams et al. (2016) and North and Fiske (2016) offer new insights into the persistent problem of age discrimination in the international workforce. In the Abrams et al. (2016) study, the descriptions of potential employees are manipulated to reflect characteristics thought to differentiate older and younger workers. As such, Abrams et al. (2016) are able to draw causal inferences about the role of age-based profiles on hiring decisions. In the studies by North and Fiske (2016), the age and behavior of presented targets are manipulated to assess how perceptions change as a result of and affect workplace discrimination. The experimental design of their study allows North and Fiske to draw causal inferences about how the age and behaviors of workers can influence perceptions. Together, Abrams et al.'s and North and Fiske's findings have the potential to inform workplace policies.

Contributors to this special issue also showcase the study of ageism with longitudinal designs across transitional periods, which together highlight a lifespan approach. Both Kooij and Zacher (2016) and Ng et al. (2016) examine age-diverse samples, allowing the authors to cast a wide net for the study of views and the effect of aging over time. Kooij and Zacher (2016) examined learning goal orientation and attitudes toward learning and development among participants ages 18 to 69 years of age at two time points over a 3-month period. The results show that the more individual's view their time remaining at work as expansive, the more likely they are to be focused on learning and have positive attitudes toward learning and development in the workplace. Ng et al. (2016) utilize a lifespan perspective in their study of participants ages 50 years and over across 23 years to examine the effect of stereotypes of aging on long-term health. Specifically, Ng et al. (2016) explore stereotypes of retirement as a time of lost meaning and devaluation in society and show that those who endorse positive stereotypes about physical health during retirement lived 4.5 years longer and those with positive stereotypes about mental health during retirement lived 2.5 years longer. These data are used as a springboard to speak to public policies and programs for reducing negative stereotypes of retirement.

The transition from work to retirement is a significant one in the ageism literature. It is also one that highlights the need to study ageism along with aging and to examine gender differences. The transition to retirement can trigger depression, and there are nontrivial gender differences such as women's differing employment patterns, including lower-paid jobs and thus lower benefits (such as social security in the United States; Price, 2000), and sometimes family and caregiver responsibilities can affect these aspects of women's employment (Duncan & Loretto, 2004). This area of research is growing with more qualitative studies, considering gender, racial/ethnic differences, and considering other transitions that may simultaneously occur such as the transition from work to retirement to volunteering, particularly examining women as there is an expectation in cultures like the United States that retired women volunteer (Nesteruk & Price, 2011). Other intervening transitions include becoming a grandparent and/or moving into a multigenerational family along with retiring and potentially shifting to volunteer work need greater study (e.g., Nesteruk & Price, 2011). With people living longer and thus potentially in longer retirement periods than ever before, there is a need for greater expansion of the study of transitions periods including the retirement period.

Expanding the study of ageism to include more experimental studies, longitudinal studies (including across transitional periods), as well as collecting qualitative and observational data will contribute to a better understanding of the causes and consequences of ageism.

Expansion of the Cross-Cultural Study of Ageism

There has been an expansion of the study of ageism around the world, which is consistent with a growing worldwide aging population (WHO, 2015). At the same time, the expanding international scope corresponds to the pursuit of both positive and negative ageism. Early research on ageism tended to be conducted in Western cultures in Europe and North America where negative ageism was predominately documented. The study of ageism has expanded to include countries such as Brazil (e.g., de Paula Couto & Koller, 2012), China (e.g., Bai et al., 2016), Colombia (e.g., Ramírez & Palacios-Espinosa, 2016), Israel (e.g., Bodner, Bergman, & Cohen-Fridel, 2012), New Zealand (e.g., O'Sullivan & Ashton, 2012), and Taiwan (e.g., Lien, Zhang, & Hummert, 2009). Some of the greatest expansion of research on ageism has been to other cultures where scholars sought to explore positive ageism as well as the coexistence of positive and negative ageism.

Historically, older people were valued and respected members of society across cultures for their vast knowledge of the culture (e.g., Palmore & Maeda, 1985). Scholars have noted a contemporary shift toward a general devaluing of older persons in modern societies especially in Western cultures (e.g., Nelson, 2005; Schoenberg & Lewis, 2005). For example, Butler (1969) in his landmark article introducing the problem of negative ageism, noted— "might it [ageism] not be especially evident in America; a society that has traditionally valued pragmatism, action, power, and the vigor of youth over contemplation, reflection, experience, and the wisdom of age" (p. 243). Moreover, the predicted East-West differences are expected to derive from Chinese traditions placing more respect on aging and obligation to care for older adults, referred to as filial piety (e.g., Schoenberg & Lewis, 2005).

Results have been somewhat mixed on these predicted cross-cultural differences (e.g., Cuddy et al., 2005). Löckenhoff et al.'s (2009) study of 26 cultures in six continents showed small, significant differences supporting prior work that study participants in Eastern cultures report more positive attitudes toward aging than those in Western cultures. But, some suggest that globalization including shifts toward Westernalization and youth culture are challenging filial piety (e.g., Schoenberg & Lewis, 2005) and there is evidence of negative attitudes toward older adults in countries such as Thailand (Sharps, Price-Sharps, & Hanson, 1998) and similar attitudes in comparison studies of countries such as China and the United States (Boduroglu, Yoon, Luo, & Park, 2006; for a review of children's attitudes, see Montepare & Zebrowitz, 2002). Further suggesting that more research is needed on these complex issues, there is long-standing research showing the coexistence of positive and negative characterizations of aging and older persons in Western cultures (e.g., Cuddy et al., 2005; Hummert et al., 1994; Kite et al., 2005; Levy et al., 2004; Palmore, 1990). More exclusively positive views of aging and older persons have been identified in societies around the world such as Taiwan (e.g., Lien et al., 2009).

Accordingly, this special issue spotlights insights from scholars in Asia (China, Bai et al., 2016), Europe (England, Abrams et al., 2016; Netherlands, Kooij & Zacher, 2016), South America (Colombia, Ramírez, & Palacios-Espinosa, 2016), and North America (Chrisler et al., 2016; Macdonald & Levy, 2016; Ng et al., 2016; North & Fiske, 2016).

Moving forward, it remains pressing to continue to expand the cross-cultural study of ageism. More research exploring the East-West similarities and differences in attitudes toward aging and ageism is needed. Research on similarities and differences between subcultures, such as those based on religion (Bergman, Bodner, & Cohen-Fridel, 2013), that exist within larger generalized East-West cultural distinctions is also needed, especially with regard to how surrounding dominant culture may or may not influence these subcultures and perceptions of older adults and aging. There are notable gaps in the literature as well. More studies are needed outside of Europe and North America (such as Bai et al., 2016, study in China; Ramírez and Palacios-Espinosa's, 2016, study in Colombia) and that investigate multiple countries within the same study (such as Kooij & Zacher, 2016, study of the Netherlands and the United States). The world population over 60 years old is expected to double from 12% to 22% between 2015 and 2050, with a large proportion of older people projected to be living in low- and middle-income countries (WHO, 2015). Additionally, in the age of globalization (e.g., Chiu, Gries, Torelli, & Cheng, 2011; Diaz & Zirkel, 2012), it is even more pressing and important to consider culture and cross-culture contact as we seek to understand the wide range of forces influencing people's beliefs and behaviors relating to age across the lifespan.

Expansion of the Within-Culture Study of Ageism

Along with the expansion of the study of ageism cross-culturally, there have been expansions in the study of the ageism within contexts within cultures. Early research on ageism tended to focus on negative stereotyping of older adults in general or in the study of negative stereotyping perpetuated by the mass media in Western cultures (e.g., see Nelson, 2002). The focus of ageism research has become more contextualized, focusing on ageism in particular contexts.

This special issue is organized into two subsections (health contexts and employment contexts) to spotlight two significant and timely contexts under study. Recent economic problems around the world, along with a surge in the aging population worldwide, have resulted in some newer and deeper challenges in terms of hiring and work longevity as well as the health care of and treatment of older adults (e.g., Coudin & Alexopoulos, 2010; Greenhouse, 2014; Rabin, 2011; Rampell, 2010, 2011). As articles in this special issue illustrate, these health and employment contexts pose substantial and timely public policy implications and the contributors articulate how such challenges translate into public policy needs such as more and better protective laws from the government as well as greater monitoring and intervention strategies. Other environments that are not covered because of space reasons include the home and school environment, which are also significant contexts in the study of ageism.

Four articles in this special issue expand our understanding of pressing issues in the ageism literature concerning the health and well-being of older adults. Good health care and supportive caregivers can help older persons work and live longer making it imperative to better understand the factors that affect the health and well-being of older adults (e.g., Rabin, 2011). As people live longer, an unprecedented majority of middle-age people will have parents who are still alive (WHO, 2015). Understanding the roles of family and community coordination and support, then, is essential (e.g., Abrams et al., 2008; Hummert, 2007). At the same time, research needs to consider the intervening roles that prevalent stereotypes play on care providers as well as directly on older persons as ageism can influence people's cognitive, mental, and physical health (e.g., Abrams et al., 2006; Hausdorff et al., 1999; Hess et al., 2003; Lamont et al., 2015; Levy, 2000; Levy, 2009; Levy et al., 2006; Swift et al., 2013). Addressing this need, contributors in the health context section of this special issue from Canada, China, Colombia, and the United States discuss empirical data speaking to the health and well-being of older adults through the lens of the effects of general cultural stereotypes as well as specific stereotypes about retirement, of discrimination during medical treatment, and perceived family and community support (Bai et al., 2016, Chrisler et al., 2016; Ng et al., 2016; Ramírez & Palacios-Espinosa, 2016).

The work environment, like the health environment, is an important contemporary and long-lasting context in the study of ageism. Adults spend a significant amount of time throughout their lives working, and the current economic situation around the world has impacted young to older workers (e.g., Gee et al., 2007). For example, there is some evidence that young workers have fared the worst during the poor economy in terms of securing jobs (e.g., Greenhouse, 2009). At the same time, there is evidence that older workers approaching retirement potentially face forced early retirement; older workers further from retirement have also been laid off from work to make room for cheaper, younger labor, presumably with superior skills, and some older workers have seen deep cuts in their pay (e.g., Rampell, 2010). The decline in world economies means that people in general have fewer resources, but older persons are unique in lacking the time to make up losses and staying unemployed longer (e.g., Rampell, 2011). Suggesting potentially worsening conditions, some predict that an increasing aging workforce will translate into a rise in age discrimination in countries such as England and the United States (e.g., Bevitt et al., 2006; see also Carrns, 2013). Some governments around the world have acknowledged this pressing problem with policies aimed at protecting workers of all ages. Moreover, some companies have launched creative solutions such as allowing older workers unique part-time work including in warmer climates (e.g., Greenhouse, 2014). In an effort to better understand ageism in the workplace and inform policies and intervention efforts, the articles in the workplace section of this special issue advance the field by focusing on factors that help or hinder successful aging in the workforce including stereotypes of younger and older workers, intergenerational tension at work, indirect everyday experiences with age discrimination at work, psychosocial factors such as age identity and work centrality and their relation to job longevity as individuals age (Abrams et al., 2016; Kooij & Zacher, 2016; Macdonald & Levy, 2016; North & Fiske, 2016).

Collectively, the international contributors from this special issue from organizational behavior, medicine, psychology, public health, and social work draw on strong theoretical traditions and sophisticated multimethods (cross-sectional, longitudinal, and experimental) to offer empirical evidence to fill gaps in our understanding, bring together emerging perspectives, and offer insights into these two key domains of health and employment.

Conclusion

People are living longer, and the world is benefitting in numerous ways from being populated by a greater number of older adults who are outstanding leaders and resources of knowledge and expertise and who help raise, mentor, and support younger individuals. This review highlights three broad, intertwined, and timely themes toward making progress on understanding ageism; studying positive and negative ageism, studying ageism as a lifespan process, and studying ageism along with aging. Several key subthemes emerge from this review as well such as the need and benefits of cross-cultural analyses and more in depth within culture analyses of contexts as well as the expansion of study designs, of study samples, and of measures of ageism. We look forward to the next wave of basic, applied, interdisciplinary, and international research on positive and negative ageism across the lifecycle that moves us closer to a fuller understanding of ageism and promoting positive aging and intergenerational relations.

References

Abrams, D., Eller, A., & Bryant, J. (2006). An age apart: The effects of intergenerational contact and stereotype threat on performance and intergroup bias. *Psychology and Aging, 21*(4), 691–702. doi: 10.1037/0882-7974.21.4.691.

Abrams, D., Crisp, R. J., Marques, S., Fagg, E., Bedford, L., & Provias, D. (2008). Threat inoculation: Experienced and imagined intergenerational contact prevents stereotype threat effects on older people's math performance. *Psychology and Aging, 23*(4), 934–939. doi: 10.1037/a0014293.

Abrams, D., Swift, H. J., & Drury, L. (2016). Old and unemployable? How age-based stereotypes affect willingness to hire job candidates. *Journal of Social Issues, 72*(1), 105–121.

American Psychological Association (2002). Resolution on ageism [online]. Available from: http://www.apa.org/about/policy/ageism.aspx

Bai, X., Lai, D. W. L., & Guo, A. (2016). Ageism and depression: Perceptions of older people as a burden in China. *Journal of Social Issues*, *72*(1), 26–46.

Bergman, Y. S., Bodner, E., & Cohen-Fridel, S. (2013). Cross-cultural ageism: Ageism and attitudes towards aging among Jews and Arabs in Israel. *International Psychogeriatrics*, *25*(1), 6–15. doi: 10.1017/S1041610212001548.

Bevitt, A., Horne, S., & Waldmann, M.A. (2006). international age discrimination – a transatlantic comparison of the UK and US approaches. *Employment Law*, *18*(9), 1–8.

Bodner, E., Bergman, Y. S., & Cohen-Fridel, S. (2012). Different dimensions of ageist attitudes among men and women: A multigenerational perspective. *International Psychogeriatrics*, *24*(6), 895–901. doi: 10.1017/S1041610211002936.

Boduroglu, A., Yoon, C., Luo, T., & Park, D. C. (2006). Age-related stereotypes: A comparison of American and Chinese cultures. *Gerontology*, *52*(5), 324–333. doi: 10.1159/000094614.

Brewer, M. B., Dull, V., & Lui, L. (1981). Perceptions of the elderly: Stereotypes as prototypes. *Journal of Personality and Social Psychology*, *41*(4), 656–670.

Butler, R. N. (1969). Age-ism: Another form of bigotry. *The Gerontologist*, *9*(4, Pt. 1), 243–246. doi:10.1093/geront/9.4_Part_1.243

Butler, R. N. (1980). Ageism: A foreword. *Journal of Social Issues*, *36*(2), 8–11. doi: 10.1111/j.1540-4560.1980.tb02018.x.

Carrns, A. (2013). Older workers say age bias is common. New York Times, http://www.bucks.blogs.nytimes.com/2013/05/08/older-workers-say-age-bias-is-common/?module=Search&mabReward=relbias%3Ar

Chiu, C., Gries, P., Torelli, C. J., & Cheng, S. Y. (2011). Toward a social psychology of globalization. *Journal of Social Issues*, *67*(4), 663–676. doi: 10.1111/j.1540-4560.2011.01721.x.

Chrisler, J. C., Barney, A., & Palatino, B. (2016). Ageism can be hazardous to women's health: Ageism, sexism, and stereotypes of older women in the healthcare system. *Journal of Social Issues*, *72*(1), 86–104.

Coudin, G., & Alexopoulos, T. (2010). "Help me! I'm old!": How negative aging stereotypes create despondency among older adults. *Aging & Mental Health*, *14*(5), 516–523. doi: 10.1080/13607861003713182.

Cuddy, A. C., Norton, M. I., & Fiske, S. T. (2005). This old stereotype: The pervasiveness and persistence of the elderly stereotype. *Journal of Social Issues*, *61*(2), 267–285. doi: 10.1111/j.1540-4560.2005.00405.x.

Davidovic, M., Djordjevic, Z., Erceg, P., Despotovic, N., & Milosevic, D. P. (2007). Ageism: Does it exist among children? *The Scientific World Journal*, *7*, 1134–1139. doi: 10.1100/tsw.2007.171.

de Paula Couto, M. C. P., & Koller, S.H. (2012). Warmth and competance: Stereotypes of the elderly among young adults and older persons in Brazil. *International Perspectives in Psychology: Research, Practice. Consultation*, *1*(1), 52–62.

Diaz, J., & Zirkel, S. (2012). Globalization, psychology, and social issues research: An introduction and conceptual framework. *Journal of Social Issues*, *68*(3), 439–453. doi: 10.1111/j.1540-4560.2012.01757.x.

Dong, X. (2014). Elder abuse: Research, practice, and health policy. The 2012 GSA Maxwell Pollack award lecture. *The Gerontologist*, *54*(2), 153–162.

Duncan, C., & Loretto, W. (2004). Never the right age? Gender and age-based discrimination in employment. *Gender, Work, and Organization*, *11*(1), 95–115. doi: 10.1111/j.1468-0432.2004.00222.x.

Garstka, T. A., Hummert, M., & Branscombe, N. R. (2005). Perceiving age discrimination in response to intergenerational inequity. *Journal of Social Issues*, *61*(2), 321–342. doi: 10.1111/j.1540-4560.2005.00408.x.

Gee, G. C., Pavalko, E. K., & Long, J. S. (2007). Age, cohort, and perceived age discrimination: Using the life course to assess self-reported age discrimination. *Social Forces*, *86*(1), 265–290. doi: 10.1353/sof.2007.0098.

Giles, H., & Reid, S. A. (2005). Ageism across the lifespan: Towards a self-categorization model of ageing. *Journal of Social Issues*, *61*(2), 389–404. doi: 10.1111/j.1540-4560.2005.00412.x.

Greenhouse, S. (2009). Young and old are facing off for jobs. *New York Times*, http://www.nytimes.com/2009/03/21/business/21age.html?pagewanted=all&module=Search&mabReward=relbias%3Aw

Greenhouse, S. (2014). The age premium: Retaining older workers. *New York Times*, http://www.nytimes.com/2014/05/15/business/retirementspecial/the-age-premium-retaining-older-workers.html?module=Search&mabReward=relbias%3Ar

Hausdorff, J. M., Levy, B. R., & Wei, J. Y. (1999). The power of ageism on physical functions of older persons: Reversibility of age-related gait changes. *Journal of the American Geriatrics Society*, *47*, 1346–1349.

Hess, T. M., Auman, C., Colcombe, S. J., & Rahhal, T. A. (2003). The impact of stereotype threat on age differences in memory performance. *Journal of Gerontology: Psychological Sciences*, *58B*, 3–11.

Hummert, M. L. (1990). Multiple stereotypes of elderly and young adults: A comparison of structure and evaluations. *Psychology and Aging*, *5*(2), 183–193.

Hummert, M. L. (2007). As family members age: A research agenda for family communication. *Journal of Family Communication*, *7*, 3–21.

Hummert, M. L., & Shaner, J. L. (1994). Patronizing speech to the elderly as a function of stereotyping. *Communication Studies*, *45*, 145–158.

Hummert, M. L., Garstka, T. A., Shaner, J. L., & Strahm, S. (1994). Stereotypes of the elderly help by young, middle-aged and elderly adults. *Journal of Gerontology: Psychological Sciences*, *49*, 240–249.

Kastenbaum, R. (2005). Theories of aging. In E. B. Palmore, L. Branch, & D. K. Harris (Eds.), *Encyclopedia of ageism* (pp. 318–327). Binghamton, NY: Haworth Pastoral Press.

Kite, M. E., Stockdale, G. D., Whitley, B. R., & Johnson, B. T. (2005). Attitudes toward younger and older adults: An updated meta-analytic review. *Journal of Social Issues*, *61*(2), 241–266. doi: 10.1111/j.1540-4560.2005.00404.x.

Kooij, D. T. A. M., & Zacher, H. (2016). Why and when do learning goal orientation and attitude decrease with age? The role of perceived remaining time and work centrality. *Journal of Social Issues*, *72*(1), 146–168.

Kwong See, S. T., & Heller, R. B. (2005). Measuring ageism in children. In E.B. Palmore, L. Branch, & D.K. Harris (Eds.) *Encyclopedia of ageism* (pp. 210–217). Binghamton, NY: Haworth Pastoral Press.

Lamont, R. A., Swift, H. J., & Abrams, D. (2015). A review and meta-analysis of age-based stereotype threat: Negative stereotypes, not facts, do the damage. *Psychology and Aging*, *30*, 180–193. doi: 10.1037/a0038586.

Levy, B. R. (2000). Handwriting as a reflection of aging self-stereotypes. *Journal of Geriatric Psychiatry*, *33*, 81–94.

Levy, B. R. (2009). Stereotype embodiment: A psychosocial approach to aging. *Current Directions in Psychological Science*, *18*, 332–336.

Levy, B. R., Kasl, S. V., & Gill, T. M. (2004). Image of aging scale. *Perceptual and Motor Skills*, *99*, 208–210.

Levy, B. R., Slade, M. D., & Gill, T. (2006). Hearing decline predicted by elders' age stereotypes. *Journal of Gerontology: Psychological Sciences*, *61*, 82–87.

Levy, B. R., Slade, M. D., Kunkel, S. R., & Kasl, S. V. (2002). Longevity increased by positive self-perceptions of aging. *Journal of Personality and Social Psychology*, *83*(2), 261–270. doi:10.1037/0022-3514.83.2.261.

Levy, S. R. (under review). Reducing ageism: PEACE (positive education about aging and contact experiences) model.

Lien, S., Zhang, Y., & Hummert, M. (2009). Older adults in prime-time television dramas in Taiwan: Prevalence, portrayal, and communication interaction. *Journal of Cross-Cultural Gerontology*, *24*(4), 355–372. doi: 10.1007/s10823-009-9100-3.

Löckenhoff, C. E., De Fruyt, F., Terracciano, A., McCrae, R. R., De Bolle, M., Costa, P. R., Aguilar-Vafaie, M. E., Ahn, CK, Ahn, H. N., Alcalay, L., Allik, J., Avdeyeva, T. V., Barbaranelli, C., Benet-Martinez, V., Blatný, M., Bratko, D., Brunner-Sciarra, M., Cain, T. R., Crawford, J. T., Lima, M. P., Ficková, E., Gheorghiu, M., Halberstadt, J., Hrebíčková M, M., Jussim, L., Klinkosz, W., Knezevic, G., de Figueroa, N. L., Martin, T. A., Marusic, I., Mastor, K. A., Miramontez, D. R., Nakazato, K., Nansubuga, F., Pramila, V. S., Puric, D., Realo, A., Reátegui,

N., Rolland, J. P., Rossier, J., Schmidt, V., Sekowski, A., Shakespeare-Finch, J., Shimonaka, Y., Simonetti, F., Siuta J, Smith, P. B., Szmigielska, B., Wang, L., Yamaguchi, M., & Yik, M. (2009). Perceptions of aging across 26 cultures and their culture-level associates. *Psychology and Aging, 24*(4), 941–954. doi: 10.1037/a0016901.

Macdonald, J. L., & Levy, S. R. (2016). Ageism in the workplace: The role of psychosocial factors in predicting job satisfaction, commitment, and engagement. *Journal of Social Issues, 72*(1), 169–190.

Martens, A., Goldenberg, J. L., & Greenberg, J. (2005). A terror management perspective on ageism. *Journal of Social Issues, 61*(2), 223–239. doi: 10.1111/j.1540-4560.2005.00403.x.

Montepare, J. M., & Zebrowitz, L. A. (2002). A social-developmental view of ageism. In T. D. Nelson (Ed.), *Ageism: Stereotyping and prejudice against older persons* (pp. 77–125). Cambridge, MA: MIT Press.

Nelson, T. D. (2002). *Ageism: Stereotyping and prejudice against older persons.* Cambridge, MA: MIT Press.

Nelson, T. D. (2005). Ageism: Prejudice against our feared future self. *Journal of Social Issues, 61*(2), 207–221. doi: 10.1111/j.1540-4560.2005.00402.x.

Nelson, T. D. (2009). Ageism. In T. D. Nelson (Ed.), *Handbook of prejudice, stereotyping, and discrimination* (pp. 431–440). New York: Psychology Press.

Nesteruk, O., & Price, C.A. (2011). Retired women and volunteering: The good, the bad, and the unrecognized. *Journal of Women and Aging, 23*(2), 99–112. doi: 10.1080/08952841.2011.561138.

Neugarten, B. L. (1974). Age groups in American society and the rise of the young-old. *The Annals of the American Academy of Political and Social Science, 415*(1), 187–198. doi: 10.1177/000271627441500114.

Ng, R., Monin, J. K., Allore, H. G., & Levy, B. R. (2016). Retirement as meaningful: Positive retirement stereotypes associated with longevity. *Journal of Social Issues, 72*(1), 69–85.

North, M. S., & Fiske, S. T. (2012). An inconvenienced youth? Ageism and its potential intergenerational roots. *Psychological Bulletin, 138*(5), 982–997. doi: 10.1037/a0027843.

North, M. S., & Fiske, S. T. (2013a). Subtyping ageism: Policy issues in succession and consumption. *Social Issues and Policy Review, 7*(1), 36–57. doi: 10.1111/j.1751-2409.2012.01042.x.

North, M. S., & Fiske, S.T. (2013b). A prescriptive, intergenerational-tension ageism scale: Succession, identity, and consumption (SIC). *Psychological Assessment, 25*(3), 706–713. doi: 10.1037/a0032367.

North, M. S., & Fiske, S. T. (2016). Resource scarcity and prescriptive attitudes generate subtle, intergenerational older-worker exclusion. *Journal of Social Issues, 72*(1), 122–145.

Nussbaum, J. F., Pitts, M. J., Huber, F. N., Krieger, J., & Ohs, J. E. (2005). Ageism and ageist language across the life span: Intimate relationships and non-intimate interactions. *Journal of Social Issues, 61*(2), 287–305. doi: 10.1111/j.1540-4560.2005.00406.x.

O'Sullivan, J., & Ashton, T. (2012). A minimum income for healthy living (MIHL) – older New Zealanders. *Ageing and Society, 32*(5), 747–768. doi: 10.1017/S0144686×11000559.

Palmore, E. B. (1979). Predictors of successful aging. *The Gerontologist, 19*(5), 427–431. doi: 10.1093/geront/19.5_Part_1.427.

Palmore, E. (1982). Attitudes toward the aged: What we know and need to know. *Research on Aging, 4*(3), 333–348. doi: 10.1177/0164027582004003004.

Palmore, E. (1990). *Ageism: Negative and positive.* New York: Springer.

Palmore, E. (1999). *Ageism: Negative and positive,* 2nd ed. New York: Springer.

Palmore, E. (2004). Research note: Ageism in Canada and the United States. *Journal of Cross-Cultural Gerontology, 19,* 41–46.

Palmore, E., & Maeda, D. (1985). *The honorable elders revisited.* Durham, NC: Duke University Press.

Patterson, L. G., Forbes, K. E., & Peace, R. M. (2009). Happy, stable and contented: Accomplished ageing in the imagined futures of young New Zealanders. *Ageing and Society, 29*(3), 431–454.

Price, C. A. (2000). Women and retirement: Relinquishing professional identity. *Journal of Aging Studies, 14*(1), 81–101. doi: 10.1016/S0890-4065(00)80017-1.

Rabin, R. C. (2011). Aging: Hearing loss is common but often ignored. *New York Times,* http://www.nytimes.com/2011/03/08/health/research/08aging.html?module=Search&mab Reward=relbias%3Ar&_r=0

Ramírez, L. F., & Palacios-Espinosa, X. (2016). Stereotypes about old age, social support, aging anxiety and evaluations of one's own health. *Journal of Social Issues, 72*(1), 47–68.

Rampell, C. (2010). In job market shift, some workers are left behind. *New York Times*, http://www.nytimes.com/2010/05/13/business/economy/13obsolete.html?pagewanted=all&_r=0

Rampell, C. (2011). Older workers without jobs face longest time out of work. *New York Times*, http://www.economix.blogs.nytimes.com/2011/05/06/older-workers-without-jobs-face-longest-time-out-of-work/?module=Search&mabReward=relbias%3Ar

Rose, B. (2010). If 65 is the new 50, how will baby boomers remake retirement? http://www.abajournal.com/news/article/if_65_is_the_new_50_how_will_baby_boomers_remake_retirement/

Rowe, J. W., & Kahn, R. L. (1987). Human aging: Usual and successful. *Science*, *237*(4811), 143–149. doi: 10.1126/science.3299702.

Schoenberg, N. E., & Lewis, D. C. (2005). Cross-cultural ageism. In E. B. Palmore, L. Branch, & D. K. Harris (Eds.), *Encyclopedia of ageism* (pp. 87–92). Binghamton, NY: Haworth Pastoral Press.

Schulz, R., & Heckhausen, J. (1996). A lifespan model of successful aging. *American Psychologist*, *51*(7), 702–714. doi: 10.1037/0003-066X.51.7.702.

Sharps, M. J., Price-Sharps, J. L., & Hanson, J. (1998). Attitudes of young adults towards older adults: Evidence from the United States and Thailand. *Educational Gerontology*, *24*(7), 655–660. doi: 10.1080/03601127980240703.

Sneed, J. R., & Whitbourne, S. K. (2005). Models of the aging self. *Journal of Social Issues*, *61*(2), 375-388. doi: 10.1111/j.1540-4560.2005.00411.x.

Swift, H. J., Abrams, D., & Marques, S. (2013). Threat or boost: Social comparison affects older people's performance differently depending on task domain. *Journals of Gerontology, Series B*, *68*, 23–30. doi: 10.1093/geronb/gbs044.

Tuckman, J., & Lorge, I. (1953). Attitudes toward old people. *The Journal of Social Psychology*, *37*(2), 249–260.

Wang, D., & Chonody, J. (2013). Social workers' attitudes toward older adults: A review of the literature. *Journal of Social Work Education*, *49*(1), 150–172.

Wolff, J. K., Warner, L. M., Ziegelmann, J. P., & Wurm, S. (2014). What do targeting positive views on ageing add to a physical activity intervention in older adults? Results from a randomised controlled trial. *Psychology & Health*, *29*(8), 915–932. doi: 10.1080/08870446.2014.896464.

World Health Organization (WHO) (2015). 10 facts on ageing and the life course. Retrieved from http://www.who.int/features/factfiles/ageing/en/

SHERI R. LEVY is an Associate Professor in the Department of Psychology at Stony Brook University. She studies factors that cause and maintain prejudice, stigmatization, and negative intergroup relations and that can be harnessed to reduce bias, marginalization, and discrimination. Her research focuses on bias based on age, ethnicity, gender, nationality, race, sexual orientation, social class, and weight. Building on her research on ageism, she founded an organization called the *Wise Owls* to bring cheer and support to our older adult community (www.thewiseowls.org; thewiseowls.org@gmail.com). Levy was Editor of *Journal of Social Issues* from 2010 to 2013.

JAMIE L. MACDONALD is a graduate student in the Department of Psychology at Stony Brook University. She studies prejudice, stereotyping, discrimination, and intergroup relations. Her research focuses on ageism, and how it affects individuals in different contexts throughout the life course.

Journal of Social Issues, Vol. 72, No. 1, 2016, pp. 26–46
doi: 10.1111/josi.12154

Ageism and Depression: Perceptions of Older People as a Burden in China

Xue Bai[*]
The Hong Kong Polytechnic University

Daniel W.L. Lai
The Hong Kong Polytechnic University

Aimei Guo
Nanjing Normal University

Traditional values and beliefs about aging and older adults appear to be changing in China, as a result of transformations in family structure and social system in the context of rapid modernization and economic growth. This study examined the effects of burden views toward Chinese older adults on their depressive symptoms based on a secondary analysis of data collected from a sample of 954 Chinese adults aged 60 and over in Jiangsu Province. After controlling for sociodemographic, health, and family relationship variables, results of hierarchical multiple regression analysis revealed that participants with stronger views of older people as a burden to family and society were at higher risk of depressive symptoms. Findings of this study can inform the development of policies and programs to address mental health challenges facing older adults in China, focusing on helping them get rid of the burden views about older people, improving family relationship quality, and fostering a positive attitude toward aging in the wider society.

Depression is a common and chronic mental health problem faced by older people (Lai, 2004; Mui & Kang, 2006), with Chinese older people of no exception (Lai & Tong, 2009; Zeng & Chan, 2010; Zeng, North, & Kent, 2012). Depressive disorders are characterized by a cluster of symptoms including fatigue, reduced energy, reduced pleasure and interest, prevailing sad mood, and increased risk of

*[*]Correspondence concerning this article should be addressed to Xue Bai, Department of Applied Social Sciences, The Hong Kong Polytechnic University, 11 Yuk Choi Road, Hunghom, Hong Kong. Tel: (852) 3400 3694 [e-mail: xuebai@polyu.edu.hk].

suicide, disability, and mortality (Chong et al., 2001; Neugebauer, 1999; Saab, El-Roueiheb, Chaaya, & Sibai, 2005). The World Health Organization (Barua, Ghosh, Kar, & Basilio, 2010; Rangaswamy, 2001) has estimated that the prevalence rate of depression among older adults in the world varies between 10% and 20% depending on cultural contexts. It is further reported that prevalence rates of depression in older people are similar across Asia, America, and Europe (Barua, Ghosh, Kar, & Basilio, 2011).

Previous studies have identified three broad categories of risk factors contributing to depressive symptoms in old age. The first category includes sociodemographic factors such as an older age (George, Landerman, Blazer, & Anthony, 1991), female gender (Kessler et al., 1994), lower socioeconomic status (Cairney & Krause, 2005; Kahn & Fazio, 2005; Mirowsky & Ross, 2003), and living alone (Mui, 1998). The second category comprises indicators of poor health including more chronic diseases (Chi et al., 2005; Gagnon & Patten, 2002), poorer self-rated health status (Han, 2002), and greater levels of functional dependence (Ormel, Rijsdijk, Sullivan, van Sonderen, & Kempen, 2002; Travis, Lyness, Shields, King, & Cox, 2004; Zeng et al., 2012). Finally, older people who have experienced stressful life events (Chi et al., 2005; Turner & Lloyd, 1999) and who lack social support (Brummett, Barefoot, Siegler, & Steffens, 2000; Lai & Tong, 2012; Travis et al., 2004) are more vulnerable to depressive symptoms. However, despite their potentially significant implications for older adults' well-being, the specific effects of family relationship quality and attitude toward aging and older people as social determinants of depressive symptoms have seldom been examined in previous studies, especially in Chinese societies.

The impact of family relationships on older adults' mental health has been widely studied in western societies. Positive aspects of family relationships and better intergenerational communications are found to contribute to older adults' mental health, while negative aspects of these relationships have detrimental effects on their well-being (Hummert, 2007; Lendon, 2012; Ward, 2008). However, very little is known about the effects of family relationship quality on older Chinese adults' depressive symptoms (Chen & Silverstein, 2000; Guo, Chi, & Silverstein, 2012). One possible explanation is that Chinese tradition and culture often emphasize respecting and valuing the contributions of older people, leading many to assume that Chinese older people enjoy prestigious familial and social status. Filial responsibility for elder care has also often been taken for granted in China, and these values and beliefs often form the basis for older Chinese adults' satisfaction and wellness. However, societal values toward older people in Chinese culture appear to be changing (Chiu & Yu, 2001). Changes in family structures and values associated with economic growth and westernization, the rise of nuclear families, and an increasing emphasis on productivity, technological advancement, and competitiveness, all form major challenges to the perceived contributions and social status of the aging population in Chinese societies (Bai, 2014; Bai, 2016;

Bai, Chan, & Chow, 2012; Chao & Roth, 2000; Chiou, Chen, & Wang, 2005; Chow & Bai, 2011; Holroyd, 2001; Lai, 2007; Ng, 2002; Zhan, 2004; Zhan & Montgomery, 2003). Under the "one-child" policy, it has become increasingly difficult for the younger generation to provide filial support in a traditional way as most of them do not have siblings to share the filial obligations. The tremendous urban–rural disparity has further pushed young people from rural areas to urban areas for better education and employment opportunities in the process of the modernization, leaving behind their older parents who have to face an empty nest (Chow & Bai, 2011). Along with an increasing acceptance of older parents living separately from adult children, by the end of 2010, the average household size had shrunk to 3.1 persons in China (Du, 2013; Sereny, 2011). This separate living arrangement may pose new challenges for adult children to provide timely support and care for their older parents, resulting in a burden view of older people.

In western societies, older people are often perceived in a negative manner, viewed as ill, mentally slower, forgetful, bothersome, sexually inactive, unproductive, a burden to society, and so forth, although it is acknowledged that some might show positive characteristics (Aaronson, 1966; Kite & Wagner, 2002; Kite, Stockdale, Whitley, & Johnson, 2005; Palmore, 2005; Levy & Macdonald, 2016). Researchers have become increasingly interested in issues of aging-related attitudes and stereotypes (Bai et al., 2012; Bugental & Hehman, 2007; Nelson, 2005; North & Fiske, 2012, 2013). Positive attitudes toward aging are found to be predictive of better memory and hearing performance (Hess, Auman, Colcombe, & Rahhal, 2003; Levy & Langer, 1994; Levy, Slade, & Gill, 2006), lower chance of cardiovascular disease (Levy, Hausdorff, Hencke, & Wei, 2000), better life satisfaction, less depression, stronger will to live, and better survival over time among older people (Dong, Simon, Beck, & Evans, 2010; Hausdorff, Levy, & Wei, 1999; Lai, 2009; Levy, Ashman, & Dror, 2000; Ng, Monin, Allore, & Levy, 2016). Compared to western countries, there are far fewer studies available in Chinese communities which have examined views of aging, among older adults themselves or by others (Bai et al., 2012; Zhang et al., 2006).

In the context of rapid modernization and population aging in China, it is of both theoretical and practical merit to investigate issues of family relationship quality and aging stereotypes, as perceived by older people themselves, and their possible impacts on depression in older Chinese adults. This study aimed to examine the effects of family relationship quality and aging stereotypes on Chinese older adults' depressive symptoms, after adjusting for their sociodemographic characteristics, as well as physical and functional health status. Implications for policy and practice are further discussed.

Theoretical Perspectives

Modernization Theory

Older people's status and esteem in society often decline as a society becomes more modernized, with health technology, scientific technology, urbanization, literacy, and mass education reflecting forces potentially contributing to older adults' declining status in "modern" society (Cowgill & Holmes, 1972). According to Cowgill (1974), modernization is defined as "the transformation of a total society from a relatively rural way of life based on animated power, limited technology, relatively undifferentiated institutions, parochial and traditional outlook and values, toward a predominantly urban way of life, based on inanimate sources of power, highly differentiated institutions, matched by segmented individual roles, and a cosmopolitan outlook which emphasizes efficiency and progress" (p. 127). In the field of gerontology, modernization theory suggests that the process of modernization serves to disadvantage older people.

China has been modernizing since 1949, in a more rapid pace after its opening up in 1978. It has been stated that China must confront the challenges of population aging before becoming an "advanced" industrial society (Calvo & Williamson, 2008; Chow & Bai, 2011). China has experienced a "compressed" form of modernization, which resulted in a modernization strategy of first developing urban areas (Sun, 2003), anticipating that benefits of modernization would spread from urban areas at the center of modernization, to rural areas in the periphery. Unfortunately, the anticipated "spread effect" has been replaced by a "backlash effect," with rich regions becoming more prosperous and underdeveloped regions becoming even poorer (Sun, 2005). Significant inequalities and resource disparities exist between urban and rural areas in contemporary China (Bai, 2016; Kanbur & Zhang, 1999). The common belief that older people in rural areas are more likely to command respect compared to their urban counterparts has become a myth in the process of modernization. It seems that rural elders have been even more upset than urban elders when being left behind by their children, as they have much less access to formal support provided by the Government (Chow & Bai, 2011).

The needs of older people in China have not been sufficiently addressed by the government, and are no longer necessarily fulfilled by informal family support. As explained above, processes of modernization and westernization including a focus on economic growth and technological advancement, have led to significant changes in family structures, as well as values and attitudes associated with aging and older people (Bai et al., 2012; Chao & Roth, 2000; Chiou et al., 2005; Chow & Bai, 2011; Holroyd, 2001; Lai, 2007; Zhan, 2004; Zhan & Montgomery, 2003), which have implications for family relationships and care. Age-related stereotypes have been worsening under modernization, as older Chinese people, especially in rural areas, are likely to be perceived as a burden to family and society, when families cannot respond to older adults' emotional, physical, and material needs, and when uneven development across China has resulted in a lack of adequate services in numerous areas. In turn, this can have direct impacts on older adults' physical and mental well-being. Modernization theory can thus provide a framework for understanding the current context in which aging stereotypes have emerged and affect perceptions and experiences of older adults in China, within their family and in the wider society.

Stereotype Internalization Theory

Facing the challenges and worsening images of aging in the process of modernization, how will older adults' self-image be affected? A number of theories, including assimilation theory (Rothermund & Brandtstädter, 2003) and internalization and self-fulfilling prophecy effects (von Hippel, Silver, & Lynch, 2000; Nelson, 2005), suggest that exposure to negative stereotypes about their group may make the stereotype target groups internalize those stereotypes, directly or indirectly causing such stereotypes to become true, and leading to a sense of inadequacy, low self-esteem, and depression (Bai & Chow, 2011; Rodin & Langer, 1980). This line of argument has its roots in cognitive theories of aging (Kuypers & Bengtson, 1973; Rodin & Langer, 1980), with scholars maintaining that older people tend to internalize age-related stereotypes (e.g., Bugental & Hehman, 2007; von Hippel et al., 2000). The views of older people in general are influenced by age-related stereotypic information with which they are confronted (Levy, 1996), and older adults' self-conceptions are also contaminated by certain types of age-stereotypic information. Sinclair, Huntsinger, Skorinko, and Hardin (2005) report that social interactions with individuals expressing stereotype-relevant views affect the self-evaluations of stereotype targets. In other words, the internalization (or "contamination") hypothesis predicts an assimilation effect whereby age-related stereotypes are incorporated into one's self-image (Bennett & Gaines, 2010; Rothermund & Brandtstädter, 2003).

This perspective is relevant given changing societal values toward older people in Chinese culture (Chiu & Yu, 2001), is linked to processes of modernization and changes in socioeconomic structure and family relationships. Older adults in China may internalize broader attitudes toward the role and value of older adults in the family and wider society. Internalization of and adaptation to these changing attitudes, and associated loss of traditional societal and familial status and value, can potentially severely affect older adults' sense of adequacy, self-esteem, and well-being. This is of relevance given previous research findings speaking to the negative impact of negative attitude toward aging on older adults' mental health (Bai et al., 2012; Bugental & Hehman, 2007; Dong et al., 2010; Hausdorff et al., 1999; Hess et al., 2003; Lai, 2009; Levy & Langer, 1994; Levy et al., 2000, 2006; Nelson, 2005; North & Fiske, 2012, 2013), however, there are far fewer relevant studies available in China than in western countries. This perspective can provide a framework for understanding the ways in which changing attitudes toward older adults are influencing older adults' perceptions of their roles and status in the family and society, as well as the potential effects of these perceptions on their mental health status.

Based on these theories, it is hypothesized that older adults' stereotypical views of older people as a group would affect their mental health status, represented by depressive symptoms, even after controlling for sociodemographic characteristics, physical and functional health status, and quality of family life. More specifically, it is hypothesized that more the older adults themselves perceive older people as a burden to family and society, the more depressive symptoms they would experience.

Methods

Research Design, Data Set, and Sampling

This study was based on a secondary analysis of data originally collected as part of a larger-scale cross-sectional study examining the general needs and well-being of a representative sample of Chinese adults aged 60 years and older in Jiangsu, an eastern coastal province of China in June 2010. Jiangsu is one of the most densely populated of the 22 provinces of China, and older population aged 65 years and over has accounted for 10.89% of its total population (Jiangsu Province Statistical Bureau, 2011). In the original study, data were collected through face-to-face interviews using a structured questionnaire that covered a range of topics including, but not limited to, basic demographics, labor participation and employment, health status, family networks, service need, and use of community services. The interviews were conducted mainly in Mandarin, by trained interviewers who were senior-year undergraduate students and graduate students in social science disciplines.

The sample was obtained using multistage proportional probability sampling, covering both urban and rural areas in Jiangsu province. As a first step, four cities and four rural counties were randomly selected as a first step (Wu Xi, Chang Zhou, Tai Zhou, Ru Gao). Sixteen districts and 16 towns were then randomly selected from urban and rural areas, respectively. Each district and town was further divided into different street clusters, and using the residents' registration system, 505 participants were selected from 19 street clusters in the four cities and 500 participants were selected from 17 street clusters in four rural counties (Dong Hai, Jiang Ning, Hongze, Binghai).The selection was proportionally based on the actual population distribution of adults 60 years and older in the selected local communities. Similarly, for the rural sample, in total, 505 urban participants (100% response rate) and 499 rural participants (99.8% response rate) were interviewed.

The high response rate was likely due to the study being sponsored by the Province, with strong collaboration and support from local governing units. Publicity at the local community level was used to promote awareness and involvement of residents. Trust in the credibility of the original study formed the basis for the positive response among the participants. Due to missing answers for some variables, only 475 urban cases and 479 rural cases were included in the secondary analysis for this study, for a total of 954 participants.

Measurement

Variables that were measured in this study included burden views toward older people and their depressive symptoms, as well as sociodemographic characteristics, physical and functional health status, and quality of family life.

Sociodemographic characteristics. Sociodemographic characteristics include urban–rural residence, age, gender, and living arrangement. The mean age of the overall sample was 72.73 years ($SD = 7.55$). Respondents were asked to report their chronological age, and it was used as a continuous variable in the correlational and regression analyses. Owing to long-lasting dichotomized and imbalanced urban–rural development in Chinese society (Sun, 2003), older people living in urban areas are generally better off in terms of both education and financial status. Urban–rural residence is therefore considered a reliable variable that can accurately assess participants' socioeconomic status (Chow & Bai, 2011). Living arrangement was measured by asking participants if they were currently living with a spouse, child, and/or significant other, or if they were living alone.

Physical and functional health status. Physical health status was determined by the number of chronic illnesses reported by participants, such as stroke or cerebrovascular diseases, rheumatism, diabetes, hypertension, cataracts, heart disease, respiratory diseases, and digestive diseases. The adapted version of the Instrumental Activities of Daily Living (IADL) scale (alpha = .92) was used to assess participants' functional capacity, including capacity or dependence in seven IADL areas: telephone use, shopping, food preparation, housekeeping, laundry, use of public transportation, and handling finances (Lawton & Brody, 1969). Participants were asked to report whether they could perform the above-mentioned tasks independently, with some assistance, or could not complete them even with assistance. Functional status was measured as totally dependent on others (1), somewhat dependent on others (2), or totally independent (3). Composite scores were calculated by summing the seven items, with higher scores indicating more optimal functional health status.

Quality of family relations. Quality of family relations was measured based on participants' perceived availability of family support and self-rated family relations, using the three-item family network subscale of Lubben's Social Network Scale (Lubben, 1988), and a single item asking participants to rate their family relations as harmonious or not, respectively. Participants were asked how many relatives they met or contacted at least once a month, how many relatives they could share innermost feelings with, and how many relatives they could turn to for help when needed, on a six-point scale (from 0 = none, 1 = one, 2 = two; 3 = three or four; 4 = five through eight; 5 = nine or more). The scale has vindicated a satisfactory level of internal consistency, with alpha = .82 for the study sample. Composite scores were obtained by summing the three items, with higher scores indicating greater perceived availability of family support. This scale pro vides quantitative information on individuals' family ties and accurately identifies persons at risk of social isolation (Lubben et al., 2006). Harmonious family relationship is often characterized by positive emotion or behavior, shared beliefs and feelings, and enduring ties among family members (Dykstra & Fokkema, 2011). Participants' self-rated family relations were classified as being either harmonious (1) or not harmonious (0).

Burden views toward older people. Participants' burden views toward older people were measured by two items. On a three-point scale, they were asked to rate the extent to which they perceived older people as a burden to family, and the extent to which they perceived older people as a burden to society (1 = "No"; 2 = "Neutral"; 3 = "Yes"). The satisfactory internal consistency of these two items was evidenced in this study, with alpha = .84. Thus, composite scores were then calculated by summing the two items, with higher scores indicating a stronger burden view toward older people.

Depressive symptoms. Participants' depressive symptoms were assessed using a 15-item short form of the Chinese version of the Geriatric Depression Scale (GDS-SF). Among the various depression screening instruments, the GDS was the first developed for the aging population (Lai, Tong, Zeng, & Wu, 2010). The 15-item GDS-SF is derived from the 30-item GDS, and is a popular depression screening tool for older adults (Brink et al., 1982; Yesavage et al., 1983). Respondents are asked to indicate whether they have experienced specific symptoms during the past week (e.g., drop activities and interests, feel that life is empty, get bored), reporting either "yes" or "no." A score range from zero to four is considered "normal," from five to nine is considered "mildly depressed," and 10 or above is considered "moderately to severely" depressed. The scale is found to carry satisfactory internal consistency for the study sample, with alpha = .80.

Data analysis.   Data entry and analysis were performed using the Statistical Package for Social Sciences version 17.0. Descriptive statistics of the key study variables, including frequencies, means, and standard deviations, were first examined. Analysis of bivariate correlations between mental health status and all independent variables was then conducted. To test the hypotheses, hierarchical multiple regression analysis was used with sociodemographic variables (urban–rural residency, age, gender, living arrangement) entered as the first block, followed by health variables, and then quality of their family life. The composite score of familial and societal burden views was entered as the final block.

Results

Characteristics of Older Participants

Sociodemographic characteristics.   Descriptive findings concerning participants' sociodemographic characteristics are presented in Table 1. Of the 954 participants aged from 60 to 94 (mean = 72.73), half were from rural areas and half were from urban areas, with 49% being male, and 51% being females. The vast majority of participants (86.7%) were currently living with their spouse, children, and/or significant others, and 13.3% were living alone.

Physical and functional health status.   On average, participants reported to be experiencing two chronic diseases, such as stroke or cerebrovascular diseases, rheumatism, diabetes, hypertension, cataract, heart disease, respiratory diseases, or digestive diseases. Concerning their functional health status, mean scores for the seven IADL domains were 2.51 for ability to use phone, 2.68 for shopping, 2.71 for food preparation, 2.79 for housekeeping, 2.58 for laundry, 2.59 for use of public transportation, and 2.63 for ability to handle finances. Most participants were able to perform these activities by themselves.

Quality of family relations.   On average, participants had three to four relatives that they would meet or contact at least once a month, two to three relatives with whom they could share their innermost feelings, and three to four relatives that they could turn to for help when needed. With respect to participants' self-rated family relations, 94.2% rated their family relations as harmonious, while only around 6% perceived family relations as not harmonious.

Burden views toward older people.   Of the 954 participants, 392 (41.9%) perceived older people as a real burden to the family, 400 (41.9%) perceived older people as somewhat of a burden on families, and only 162 (17.0%) did not think that older people were a burden on families. A similar trend was observed in their perception of older people as a burden for society, with only 186 participants

Table 1. Descriptive Statistics of Older Participants' Characteristics ($N = 954$)

Characteristics	Categories/items	Frequency (%)	Mean (*SD*)
Residence	Rural (0)	479 (50.2%)	
	Urban (1)	475 (49.8%)	
Age	Range: 60–94		72.73(7.55)
Gender	Female (0)	467 (49.0%)	
	Male (1)	487 (51.0%)	
Living arrangement	Not living alone (0)	827 (86.7%)	
	Living alone (1)	127 (13.3%)	
Number of chronic diseases	Range: 0–11		1.89 (1.78)
Function health	IADL composite score (range: 7–21)		18.49 (3.85)
	Ability to use phone (range: 1–3)		2.51 (.77)
	Shopping (range: 1–3)		2.68 (.64)
	Food preparation (range: 1–3)		2.71 (.63)
	Housekeeping (range: 1–3)		2.79 (.55)
	Laundry (range: 1–3)		2.58 (.70)
	Use of public transportation (range: 1–3)		2.59 (.70)
	Ability to handle finances (range: 1–3)		2.63 (.71)
Availability of family support	Lubben's family support composite score (range: 0–15)		8.39 (3.35)
	Number of relatives who would be met or contacted at least once a month (range: 0–5)		3.03 (1.23)
	Number of relatives who can share innermost feelings with (range: 0–5)		2.47 (1.28)
	Number of relatives who can offer help when needed (range: 0–5)		2.88 (1.38)
Self-rated family relations	Not harmonious (0)	55 (5.8%)	
	Harmonious (1)	899 (94.2%)	
Burden views of older people	Composite score (range: 2–6)		3.98 (1.68)
	Perceive older people as burden to family (range: 1–3)		2.01 (.91)
	Perceive older people burden to society (range: 1–3)		1.97 (.90)
Depression	GDS composite score (range: 0–15)		3.98 (1.68)
	Normal (range: 0–4)	562 (58.9%)	
	Mild depression (range: 5–9)	293 (30.7%)	
	Moderate to severe depression (range: 10–15)	99 (10.4%)	

Note. SD = standard deviation.

Table 2. Bivariate Correlation Coefficients for Independent Variables and Depression

	Correlation coefficient
Rural–urban residence	$-.15^{***}$
Age	$.17^{***}$
Gender	$-.11^{**}$
Living arrangement	$.04$
Number of chronic diseases	$.18^{***}$
Functional health status	$-.43^{***}$
Availability of family support	$-.18^{***}$
Self-related family relations	$-.21^{***}$
Burden views of older people	$.33^{***}$

Note. *p $< .05$; **p $< .01$; ***p $< .001$.

(19.5%) disagreeing with the statement that older people were a burden for society. Other participants either strongly agreed (41.8%) or somewhat agreed (38.7%) that older people were a burden for society.

Mental health status.   The mean GDS score for study participants was 3.98 ($SD = 1.68$), with 30.7% experiencing mild depression and 10.4% experiencing moderate to severe depressive symptoms.

Correlations between Potential Predictors and Mental Health

Bivariate analysis was performed in order to identify correlations between participants' depressive symptoms and all independent variables. As shown in Table 2, mental health status, represented by GDS score, was significantly correlated with rural–urban residence, age, gender, number of chronic diseases, functional health status, availability of family support, self-rated family relations, and burden views toward older people.

Hierarchical Regression Analysis of Mental Health

Table 3 presents the regression analysis for all potential predictors when depressive symptoms was treated as the dependent variable. The final model explained 31% of variance in depressive symptoms. The four blocks of variables introduced respective increases of 7% ($p < .001$), 14% ($p < .01$), 6% ($p < .001$), and 5% ($p < .001$) in explained variance of depressive symptoms. In the first model, sociodemographic variables, including urban–rural residence, age, gender, and living arrangement, were entered. With the exception of living arrangement, these variables were significantly associated with depressive symptoms. Urban

Table 3. Hierarchical Multiple Regression Analysis of Participants' Depressive Symptoms

	Model 1 Beta	Model 2 Beta	Model 3 Beta	Model 4 Beta
Sociodemographic variables				
Urban–rural residence (0 = rural; 1 = urban)	−0.17***	−0.14***	−0.15***	−0.08**
Age	0.17***	−0.03	0.00	0.01
Gender (0 = female; 1 = male)	−0.12***	−0.06*	−0.07*	−0.05
Living arrangement (0 = not living alone; 1 = living alone)	−0.03	0.12	0.01	0.00
Physical and functional health variables				
Number of chronic diseases		0.07*	0.07*	0.09**
Functional health status		−0.40***	−0.38***	−0.33***
Family-related variables				
Availability of family support			−0.14***	−0.13***
Self-rated family relations (0 = not hamonious; 1 = harmonious)			−0.20***	−0.19***
Burden views of older people				
The extent of perceiving older people as a burden to family and society				0.23***
R^2 change	0.07***	0.14***	0.06***	0.05***
R^2	0.07	0.21	0.27	0.32
Adjusted R^2	0.06	0.20	0.26	0.31

Notes. ΔR^2 = Change of explained variance. For each model, F change = 16.58 (df = 4 and 949, $p <$ .001), F change = 83.19 (df = 2 and 947, $p <$ .001), F change = 40.90 (df = 2 and 945, $p <$ .001), and F change = 64.31 (df = 1 and 944, $p <$ .001), respectively.
*$p <$ .05; **$p <$ .01; ***$p <$ .001.

residence, younger age, and male gender were found to predict better mental health with less depressive symptoms. In the second model, variables measuring physical and functional health status were added. Age was no longer significant in predicting mental health in this model. Those who reported less chronic diseases and better functional health status were less likely to suffer depressive symptoms.

In the third model, quality of family relations, including availability of family support and self-rated family relations, was added into the regression. After controlling for sociodemographic characteristics, and physical and functional health status, the availability of family support and better self-rated family relations were associated with more favorable mental health. The final regression model examined whether participants' perception of older people as a burden on family and society was significantly associated with depressive symptoms, independent of the first three blocks of predictors. The final model revealed that those who held burden views toward older people were more likely to suffer more depressive symptoms, indicating poorer mental health status. Other significant predicting factors included living in rural areas, reporting more chronic diseases, being more dependent on others in dealing with daily activities, having limited family support, and poorer family relations.

Discussion and Implications

The findings of this study show that in general, older Chinese adults often face a number of challenges with respect to maintaining a positive view of themselves as a group. When asked whether they perceived older people as a burden to family and to society, participants reported a mean score of two, on a scale of one to three. This may reflect that the images of aging and of older people are changing in contemporary China, to the extent that many older people have started to perceive themselves as a bit of a burden for both family and society, especially when they lack capability and necessary resources to stand on their own feet (Chow & Bai, 2011). This is consistent with modernization theory hypotheses as well as with stereotype internalization hypotheses. Through exposure to negative stereotypes about their group, in the context of rapid modernization, older people are likely to internalize these views into their self-image (Bai, 2014; Bennett & Gaines, 2010; Cowgill, 1974; von Hippel et al., 2000).

Aging stereotypes held by older participants were identified as an important predictor of depressive symptoms after controlling for sociodemographic characteristics, physical and functional health status, and family relationship quality. Confirming the most important hypothesis of this study, those with stronger burden views toward older people were found to be at higher risk of mental health challenges, notably depression. Age-based stereotypes and discrimination are embedded in our society and manifested through various aspects of daily life (Bai, 2014; Nelson, 2005). According to the stereotype internalization perspective, older peoples' self-image may deteriorate when they internalize such negative stereotypes. This is consistent with findings of previous studies, that positive attitudes toward aging are associated with positive effects on well-being, including depression (Dong et al., 2010; Hausdorff et al., 1999; Lai, 2009; Levy et al., 2000). This means that addressing aging stereotypes and older adults' self-image may be effective in the prevention of depressive symptoms. It is worthwhile to encourage late-middle-aged adults to take active preparation efforts before they virtually enter into old age, with the assistance of family, friends, and governments at all levels. Such preparation should at least include plans for financial security, appropriate social functioning, health maintenance, adaptation to relationship change with other family members, and future care arrangement. Based on the results of previous studies (e.g., Kim, Kwon, & Anderson, 2005; Lee & Law, 2004), we have reasons to expect that those who have paid more effort in getting prepared for retirement are more likely to adjust better to old age, have more optimal self-esteem, experience less anxiety and depression, and be more confident in taking up future challenges.

As the number and proportion of older persons will continue to increase over the next few decades in China, and in many other countries and regions, negative attitudes toward aging must be addressed, among older adults and the general public. This can enable a more pleasant, productive, and positive aging experience, and reduce risk of mental health challenges such as depression. Older adults should be guided to protect their self-concept against the contaminating effects of stereotyped expectations of "typical" older people (Bai & Chow, 2011). For example, counseling activities with older adults might address their negative self-image, in addition to clinical symptoms associated with depression. Programs could provide opportunities for older adults to identify and explore positive aspects of aging, such as leisure or recreational opportunities, which might shift their attitudes toward aging. Participation in voluntary activities might also shift perceptions of older adults as a "burden" to society and improve their self-image. Social workers could also take on an advocacy role with older adults, with an empowerment focus intended to promote self-esteem and self-image (Kelchner, 1999).

Older adults' attitudes toward aging are a reflection of broader societal attitudes. Policy and program efforts should therefore actively address issues related to ageism (Kelchner, 1999; Nelson, 2005). Community education efforts should aim to create a positive social and community environment for the aging population, focusing on the positive aspects of aging and dispelling myths. Programs might also facilitate intergenerational understanding and respect through the development of relationships between older adults and members of the younger generations. Leisure, recreational, and voluntary activities might provide opportunities for developing such relationships.

In addition to burden views toward older adults, this study identified other factors associated with older adults' depressive symptoms. Perceived availability of family support and better self-rated family relations were found to be associated with more favorable mental health status among older participants, after adjusting for sociodemographic and health characteristics. This is consistent with previous evidence that positive family relations contribute to older peoples' mental health, while negative aspects of family relations have detrimental effects (Lendon, 2012; Ward, 2008). Perceived availability of family support and harmonious family relationships can buffer the negative effects of stressful events on older people's mental health (Lang & Schütze, 2002; Ward, 2008). As family members have traditionally been responsible for the well-being of older people in Chinese society, the impact of these changes in family structure and roles associated with modernization are particularly great. Efforts to enhance the mental health of older Chinese adults should focus on strategies or programs to improve family relationships, develop family support, and expand and strengthen older adults' social support networks. Older adults' sense of self is often tied to their role in their family and to their relations with family members, particularly in Chinese culture. As such, the development and strengthening of family relationships may contribute to the enhancement of older adults' self-image and improve their views of aging (Gergen & Gergen, 2001).

Inasmuch as Chinese society is often described as founded on social relationships and interlocking social networks of familiarity (Fei, 1998), and as kinship relationships form an essential element in the community from which the elderly in China can receive care and support, the family network might be extended to friends, peers, and ideally to the whole caring community (Wang, 2005). More adequate provision of community services would help to share the responsibility in taking care of older people. Other sources of assistance should also be explored and organized. To ease the empty-nesters' problem of lack of sufficient care, they should be provided with more access to in-home services, day care centers, and residential care facilities (Yao, 2006).

Among participants, mental health challenges, measured by depressive symptoms, were associated with poorer physical and functional health and with rural residence (Chow & Bai, 2011; Sun, 2005). The contribution of health variables to variance in the dependent variable is more important than that of sociodemographic variables. These findings align with previous studies, which have reported that predictors of depression among older adults include rural residence (Chen et al., 2005; Lim et al., 2011), lower socioeconomic status and financial strain (Cairney & Krause, 2005; Chi et al., 2005; Kahn & Fazio, 2005; Lim et al., 2011; Mirowsky & Ross, 2003), and poorer health and functional status (Chi et al., 2005; Gagnon & Patten, 2002; Han, 2002; Ormel et al., 2002; Travis et al., 2004; Zeng et al., 2012). Previous research has also reported that better physical and mental health and socioeconomic status are linked to more positive attitudes toward aging (Lai, 2007).

Efforts to address depressive symptoms among older adults in China should include the development of adequate health care and health promotion services for the aging population (Travers, Martin-Khan, & Lie, 2009), including prevention, early detection, and intervention programs to reduce risks associated with chronic diseases and deterioration of functional capacity as adults enter into old age. The community-based healthcare teams need to be more effectively organized to pay frequent home visits to needy elderly members, especially those who are living alone, or with chronic diseases. Policy efforts could also focus on enhancing rural elders' financial situation, though multipillar retirement pension schemes. Older adults, and society in general, view aging negatively when it is associated with expected outcomes such as poor health and loss of independence, as opposed to being viewed as a meaningful and positive process (Gergen & Gergen, 2001; Nelson, 2005; Chrisler, Barney, & Palatino, 2016; Ramírez & Palacios-Espinosa, 2016). If these expectations and perceived outcomes can be improved, people may view aging in a more positive way, which can in turn improve older adults' mental health status (Kim, 2009; Gergen & Gergen, 2001). It is also imperative that health and mental health professionals, social workers, and other service providers get rid of their stereotypes and biases toward aging and older people (Kelchner, 1999; Nelson, 2005).

Limitations

There are several limitations in this study that should be acknowledged. First, this study was based on data from one province, and as such, one should be cautious about generalizing the findings to older adult populations in other parts of China. Second, as this study was based on secondary analysis of data originally collected as part of a larger-scale cross-sectional study, the measurements used were limited by the availability of variables in the original data set. More sophisticated measurements of aging stereotypes could be used in future studies, and the inclusion of both subjective and objective measures of aging stereotypes in both positive and negative directions would be desirable. Third, viewing older people as a burden only explained 5% of variance in depression in the final regression model, much lower than the explanation power of physical and functional health variables, indicating that burden views toward older people represent an important but not necessarily critical variable in predicting mental health outcomes. While physical and functional health are also important predictors of depressive symptoms the study findings raise questions about the potential role that ageism might play in older adults' access to health and community support services, which could have significant impacts on older adults' health and mental health outcomes. Thus, further research on the interaction between ageism and service access in aging population is recommended.

References

Aaronson, B. S. (1966). Personality stereotypes of aging. *Journal of Gerontology, 21*(3), 458–462. doi: 10.1093/geronj/21.3.458.

Bai, X. (2014). Images of ageing in society: A literature review. *Journal of Population Ageing, 7*, 231–253.

Bai, X. (2016). Alignment or struggle? Exploring socio-demographic correlates of individual modernity in Chinese older people. *Ageing and Society, 36*(1), 133–159.

Bai, X., & Chow, N. (2011). How is the self-image formed and enhanced among older Chinese people: Through assimilation or contrast? *Asian Journal of Gerontology and Geriatrics, 6*, 22–28.

Bai, X., Chan, S., & Chow, N. (2012). Validation of self-image of aging scale for Chinese elders. *International Journal of Aging and Human Development, 74*(1), 67–86. doi: 10.2190/AG.74.1.d.

Barua, A., Ghosh, M. K., Kar, N., & Basilio, M. A. (2010). Distribution of depressive disorders in the elderly. *Journal of Neurosciences in Rural Practice, 1*(2), 67–73.

Barua, A., Ghosh, M. K., Kar, N., & Basilio, M. A. (2011). Prevalence of depressive disorder in the elderly. *Annals of Saudi Medicine, 31*(6), 620–624. doi: 10.4103/0256-4947.87100.

Bennett, T., & Gaines, J. (2010). Believing what you hear: The impact of aging stereotypes upon the old. *Educational Gerontology, 36*(5), 435–445. doi: 10.1080/03601270903212336.

Brink, T. L., Yesavage, J. A., Lum, O., Heersema, P., Adey, M., & Rose, T. L. (1982). Screening tests for geriatric depression. *Clinical Gerontologist, 1*, 37–43. doi: 10.1300/J018v01n01_06.

Brummett, B. H., Barefoot, J. C., Siegler, I. C., & Steffens, D. C. (2000). Relation of subjective and received social support to clinical and self-report assessments of depressive symptoms in an elderly population. *Journal of Affective Disorders, 61*(1), 41–50. doi: 10.1016/S0165-0327(99)00191-3.

Bugental, D. B., & Hehman, J. A. (2007). Ageism: A review of research and policy implications. *Social Issues and Policy Review, 1*(1), 173–216. doi: 10.1111/j.1751-2409.2007.00007.x.

Cairney, J., & Krause, N. (2005). The social distribution of psychological distress and depression in older adults. *Journal of Aging and Health, 17*(6), 807–835. doi: 10.1177/0898264305280985.

Calvo, E., & Williamson, J. B. (2008). Old-age pension reform and modernization pathways: Lessons for China from Latin America. *Journal of Aging Studies, 22*, 74–87. doi: 10.1016/j.jaging.2007.02.004.

Chao, S. Y., & Roth, P. (2000). The experiences of Taiwanese women caring for parents-in-law. *Journal of Advanced Nursing, 31*(3), 631–638. doi: 10.1046/j.1365-2648.2000.01319.x.

Chen, X., & Silverstein, M. (2000). Intergenerational social support and the psychological well-being of older parents in China. *Research on Ageing, 22*(1), 43–65. doi: 10.1177/0164027500221003.

Chen, R., Li, W., Zhi, H., Xia, Q., Copeland, J. R., & Hemingway, H. (2005). Depression in older people in rural China. *Archives of Internal Medicine, 165*, 2019–2025. doi: 10.1001/archinte.165.17.2019.

Chi, I., Chiu, H. F. K., Chou, K. L., Chan, K. S., Kwan, C. W., Conwell, Y., & Caine, E. (2005). Prevalence of depression and its correlates in Hong Kong's Chinese older adults. *American Journal of Geriatric Psychiatry, 13*(5), 409–416. doi: 10.1097/00019442-200505000-00010.

Chiou, C. J., Chen, J. P., & Wang, H. H. (2005). The health status of family caregivers in Taiwan: An analysis of gender differences. *International Journal of Geriatric Psychiatry, 20*(9), 821–826. doi: 10.1002/gps.1364.

Chiu, S., & Yu, S. (2001). An excess of culture: The myth of shared care in the Chinese community in Britain. *Ageing and Society, 21*(6), 681–699. doi: 10.1017/S0144686X01008339.

Chong, M. Y., Chen, C. C., Tsang, H. Y., Yeh, T. L., Chen, C. S., Lee, Y. H., Tang, H. Y., & Lo, H. Y. (2001). Community study of depression in old age in Taiwan: Prevalence, life events and socio-demographic correlates. *British Journal of Psychiatry, 178*, 29–35. doi: 10.1192/bjp.178.1.29.

Chow, N., & Bai, X. (2011). Modernization and its impact on Chinese older people's perception of their own image and status. *International Social Work, 54*(6), 800–815. doi: 10.1177/0020872811406458.

Chrisler, J. C., Barney, A., & Palatino, B. (2016). Ageism can be hazardous to women's health: Ageism, sexism, and stereotypes of older women in the health care system. *Journal of Social Issues, 72*(1), 86–104.

Cowgill, D. O. (1974). Aging and modernization: A revision of the theory. In J. F. Gubrium (Ed.), *Late Life* (pp. 123–145). Springfield, IL: Thomas.

Cowgill, D. O., & Holmes, L. D. (1972). *Aging and modernization.* New York: Appleton-Century-Crofts.

Dong, X., Simon, M., Beck, T., & Evans, D. (2010). A cross-sectional population-based study of elder self-neglect and psychological, health, and social factors in a biracial community. *Aging and Mental Health, 14*(1), 74–84. doi: 10.1080/13607860903421037.

Du, P. (2013). Intergenerational solidarity and old-age support for social inclusion of elders in Mainland China: The changing roles of family and government. *Ageing and Society, 33*(1), 44–63.

Dykstra, P. A., & Fokkema, T. (2011). Relationships between parents and their adult children: A West European typology of late-life families. *Ageing and Society, 31*, 545–569.

Fei, X. T. (1998). *From the soil.* Beijing: Peking University Press.

Gagnon, L. M., & Patten, S. B. (2002). Major depression and its association with long-term medical conditions. *Canadian Journal of Psychiatry, 47*, 149–152.

George, L. K., Landerman, R., Blazer, D. G., & Anthony, J. C. (1991). Cognitive impairment. In L. N. Robins & D. A. Reiger (Eds.), *Psychiatric disorders in America: The Epidemiologic Catchment Area Study* (pp. 291–327). New York: Free Press.

Gergen, M. M., & Gergen, K. J. (2001). Positive aging: New images for a new age. *Ageing International, 27*(1), 3–23. doi: 10.1007/s12126-001-1013-6.

Guo, M., Chi, I., & Silverstein, M. (2012). The structure of intergenerational relations in rural China: A latent class analysis. *Journal of Marriage and Family, 74*(5), 1114–1128. doi: 10.1111/j.1741-3737.2012.01014.x.

Han, B. (2002). Depressive symptoms and self-rated health in community-dwelling older adults: A longitudinal study. *Journal of the American Geriatric Society, 50,* 1549–1556. doi: 10.1046/j.1532-5415.2002.50411.x.

Hausdorff, J. M., Levy, B., & Wei, J. Y. (1999). The power of stereotypes on gait of older persons: Reversibility of age-related changes. *Journal of the American Geriatrics Society, 47*(9), S5.

Hess, T. M., Auman, C., Colcombe, S. J., & Rahhal, T. A. (2003). The impact of stereotype threat on age differences in memory performance. *The Journals of Gerontology Series B: Psychological Sciences and Social Sciences, 58*(1), P3–P11. doi: 10.1093/geronb/58.1.P3.

Holroyd, E. (2001). Hong Kong Chinese daughters' intergenerational caregiving obligations: A cultural model approach. *Social Sciences and Medicine, 53*(9), 1125–1134. doi: 10.1016/S0277-9536(00)00406-8.

Hummert, M. L. (2007). As family members age: A research agenda for family communication. *Journal of Family Communications, 7*(1), 3–21.

Jiangsu Province Statistical Bureau (2011). Major figures for Jiangsu Province from the 2010 National Population Census. Available from http://www.jssb.gov.cn/jstj/djgb/qsndtjgb/201105/t20110503_115227.htm.

Kahn, J. R., & Fazio, E. M. (2005). Economic status over the life course and racial disparities in health. *The Journals of Gerontology Series B: Psychological Sciences and Social Sciences, 60*(2), S76–S84. doi: 10.1093/geronb/60.Special_Issue_2.

Kanbur, R., & Zhang, X. (1999). Which regional inequality? The evolution of rural-urban and inland-coastal inequality in China from 1983 to 1995. *Journal of Comparative Economics, 27,* 686–701. doi: 10.1006/jcec.1999.1612.

Kelchner, E. S. (1999). Ageism's impact and effect on society: Not just a concern for the old. *Journal of Gerontological Social Work, 32*(4), 85–100. doi: 10.1300/J083v32n04_07.

Kessler, R. C., McGonagle, K. A., Zhao, S., Nelson, C. B., Hughes, M., & Eshleman, S. (1994). Lifetime and 12-month prevalence of DSM-III-R psychiatric disorders in the United States: Results from the National Comorbidity Survey. *Archives of General Psychiatry, 51,* 8–19. doi: 10.1001/archpsyc.1994.03950010008002.

Kim, S. H. (2009). Older people's expectations regarding ageing, health-promoting behaviour and health status. *Journal of Advanced Nursing, 65*(1), 84–91. doi: 10.1111/j.1365-2648.2008.04841.x.

Kim, J., Kwon, J., & Anderson, E. A. (2005). Factors related to retirement confidence: Retirement preparation and workplace financial education. *Financial Counseling and Planning, 16*(2), 77–89.

Kite, M. E., & Wagner, L. S. (2002). Attitudes towards older adults. In T. D. Nelson (Ed.), *Ageism: Stereotyping and prejudice against older persons* (pp. 129–161). Cambridge, MA: MIT Press.

Kite, M. E., Stockdale, G. D., Whitley, B. E, & Johnson, B. T. (2005). Attitudes towards older and younger adults: An updated meta-analytic review. *Journal of Social Issues, 61*(2), 241–266. doi: 10.1111/j.1540-4560.2005.00404.x.

Kuypers, J. A., & Bengtson, V. L. (1973). Social breakdown and competence: A model of normal aging. *Human Development, 16,* 181–201. doi: 10.1159/000271275.

Lai, D. W. L. (2004). Impact of culture on depressive symptoms of elderly immigrants. *Canadian Journal of Psychiatry, 49*(12), 820–827.

Lai, D. W. L. (2007). Attitudes of elderly Chinese toward aging: An international comparison. *International Journal of Sociology of the Family, 33*(1), 79–94.

Lai, D. W. L. (2009). Older Chinese attitudes toward aging and the relationship to mental health: An international comparison. *Social Work in Health Care, 48*(3), 243–259. doi: 10.1080/00981380802591957.

Lai, D. W. L., & Tong, H. M. (2009). Comparison of social determinants of depressive symptoms among elderly Chinese in Guangzhou, Hong Kong and Taipei. *Asian Journal of Gerontology & Geriatrics, 4,* 58–65.

Lai, D. W. L., & Tong, H. M. (2012). Effect of social exclusion on attitude toward ageing in older adults living alone in Shanghai. *Asian Journal of Gerontology & Geriatrics, 7,* 88–94.

Lai, D. W. L., Tong, H. M., Zeng, Q., & Xu, W. Y. (2010). The factor structure of a Chinese geriatric depression scale-SF: Use with alone elderly Chinese in Shanghai, China. *International Journal of Geriatric Psychiatry, 25,* 503–510. doi: 10.1002/gps.2369.

Lang, F. R., & Schütze, Y. (2002). Adult children's supportive behaviors and older parents' subjective well-being: A developmental perspective on intergenerational relationships. *Journal of Social Issues, 58*(4), 661–680. doi: 10.1111/1540-4560.00283.

Lawton, M. P., & Brody, E. M. (1969). Assessment of older people: Self-maintaining and instrumental activities of daily living. *Gerontologist, 9,* 179–186.

Lee, W., & Law, K. (2004). Retirement planning and retirement satisfaction: The need for a national retirement program and policy in Hong Kong. *Journal of Applied Gerontology, 23*(3), 212–233.

Lendon, J. P. (2012). *The measurement, life course patterns, and outcomes of intergenerational ambivalence among parent-adult child dyads.* Doctoral Thesis. Retrieved from ProQuest Dissertations and Theses Database. (Publication No. 3514231).

Levy, B. (1996). Improving memory in old age through implicit self-stereotyping. *Journal of Personality and Social Psychology, 71*(6), 1092–1107. doi: 10.1037/0022-3514.71.6.1092.

Levy, B., & Langer, E. (1994). Aging free from negative stereotypes: Successful memory in China among the American deaf. *Journal of Personality and Social Psychology, 66*(6), 989–997. doi: 10.1037/0022-3514.66.6.989.

Levy, S. R., & Macdonald, J. L. (2016). Progress on understanding ageism. *Journal of Social Issues, 72*(1), 5–25. doi: 10.1111/josi.12153.

Levy, B., Ashman, O., & Dror, I. (2000). To be or not to be: The effects of aging stereotypes on the will to live. *OMEGA-Journal of Death and Dying, 40*(3), 409–420. doi: 10.2190/Y2GE-BVYQ-NF0E-83VR.

Levy, B. R., Hausdorff, J. M., Hencke, R., & Wei, J. Y. (2000). Reducing cardiovascular stress with positive self-stereotypes of aging. *The Journals of Gerontology Series B: Psychological Sciences and Social Sciences, 55*(4), P205–P213. doi: 10.1093/geronb/55.4.P205.

Levy, B. R., Slade, M. D., & Gill, T. M. (2006). Hearing decline predicted by elders' stereotypes. *The Journals of Gerontology Series B: Psychological Sciences and Social Sciences, 61*(2), P82–P87.

Lim, L. L., Chang, W. N., Yu, X., Chiu, H., Chong, M. Y., & Kua, E. H. (2011). Depression in Chinese elderly populations. *Asia-Pacific Psychiatry, 3,* 46–53. doi: 10.1111/j.1758-5872.2011.00119.x.

Lubben, J. E. (1988). Assessing social networks among elderly populations. *Family and Community Health, 11*(3), 42–52.

Lubben, J. E., Blozik, E., Gillmann, G., Iliffe, S., Cruse, W. R., Beck, J. C., & Stuck, A. E. (2006). Performance of an abbreviated version of the Lubben social network scale among three European community-dwelling older adult populations. *Gerontologist, 46*(4), 503–513. doi: 10.1093/geront/46.4.503.

Mirowsky, J., & Ross, C. E. (2003). *Education, social status and health.* New York: Walter de Gruyter.

Mui, A. C. (1998). Living alone and depression among older Chinese immigrants. *Journal of Gerontological Social Work, 30*(3–4), 147–166. doi: 10.1300/J083v30n03_12.

Mui, A. C., & Kang, S. Y. (2006). Acculturation stress and depression among Asian immigrant elders. *Social Work, 51*(3), 243–255. doi: 10.1093/sw/51.3.243.

Nelson, T. D. (2005). Ageism: Prejudice against our feared future self. *Journal of Social Issues, 61*(20), 207–221. doi: 10.1111/j.1540-4560.2005.00402.x.

Neugebauer, R. (1999). Mind matters: The importance of mental disorders in public health's 21st century mission. *American Journal of Public Health, 89,* 1309–1311.

Ng, S. H. (2002). Will families support their elders? Answers from across cultures. In T. D. Nelson (Ed.), *Ageism: Stereotyping and prejudice against older persons* (pp. 295–309). Cambridge, Mass: MIT Press.

Ng, R., Monin, J. K., Allore, H. G., & Levy, B. R. (2016). Retirement as meaningful: Positive retirement stereotypes associated with longevity. *Journal of Social Issues, 72*(1), 69–85.

North, M. S., & Fiske, S. T. (2012). An inconvenienced youth? Ageism and its potential intergenerational roots. *Psychological Bulletin, 138*(5), 982–997. doi: 10.1037/a0027843.

North, M. S., & Fiske, S. T. (2013). Act your (old) age: Prescriptive, ageist biases over succession, consumption, and identity. *Personality and Social Psychology Bulletin, 39*(6), 720–734. doi: 10.1177/0146167213480043.

Ormel, J., Rijsdijk, F. V., Sullivan, M., van Sonderen, E., & Kempen, G. I. J. M. (2002). Temporal and reciprocal relationship between IADL/ADL disability and depressive symptoms in late life. *The Journals of Gerontology Series B: Psychological Sciences and Social Sciences, 57*, 338–347. doi: 10.1093/geronb/57.4.P338.

Palmore, E. (2005). Three decades of research on ageism. *Generations, 29*(3), 87–90.

Ramírez, L. F., & Palacios-Espinosa, X. (2016). Stereotypes about old age, social support, aging anxiety and evaluations of one's own health. *Journal of Social Issues, 72*(1), 47–68.

Rangaswamy, S. M. (2001). *World health report: Mental health: New understanding, new hope.* Geneva: World Health Organization.

Rodin, J., & Langer, E. J. (1980). Ageing labels: The decline of control and the fall of self-esteem. *Journal of Social Issues, 36*, 12–29. doi: 10.1111/j.1540-4560.1980.tb02019.x.

Rothermund, K., & Brandtstädter, J. (2003). Age stereotypes and selfviews in later life: Evaluating rival assumptions. *International Journal of Behavioral Development, 27*, 549–554. doi: 10.1080/01650250344000208.

Saab, B. R., El-Roueiheb, Z., Chaaya, M., & Sibai, A. M. (2005). Determinants of depression among poor elderly women: Findings from refugee and non-refugee communities in the outskirts of Beirut, Lebanon. *Europe's Journal of Psychology, 1*(3). Retrieved from http://ejop.psychopen.eu/article/view/374

Sereny, M. (2011). Living arrangements of older adults in China: The interplay among preferences, realities, and health. *Research on Aging, 33*(2), 172–204.

Sinclair, S., Huntsinger, J., Skorinko, J., & Hardin, C. D. (2005). Social tuning of the self: Consequences for the self-evaluations of stereotype targets. *Journal of Personality and Social Psychology, 89*, 160–175. doi: 10.1037/0022-3514.89.2.160.

Sun, L. P. (2003). *Rupture: The Chinese society after 1990.* Beijing: Social Science Academic Press (in Chinese).

Sun, L. P. (2005). *Modernization and social transformation.* Beijing: Peking University Press (in Chinese).

Travers, C., Martin-Khan, M., & Lie, D. (2009). Barriers and enablers of health promotion, prevention and early intervention in primary care: Evidence to inform the Australian national dementia strategy. *Australasian Journal on Ageing, 28*(2), 51–57. doi: 10.1111/j.1741-6612.2009.00359.x.

Travis, L. A., Lyness, J. M., Shields, C. G., King, D. A., & Cox, C. (2004). Social support, depression, and functional disability in older adult primary-care patients. *American Journal of Geriatric Psychiatry, 12*(3), 265–271. doi: 10.1097/00019442-200405000-00005.

Turner, R. J., & Lloyd, D. A. (1999). The stress process and the social distribution of depression. *Journal of Health and Social Behaviour, 40*, 374–404.

von Hippel, W., Silver, L. A., & Lynch, M. E. (2000). Stereotyping against your will: The role of inhibitory ability in stereotyping and prejudice among the elderly. *Personality and Social Psychology Bulletin, 26*, 523–532. doi: 10.1177/0146167200267001.

Wang, Y. X. (2005). Pay attention to elderly care issue in rural empty-nest families. *China Population Science*, Supplement, 160–165.

Ward, R. A. (2008). Multiple parent-adult child relations and well-being in middle and later life. *Journals of Gerontology Series B: Psychological Sciences and Social Sciences, 63*, 239–247.

Yao, Y. M. (2006). Care for rural empty-nest elderly in relatively developed regions: A case study of rural Zhejiang province. *Population Research, 30*(6), 38–46.

Yesavage, J. A., Brink, T. L., Rose, T. L., Lum, Q., Huang, V., Adey, M., & Leirer, V. O. (1983). Development and validation of a geriatric depression screening scale: A preliminary report. *Journal of Psychiatric Research, 17*(1), 37–49. doi: 10.1016/0022-3956(82)90033-4.

Zeng, W., & Chan, M. F. (2010). Investigating factors related to depression among older persons in Macau. *Macau Journal of Nursing, 9*, 1–9.

Zeng, W., North, N., & Kent, B. (2012). A framework to understand depression among older persons. *Journal of Clinical Nursing, 21*, 2399–2409. doi: 10.1111/j.1365-2702.2011.04049.x.

Zhan, H. J. (2004). Through gendered lens: Explaining Chinese caregivers' task performance and care reward. *Journal of Women and Aging, 16*(1/2), 123–142. doi: 10.1300/J074v16n01_09.

Zhan, H. J., & Montgomery, J. V. (2003). Gender and elder care in China: The influence of filial piety and structural constraints. *Gender and Society, 17*(2), 209–229. doi: 10.1177/0891243202250734.

Zhang, Y. B., Harwood, J., Williams, A., Ylanne-McEwen, V., Wadleigh, P. M., & Thimm, C. (2006). The portrayal of older adults in advertising: A cross-national review. *Journal of Language and Social Psychology, 25*(3), 264–282. doi: 10.1177/0261927X06289479.

XUE BAI is Assistant Professor at the Department of Applied Social Sciences, Hong Kong Polytechnic University. Her research and teaching expertise includes images of aging, health and wellness of aging population, policy and service evaluation for older people, and long-term care issues.

DANIEL W. L. Lai is Professor at the Faculty of Social Work, University of Calgary, with years of research and teaching experience in health and aging, immigration and aging, cultural diversity and aging, and attitudes toward aging in Chinese societies.

AIMEI GUO is Professor at the Ginling Women's College, Nanjing Normal University, with years of research and teaching experience in gerontology, women's studies, psychology, and labor issues. The data set used in this study belongs to Dr Aimei Guo's research project funded by the Jiangsu Province Philosophy and Social Sciences Research Program (2011ZDXM016).

Journal of Social Issues, Vol. 72, No. 1, 2016, pp. 47–68
doi: 10.1111/josi.12155

Stereotypes about Old Age, Social Support, Aging Anxiety and Evaluations of One's Own Health

Luisa Ramírez* **and Ximena Palacios-Espinosa**

Universidad del Rosario

As the aging population in Colombia grows, caring for older adults falls not just to family but also to the community including friends and religious organizations. While there is very little research on ageism in Colombia, it is increasingly urgent to understand the role of social support of the growing older population. Two studies were conducted with a community sample in Bogotá, Colombia. In a pilot study, we developed a measure of positive and negative stereotyping of older adults. In the main study with participants aged between 54 and 83, we explored the relations among endorsement of positive and negative stereotypes, anxiety about aging, perceived and expected physical and mental health, and expectations of social support. We found that perceived lack of social support and negative stereotyping significantly predict more anxiety towards aging, while positive evaluations of one's own mental health predict less anxiety. Surprisingly, greater expectations of social support predict more aging anxiety. In turn, aging anxiety and positive stereotyping predicted evaluations of mental (but not physical) health. Additionally, poorer evaluations of physical health, aging anxiety and negative stereotyping (though only marginally) significantly predict greater expectations of social support. Implications of the findings are discussed.

Worldwide, the population of older adults has grown and thus their treatment and welfare is increasingly becoming an urgent social issue (e.g., Levy & Macdonald, 2016; Nelson, 2009; Palmore, 1999; WHO, 2014). By 2050, there are expected to be almost 400 million people aged 80 and older, which means that many young and middle-age persons will be caring for older adults (WHO, 2014). Colombia is no exception to the world trends. Like other third world countries, it is

---

*Correspondence concerning this article should be addressed to Luisa Ramírez, Programa de Psicología, Escuela de Medicina y Ciencias de la Salud (Psychology Department, Medicine and Health Sciences School), Universidad del Rosario, Bogotá, Colombia. Tel: 57(1) 2970200 [e-mail: luisa.ramirez@urosario.edu.co].

47

experiencing important changes in the population growth dynamics. For example, in the last few decades, the number of newborn babies has decreased by 27.5%. Foreseeable life expectancy in Colombia is predicted to be around 79.4 for women and 73.8 for men in 2020. By that time, the population of young people (between 15 and 20 years of age) in the pyramidal distribution of the population will decrease by 18%. In contrast, the population older than 60 years of age will increase by 42.1% resulting in an inversion of the age distribution towards the predominance of the elderly (National Department of Statistics [DANE], 2010). Thus, it is vitally important to address the timely issue of studying the treatment, perceptions, and expectations about aging among the Colombian population. Below, we review the literature that laid the foundation for this investigation.

Aging in Colombia

In the past few decades, interest in the older population in Colombia has increased. For the first time in 1979, the health ministry designed an attention plan focused on people over 55 years of age. By that time the plan included, along with other goals, working for the recognition of the elderly as interdependent and respectful human beings, capable of actively taking part in the country's social, economic and political development. The creation of the social security system took place in 1993 (Ley 100, 1993), backed by the reform of the Colombian Constitution that took place in 1991, which emphasized the need to protect and support older adults among other groups of the population. Since then, more of the senior population has had access to social benefits such as a pensions and better access to the health care system (Aging and Old Age Policy 2007–2019, 2007). In 1995, the National Council on Economic and Social Policy signed a new policy (CONPES 2793) acknowledging the difficulties of the older population in Colombia, highlighting the lack of an adequate income, the greater frequency of disease, limitations of access to the social security system, and the lack of efficacy of institutional services, all of which have an impact on the well-being of older adults. The policy saw the need to intervene not only by improving institutional services, income, and access to the health care system, but also by promoting beliefs and attitudes where older adults would become symbols of experience, wisdom, and respect, as a strategy that would help diminish discrimination and segregation of the older population. Once again in 2007, the new Aging and Old Age Policy (2007–2019) acknowledged the difficult conditions for an important portion of the aging population and emphasized the need to work on improving the surrounding environment, and the fact that it is today's younger population that will become the caregivers of aging people.

Accordingly, some have argued in Colombia that it is necessary to work toward changing the existing mentality about aging as well as the tendency to disregard the old as obsolete, thus promoting a more positive outlook of the aging process (Nieto & Alonso, 2007).

Social Support and Aging

Indeed, there is increasing awareness of the need to create and strengthen support mechanisms for elders through public policy. New services and support staff are needed as well as knowledge and education on the process of aging in order to adequately address the increasing needs of the aging population. However, for public policy to be effective, understanding the surrounding context becomes a matter of importance. Thus, it is essential to understand the positive and negative roles that family and community coordination and support are playing in assisting their aging population (e.g., Hummert, 2007; Pope, 2012), but also the way in which people's outlook towards aging changes, as their expectations about attention and care for this group of the population become increasingly important. Yet, insufficient attention has been paid to the aging process, possibly because older adults are usually seen as a minority group, occupying a lower status in society (Gonçalves, 2009).

Nevertheless, available evidence suggests that good health care and supportive caregivers can help older persons work and live longer, while lack of social support, among other things, leads to greater difficulty on an increased number of activities of daily living (Buchman et al., 2010; Perissinotto, Stijacic Cenzer, & Covinsky, 2012), greater risk of increased blood pressure (Hawkley, Thisted, Masi, & Cacioppo, 2010), engaging in multiple health-risk behaviors such as smoking (Shankar, McMunn, Banks, & Steptoe, 2011), and ultimately death (Perissinotto et al., 2012).

Some research also suggests that social support plays a very important role not only for the well-being of older adults, but also in shaping their attitudes toward the aging process (Beyene, Becker, & Mayen, 2002; Giraldo, Franco, Correa, Salazar, & Tamayo, 2005; Montero-López & Rivera-Ledesma, 2009). For example, Beyene et al. (2002) conducted a qualitative study in the United States including African Americans, Filipino Americans, Cambodians and Latinos and concluded that social support can take many forms due to cultural differences. Among Hispanic communities in particular, family seems to play a fundamental role in social life, as well as when it comes to providing care for older persons. Among Latino communities the extended family, including their elders, constitutes not only a fundamental institution for society but it is at the core of their well being. Thus children feel morally and socially obligated to support their parents as they age (Beyene et al., 2002).

When social support is sufficient and of good quality, older adults feel appreciated, respected and see themselves as a source of security for their families (Beyene et al., 2002). In fact, evidence from Mexico suggests that feelings of security derived from knowing that someone will be there to help, take care and provide advice to them in the future may help reduce anxiety towards aging (Montero-López & Rivera-Ledesma, 2009). Nevertheless, to the extent that older adults are thought to be less suited for the workforce, their risk of living in poverty increases, not only for them but for their whole family (Da Silva & Peixoto Besa, 2008).

The Role of Stereotyping

Researchers have noted that lack of social support (loneliness and isolation) may affect health, including health-related behavioral and biological factors (Buchman et al., 2010; Hawkley et al., 2010; Perissinotto et al., 2012). However, research also needs to consider the intervening roles that prevalent stereotypes play on healthcare providers, as well as directly on older persons.

Stereotypes have been shown to play an important role in shaping attitudes and interactions among people in at least two ways. First, stereotyping may affect the developmental context for older people by influencing people's behavior towards them (Kornadt & Rothermund, 2015). For instance, stereotyping and ageism may lead to isolation through one of two forms of discriminatory treatment: (1) older people are perceived to be incapable, dependent, and childish or (2) they are perceived to be deteriorating and close to death (Bennett & Gaines, 2010; Levy, Housdorff, Hencke, & Wei, 2000). Second, self-stereotyping and internalization of ageism influences people's attitudes towards their own age and aging: expectations about retirement, health, concerns about death, and ultimately one's own longevity (e.g., Bai, Lai, & Guo, 2016). Levy (2009) and Kornadt and Rothermund (2015) propose some mechanisms through which stereotyping may affect people's wellbeing. Levy's (2009) Stereotype Embodiment Theory proposes that stereotypes are embodied through the assimilation of the surrounding culture, which leads to a self-definition that influences both functioning and health. Accordingly, Ng, Monin, Allore, and Levy (2016) found that positive stereotypes about mental and physical health during retirement predict greater longevity among older adults. Notwithstanding, Kornadt and Rothermund (2015) underscore the fact that views of aging are complex and multidimensional, "they comprise gains as well as losses, and they relate to different areas of functioning and attributes" (p. 122) like health or work, and therefore aren't completely negative or completely positive.

Thus, stereotyping and ageism may exert an influence upon older people themselves (Bennett & Gaines, 2010; Kornadt & Rothermund, 2015; Levy, 2009; Levy, Slade, & Gill, 2006). As pointed out by Ng et al. (2016) negative attitudes toward aging do predict worse mental health during the senior years. Health-wise, positive attitudes toward aging relate to better memory and hearing (Hess, Auman, Colcombe, & Rahhal, 2003; Levy et al., 2006), lower chance of cardiovascular disease (Levy et al., 2000), and greater life satisfaction (Kornadt & Rothermund, 2015). More impressively, in the long run they relate to more longevity (Lakra,

Ng, & Levy, 2012). On the contrary, negative attitudes toward aging adversely affect older adults' health and general performance.

In all, evidence suggests that people's outlook on the aging process influences the well being of older adults. Thus, identifying people's outlook on aging, and its relationship with people's perceptions and expectations about their wellbeing, remains an important contribution in the process of learning about the developmental context of aging.

Research on Aging, Social Support, and Stereotyping in Colombia

Help Age International's (2007) report on aging and development indicates that as life expectancy increases in Latin America, a significant proportion of seniors spend the last years of their lives in poverty. In addition, a study that collected information among several countries in Latin America, including Colombia, found a significant relationship between having some sort of income (job, pension, etc.) and stereotypes among the older population. That is, older people who had access to income, held more positive stereotypes about older adults (Lasagni et al., 2013). Nonetheless, despite evidence of the contribution of the older population to reducing household poverty either by increasing household income or by taking care of their grandchildren, some findings suggest an association between a negative outlook on aging and discrimination among the elderly in Colombia. For instance, Castellanos and Lopez (2010) conducted a qualitative study in Colombia among 39 older adults living in poor areas from Bogotá, and found that aging is more likely to be associated with negative traits like illness, dependency and other deficits than it is with wisdom.

As such, this research addresses the timely issue of studying perceptions, and expectations about aging, health and social support, among a community sample from a Colombian population. We focus on people's attitudes towards aging as they approach the elderly years. To our knowledge, this will be one of the first explorations of aging adults in Latin America, and how their outlooks on aging affect their health and expectations of social support.

Overview

This research is exploratory. It includes a pilot study and a main study, both with a community sample of Colombians from Bogotá, the largest city in Colombia. In both studies, we used methodological tools that allowed for the assessment of both positive and negative views of older adults. We explored how participants' endorsement of positive and negative stereotypes impacts their anxiety about aging, health and expectations of social support. In light of prior work suggesting women may be the target of more negative ageism than men, as ageism and sexism may intertwine and impact older women's health and well-being (e.g., Chrisler,

Barney, & Palatino, 2016; Kite, Stockdale, Whitley, & Johnson, 2005; Lauzen & Dozier, 2005; Travis, Howerton, & Szymanski, 2012), we tested for gender differences as well. Other secondary variables explored include participants' age, socioeconomic status, work status and marital status.

Method

Participants

Participants in the pilot study included 43 people whose ages ranged between 21 and 78 years of age ($M = 42.8$ and $SD = 20.35$), 21 men and 21 women (1 n.d.). Participants in the main study included 215 men ($n = 95$) and women ($n = 120$) whose ages ranged between 44 and 89 years of age, from a community sample in Bogota, Colombia and were recruited using a convenience sampling technique. Men's mean age was 60.2 ($SD = 8.2$), 68.4% reported being currently working and 78% were married. Women's mean age was 59.2 ($SD = 9.38$), 50.8% reported being currently working and 75.4% were married (see Table 1 for a summary of sample demographics).

Measures

With the exception of the stereotyping measures, which were developed in Spanish for this study, all measures were translated and back-translated from English to Spanish by two bilingual translators.

Stereotyping measure.   The stereotyping measure was modeled off of the Levy, Kasl, and Gill (2004) Image of Aging Scale. To develop the stereotyping measure, we first conducted a pilot study. Participants were provided with two sheets of paper, each containing the following instructions: "Please list the first 10 positive/negative words or phrases that come to mind when you think of an old person" and enough space to list at least 10 traits. Specifically, we asked them to think of a 65-year-old person. The authors along with a research assistant reviewed all responses and came to a consensus after each independently reviewing all the responses. Traits under the same label were grouped whenever they happened to be synonyms ("being patient" was merged with "tolerant") or whenever one could be said to be contained in another ("having history" was merged with "experi-enced"). Among the resulting list we selected eight positive (loving, enjoys life moments, experienced, wise, patient, calm, family oriented, generous) and eight negative traits (sick, stubborn, lonely, grumpy, forgetful, sad, tired, dying) that appeared most frequently and included them in the stereotyping measure.

Participants in the main study were asked to rate to what extent they believed these 16 traits described a 65 year old person on a seven point scale (0 = *not at all*

Table 1. Demographics

($n = 231$)		
Gender		
Women	123	53.2
Men	107	46.3
Age		
55 or less	83	38.6
56 to 65	78	33.8
66 or more	54	23.4
N.d.	1	0.4
Marital status		
Not married	74	32.0
Married	144	62.3
N.d.	13	5.6
Work status		
Not working	90	39.0
Currently working	128	55.4
N.d.	13	5.6
Education level		
High school or less	65	28.1
Technical studies	23	10.0
University	91	39.4
Postgraduate studies	45	19.5
N.d.	7	3.0
Socioeconomic status		
Lower class	2	0.9
Lower middle class	11	4.80
Middle class	129	55.8
Upper middle class	76	32.9
Wealthy	5	2.2
N.d.	8	3.5

characteristic and $7 = $ *very characteristic*). Both scales had very strong internal reliability; positive stereotyping ($\alpha = .86$) and negative stereotyping ($\alpha = .85$).

Perceived social support. To assess perceived social support, we used eight items which were measured on a six point scale ($0 = $ *Never*; $1 = $ *Almost never*; $2 = $ *Rarely*; $3 = $ *Sometimes*; $4 = $ *Often*; $5 = $ *Very often*; $6 = $ *Always*) the extent to which participants perceive that they can rely on coworkers, friends, family and other church members for social support ("How often are your X willing to listen to your problems"; "How often do you get help and support from your X"). This version of the scale was adapted from Bosma et al. (1997) and from Macdonald and Levy (2016), and had good internal reliability ($\alpha = .78$).

Expected social support.   To assess people's expectations of social support in the future we used a 3-item scale asking the extent to which they expect family, friends, or church members to take care of them when they are older ("I expect that my X will take care of me when I get older") on a 7-point scale of (0 = *Strongly disagree*; 1 = *Disagree*; 2 = *Disagree a little bit*; 3 = *Neutral*; 4 = *Agree a little bit*; 5 = *Agree*; 6 = *Strongly*). The internal reliability for this scale was acceptable (α = .58). This version of the scale was adapted from Bosma et al. (1997) and had good internal reliability (α = .78).

Aging anxiety.   Anxiety about aging was assessed using a 3-item Likert scale ("I do not want to get old because it means that I am closer to death"; "I am worried that I will lose my independence when I am old," and "I am concerned that my abilities will suffer when I am old"), adapted from Bousfield and Hutchinson (2010). Participant's ratings were recorded on a 6-point Likert scale (0 = *Strongly disagree*; 1 = *Disagree*; 2 = *Disagree a little bit*; 3 = *Neutral*; 4 = *Agree a little bit*; 5 = *Agree*; 6 = *Strongly*). The internal reliability for this scale was acceptable (α = .62).

Perceived and expected health.   To assess participants perceptions of current and expected health, we used two separate items to evaluate their own physical and mental health (e.g. "In general, right now how is your physical [mental] health?"), as well as two separate items to evaluate their expectations for future physical and mental health (e.g., "In general, how do you expect your physical [mental] health to be when you are old?"). Participant's evaluations of their own physical and mental health were recorded on a 5-point scale (0 = *Poor*; 1 = *Fair*; 2 = *Good*; 3 = *Very good*; 4 = *Excellent*)

Finally, we also included a demographics questionnaire to collect information about gender, current occupation, marital status, education level, and perceived socioeconomic status.

Procedure

In the pilot study, researchers and research assistants asked community members from Bogota and the university community to complete a brief survey. The survey asked them to write down positive and negative stereotypes of older persons in Colombia and to provide their age and gender. We used the findings from the pilot study to create the stereotyping measure for the main study. In the main study, we collected data again from the community with the help of three research assistants. Community members were approached in public parks, malls and bus terminals. Participants were asked for consent and then provided with a survey packet that contained the measures to evaluate positive and negative stereotypes of older persons and respond to previously described measures about aging anxiety,

Table 2. Summary of Intercorrelations, Means, and *SD* for Main Study Variables

	1	2	3	4	5	6	7	8	9
1. Positive stereotype	1								
2. Negative Stereotype	0.02	1							
3. Age anxiety	0.02	0.18^{**}							
4. Current physical health	0.15^{*}	−0.07	−0.10	1					
5. Current mental health	0.25^{**}	0.06	−0.12	0.57^{**}	1				
6. Expected physical health	0.11	0.01	−0.08	0.44^{**}	0.43^{**}	1			
7. Expected mental health	0.17^{*}	−0.05	−0.01	0.34^{**}	0.55^{**}	0.74^{**}	1		
8. Perceived social support	0.21^{**}	−0.06	−0.09	0.14^{*}	0.08	0.16^{*}	0.15^{*}	1	
9. Expected social support	0.08	0.13	0.12	0.04	0.00	0.08	0.05	0.26^{**}	1
Mean	4.49	3.46	3.98	2.27	2.74	2.49	2.69	3.46	1.94
SD	0.89	1.1	1.23	0.927	0.914	0.081	0.081	1.06	1.29
N	218	218	216	228	229	226	227	225	216

Note. $^{*}p < .05,$ $^{**}p < .01.$

actual and expected physical and mental health status, and actual and expected social support. Participants were given enough space to answer privately; however, research assistants who provided the survey remained nearby in case participants needed help. These measures were followed by a demographic questionnaire that asked information about gender, marital status, work status, education level and socioeconomic status.

Results

Table 2 includes the intercorrelations among all the variables. We then conducted a series of regression analyses to explore predictors of aging anxiety, social support, and health.

First, we reasoned that evaluations of current health, perceptions of current social support but also expectations of future social support and stereotyping of older adults would likely generate aging anxiety as suggested from the literature review above. We proceeded with a sequential regression analysis predicting aging anxiety (Table 3). Thus, we progressively introduced demographic variables (age, gender, working status, marital status, socioeconomic status (Model 1a), perceived physical and mental health (Model 1b), next our measures of expected physical and mental health (Model 3a), perceived and expected social support (Model 4a), and then positive and negative stereotyping (Model 5a) as predictor variables. We found that perceptions of having social support as well as people's positive evaluations of their own mental health and positive expectation of physical health in the future significantly predicted less anxiety toward aging (Model 4a and 5a). In contrast, negative stereotyping, and greater expectations of social support

Table 3. Standardized Coefficients and Significance Levels for Aging Anxiety

Predictors	Model 1a β	Model 2a β	Model 3a β	Model 4a β	Model 5a β
Age	.034	.024	.030	.029	.027
Gender	−.120	−.112	−.108	−.132	−.123
Currently working	.024	.029	.034	.062	.035
Marital status	.048	.051	.046	.033	.040
Socioeconomic status	.081	.090	.101	.107	.117
Perceived physical health		−.018	.032	.082	.118
Perceived mental health		−.115	−.170	−.180$^+$	−.245*
Expected physical health			−.194	−.220*	−.251*
Expected mental health			.193	.206$^+$	.248*
Perceived social support				−.172*	−.169*
Expected social support				.212**	.176
Positive stereotype					.076
Negative stereotype					.179*
R	.144	.190	.231	.327	.376
R^2	.021	.036	.053	.107	.141
Adj. R^2	.004	.001	.009	.055	.082

Note. $^*p < .05$, $^{**}p < .01$, $^+p < .075$. Model 1a, $F(5,196) = .830$, $p < $ n.s.; Model 2a, $F(7, 194) = 1.042$, $p = $ n.s.; Model 3a, $F(9,192) = 1.202$, $p = $ n.s.; Model 4a, $F(11,190) = 2.073$, $p = .024$; Model 5a, $F(13, 188) = 2.384$, $p = .006$. Change was significant for Models 4a and 5a.

and positive perceived mental health significantly predicted more anxiety toward aging.

Next, in light of previous findings that underscore the role of stereotypes and social support on health, we included a model where we regressed perceived physical health (Table 4) and mental health (Table 5) on perceived social support, age anxiety and stereotyping, including perceptions of physical health (when predicting perceptions mental health) or perceptions of mental health (when predicting perceptions physical health) as predictors in addition to the already mentioned control variables. All Models predicting physical health were significant, ($p < .01$; see Table 4). However, none of the hypothesized variables (perceived social support, aging anxiety, and stereotyping) appeared to be significant, except for age. Only in Model 5 when controlling for current perceptions of mental health, negative stereotyping had a significant effect on predicting perceptions of physical health.

When the same analysis was performed introducing mental health as the predicted variable (Table 5), we found marginally significant results for aging anxiety in Model 5 and significant results for stereotyping and perceptions of physical health (Model 4c). Thus, while anxiety toward aging predicts poorer evaluations of

Table 4. Standardized Coefficients and Significance Levels for Perceived Physical Health

Predictors	Model 1b β	Model 2b β	Model 3b β	Model 4b β	Model 5b β
Age	−.186[*]	−.187[*]	−.184[*]	−.154[*]	−.152[*]
Gender	.127	.127	.118	.099	.099
Currently working	.067	.057	.060	.047	.059
Marital status	−.011	−.005	−.003	−.019	−.023
Socioeconomic status	.146[*]	.125	.134	.107	.1
Perceived social support		.070	.060	.032	.033
Age anxiety			−.072	−.011	.014
Perceived mental health				.524[***]	.543[***]
Positive stereotype					−.028
Negative stereotype					−.118[*]
R	.292	.300	.308	.600	.612
R^2	.085	.90	.095	.360	.374
Adj. R^2	.062	.62	.062	.334	.342

Note. [*]$p < .05$, [**]$p < .01$, [***]$p < .001$. Model 1b, $F(5, 197) = 3.683$, $p = .003$; Model 2b, $F(6, 196) = 3.225$, $p = .005$; Model 3b, $F(7, 195) = 2.919$, $p = .006$; Model 4b, $F(8, 194) = 13.660$, $p = .000$; and Model 5b, $F(10,192) = 11.479$, $p = .000$. Change was significant for Model 4.

Table 5. Standardized Coefficients and Significance Levels for Perceived Mental Health

Predictors	Model 1c β	Model 2c β	Model 3c β	Model 4c β	Model 5c β
Age	−.061	−.062	−.058	.045	0.18
Gender	.052	.052	.038	−.028	−.017
Currently working	.029	.020	.025	−.009	−.048
Marital status	.022	.028	.032	.033	.046
Socioeconomic status	.058	.037	.051	−.024	−.017
Perceived social support		.069	.054	−.022	−.009
Age anxiety			−.117	−.077	−.112[+]
Perceived physical health				.560[***]	.546[***]
Positive stereotype					.199[**]
Negative stereotype					.137[*]
R	.119	.136	.178	.562	.610
R^2	.014	.018	.032	.316	.372
Adj. R^2	−.011	−.012	.003	.287	.339

Note. [*]$p < .05$, [**]$p < .01$, [***]$p < .001$. Model 1c, $F(5, 197) = 0.563$, $p = $ n.s.; Model 2c, $F(6, 196) = 0.612$, $p = $ n.s; Model 3c, $F(7, 195) = 0.910$, $p < $ n.s., and Model 4c, $F(8, 194) = 11.185$, $p < .000$; and Model 5c, $F(10, 192) = 11.351$, $p = .000$. Change was significant for Models 4c and 5c.

Table 6. Standardized Coefficients and Significance Levels for Expected Physical Health

Predictors	Model 1d β	Model 2d β	Model 3d β	Model 4d β	Model 5d β	Model 6d β
Age	−.081	−.086	−.084	−.010	.022	.028
Gender	−.062	−.069	−.084	−.137*	−.036	−.036
Currently working	.014	−.001	.005	−.018	.021	.015
Marital status	−.053	−.040	−.036	−.042	−.029	−.027
Socioeconomic status	.096	.041	.052	−.009	.046	.052
Perceived social support		.126	.106	.064	−.016	−.011
Expectation of social support		.084	.107	.148*	.083	.068
Age anxiety			−.114	−.071	−.096*	−.112*
Perceived mental health				.221**	−.150*	−.174**
Perceived physical health				.338***	.285***	.299***
Expected mental health					.713***	.727***
Positive stereotype						−.005
Negative stereotype						.098*
R	.145	.214	.240	.531	.781	.786
R^2	.021	.046	.058	.282	.610	.618
Adj. R^2	−.004	.011	.019	.245	.587	.592

Note. $^*p < .05$, $^{**}p < .01$, $^{***}p < .001$. Model 1d, $F(5, 196) = 0.837$, $p = $ n.s.; Model 2d, $F(7, 194) = 1.326$, $p = $ n.s.; Model 3d, $F(8, 193) = 1.156$, $p = $ n.s.; Model 4d, $F(10, 191) = 4.533$, $p = .000$; Model 5d, $F(11, 190) = 26.980$, $p = .000$; and Model 6d, $F(13, 188) = 23.431$, $p = .000$. Change was significant for Models 2 and 5.

mental health, positive evaluations of physical health and stereotyping positively relate to mental health.

We reasoned from the literature review that expectations of future health would be affected by current evaluations of well being and social support. We anticipated also that expectations of social support in the future would affect people's expectations of health, particularly pertaining to mental health. Hence, we conducted another series of sequential regressions predicting expected physical health (Table 6) and mental health (Table 7), including social support (perceived and expected), aging anxiety, current evaluations of mental and physical health, stereotyping, as well as either expected physical health (when predicting expected mental health) or expected mental health (when predicting expected physical health) as predictors. We found significantly negative relations for age anxiety and perceptions of mental health. Additionally, we found significantly positive relations between perceptions of physical health, expectations of mental health, and negative stereotyping. In addition, when attempting to predict people's expectations of mental health (Table 7) we found significant positive effects for current perceptions of health and expectations of physical health (Models 4e and

Table 7. Standardized Coefficients and Significance Levels for Expected Mental Health

Predictors	Model 1e β	Model 2e β	Model 3e β	Model 4e β	Model 5e β	Model 6e β
Age	−.083	−.088	−.088	−.045	−.038	−.048
Gender	−.102	−.108	−.112	−.142*	−.055	−.050
Currently working	−.022	−.041	−.039	−.055	−.044	−.037
Marital status	−.017	−.002	.000	−.018	.009	.007
Socioeconomic status	.019	−.042	−.039	−.077	−.71	−.078
Perceived social support		.152*	.147+	.113	.071	.061
Expectation of social support		.077	.083	.091	−.004	.012
Age anxiety			−.031	.035	.081	.097+
Perceived mental health				.520***	.379***	.394***
Perceived physical health				.074	−.042*	−.160**
Expected physical health					.640***	.643***
Positive stereotype						.022
Negative Stereotype						−.116**
R	.135	.222	.223	.597	.806	.814
R^2	.018	.049	.050	.356	.650	.663
Adj. R^2	−.007	.015	.011	.322	.629	.639

Note. *$p < .05$, **$p < .01$, ***$p < .001$. Model 1e, $F(5, 196) = 0.732$, $p =$ n.s.; Model 2e, $F(7, 194) = 1.430$, $p =$ n.s.; Model 3e, $F(8, 193) = 1.268$, $p =$ n.s.; Model 4e, $F(10, 191) = 10.560$, $p = .000$; Model 5e, $F(11, 190) = 32.036$, $p = .000$; and Model 6e, $F(13, 188) = 28.393$, $p = .000$. Change was significant for Models 2e, 4e, 5e, and 6e.

5e), but also negative effects for negative stereotyping. That is, people who hold more negative stereotypes of the elderly tend to expect worse mental health in the future.

Finally, we conducted another sequential regression analysis predicting people's expectations of social support (Table 8). Like in previous models, first, we introduced the control variables (Model 1f); then progressively we introduced evaluations of one's physical and mental health (Model 2f), expected physical and mental health (Model 3f), perceived social support (Model 4f), anxiety toward aging (Model 5f) and stereotyping (Model 6f). Models 4f and 5f had a significant fit ($p < .05$). Socioeconomic status was significant in most models, and so was gender in Models 5f and 6f. In addition, people who reported better evaluations of their current mental health appeared to be less concerned about their social support in the future. Consistently, people who were more anxious about aging and those who held more negative stereotypes (though the later only marginally significant) reported greater expectations of social support, and (not surprisingly) so did those that reported currently having social support.

Table 8. Standardized Coefficients and Significance Levels for Expected Social Support

Predictors	Model 1f β	Model 2f β	Model 3f β	Model 4f β	Model 5f β	Model 6f β
Age	.049	.023	.027	.022	.015	.019
Gender	.084	.100	.126	.123	.144[*]	.141[*]
Currently working	−.032	−.023	−.018	−.046	−.057	−.069
Marital status	−.016	−.020	−.010	.007	.000	.004
Socioeconomic status	.196[**]	.216[**]	.212[**]	.154[*]	.127	.135[+]
Perceived mental health		−.163+	−.213[*]	−.218[*]	−.225[*]	−.193[*]
Perceived physical health		.079	.011	.020	.055	.008
Expected physical health			.146	.140	.178	.145
Expected mental health			.062	.033	−.009	.030
Perceived social support				.196[**]	.222[**]	.219[**]
Age anxiety					.198[**]	.168[*]
Positive stereotype						.026
Negative Stereotype						.132[+]
R	.228	.263	.311	.360	.408	.427
R^2	.052	.069	.096	.130	.166	.182
Adj. R^2	.028	.036	.054	.084	.118	.126

Note. [*]$p < .05$, [**]$p < .01$, [+]$p < .07$. Model 1f, $F(5, 196) = 2.159$ $p =$ n.s.; Model 2f, $F(7, 194) = 2.059$, $p = .05$, Model 3f, $F(9, 192) = 2.277$, $p = .019$; Model 4f, $F(10, 191) = 2.845$, $p = .003$; Model 5f, $F(11, 190) = 3.443$, $p = .000$; and Model 6f, $F(13, 188) = 3.226$, $p = .000$. Change was significant for Models 4f and 5f.

Discussion

Changes in the population dynamics in the past few decades have led to the need for a better understanding of factors that influence the context in which the aging process takes place in Colombia, including attitudes and expectations about aging and old age among a Colombian population. In particular, we explored the relationship between stereotyping, anxiety toward aging, people's evaluations of their current and expected health (mental and physical), as well as perceived and expected social support. We attempted to address previous research gaps such as the fact that most research in the field comes from Western cultures by studying Colombia. Also, past research has tended to focus on college students and persons aged 65 and older (e.g., see Levy & Macdonald, 2016). We addressed this issue by collecting information from a community sample in the capital city of Bogotá.

Our evidence supports previous findings suggesting a strong and persistent relation between stereotyping and aging anxiety, such that negative stereotyping was related to a greater concern with aging (losing independence and abilities, and rejection of the aging process; Table 3), supporting past findings from Harris and Dollinger (2001), and Levy (2001) among others. We reasoned that people's evaluations of their physical and mental health (current and expected) may relate to aging anxiety and found that at least in the case of current evaluations of mental health and expected evaluations of physical health it appeared to be a reasonable expectation, suggesting that given better evaluations of mental health and better expectations of physical health in the future people feel more relaxed about aging. In addition, we found that greater expectations of social support relate to greater anxiety towards aging, which at first glance may seem contradictory, A closer look may suggest that current perceptions of having a social network help reduce anxiety, while greater concerns with having a social network in the future relates to the anxiety resulting from growing older.

In another model, we attempted to predict two health variables (physical and mental) by regressing them on anxiety toward aging, social support, and stereotyping, while controlling for the remaining health variables. We found significant results whereby perceived mental health and negative stereotyping predicted current evaluations of physical health. In line with previous research findings, negative stereotyping leads to worse evaluations of one's physical health. In contrast, positive evaluations of one's mental health relate to positive evaluations of physical health. We also found that aging anxiety (although marginally) was related to evaluations of current physical health and stereotyping (positive and negative) and significantly related to people's evaluations of their current mental health, suggesting that feeling less anxious about aging and holding stereotypes (positive and negative) about old age relate to better evaluations of one's own mental health. This finding is rather surprising in light of literature suggesting that negative stereotypes relate to worse health outcomes. Thus, these results bring only partial support for previous findings correlating stereotyping and health outcomes (e.g., Hausdorff, Levy, & Wei, 1999; Hess et al., 2003; Levy et al., 2000, 2006; Levy, 2009). That is, stereotypes appear to relate to current health outcomes, however not necessarily in the expected direction.

Nevertheless, we were looking at present day self-report evaluations of health and it is possible that the relationship between stereotyping and health is not yet as relevant as it is expected to be in the future. For instance, according to Levy's (2009) Stereotype Embodiment Theory (SET), old age stereotypes become increasingly relevant to people as they get closer to this stage in their lives.

Thus, the next part of the analysis concentrated on exploring the relationship between predictor variables and expected health outcomes. Model 4d suggests that people's expectations of social support in the future along with their evaluations of current health performance positively relate to their expected performance on physical health. Even so, the effect of expected social support became nonsignificant when other variables like expected mental health (Model 5d) and stereotyping (Model 6d) were introduced. Along the lines of previous findings from the literature, we found that anxiety toward aging negatively predicted expected physical health (Models 5d and 6d). Yet our finding that negative stereotyping positively predicts better expectations of physical health was surprising (Table 7). Nevertheless, in contrast with findings about physical health, negative stereotyping significantly predicted poorer expectations of mental health.

Taken together, our findings suggest that it is not enough to establish better and more efficient interventions for the treatment of chronic illnesses that typically develop during the aging process or to improve income for the elderly. It is necessary to create policies for the care of the elderly up to the end of life. Better and more effective policies for the aging population would make anticipated support attainable (Krause, 2007), leading to the belief that there are people that can help and assist when required. This is important because it diminishes the functional deterioration of the elderly by creating a sense of control and security that promotes their autonomy. The State should be able to reassure the aging population by creating a more efficient network of institutionalized care, as well as fostering the developmental context of aging, thus promoting the wellbeing of older people. Below, we discuss the implications of our findings.

Getting old is a common concern among humans; people worry about losing their abilities and have a hard time tolerating the idea of aging (Aguerre & Bouffard, 2008). The process of aging often brings along physical and cognitive deterioration, and it is possible that the characteristics of the surrounding environment in Colombia are not making the process any easier. Consistently, we did find that controlling for the effect of stereotyping and people's evaluations of current and expected health, perceptions of social support (current and expected) independently predicted aging anxiety, suggesting that social networks are crucial.

Indeed, having a social network constitutes an important asset in the process of aging. This has been known for several decades (see for instance Berkman & Syme, 1979). On the basis of evidence from Latin American communities, it has been hypothesized that social support reduces anxiety due to the feelings of security derived from knowing that someone will be there to help, take care and provide advice in the future (Montero-López & Rivera-Ledesma, 2009). Our findings support this notion.

It appears nonetheless that the support provided by informal networks has decreased due to socioeconomic changes in developing countries. According to Help Age International (2007), despite their active contribution through informal employment and childcare to the family economy, the efforts of older adults are socially undervalued, and family does play an important role in the exclusion of older adults, usually associated with gender and material possessions.

Past evidence suggests that, not only because women have a higher life expectancy than men, but also because in developing countries women are involved in the care of older adults, sick family members and children, policy adjustments are necessary in order to take into account the needs of aging women. Men on the other hand, have a higher risk of losing family leadership and social support from sources other than family once they retire (Help Age International, 2007). Our findings did not show gender differences in relation to aging anxiety, evaluations of health, or expectations of health for the future. We did, however, find differences between men's and women's expectations of social support, such that men had higher expectations of social support for the future than women, which is consistent with women's longer expectations for longevity. However, more research is needed to better explain the implications of this finding.

Given the importance of social support in predicting anxiety toward aging, we set out to explore whether our measured variables had a predictive capacity on people's expectations of social support. We reasoned that people's evaluations of their current health, their level of endorsement of positive and negative stereotypes, their perceptions of social support, and their levels of anxiety towards aging, could predict their expectations of social support in the future. We did find that expectations of social support were positively predicted by socioeconomic status such that people who reported higher socioeconomic status appeared to have better expectations of social support in the future. Additionally, we found that expectations of social support were positively predicted by anxiety toward aging and marginally by negative stereotyping. Further studies are needed to evaluate these relationships. People who reported better evaluations of current mental health reported lower expectations of social support in the future, coming from family, friends, and church. In contrast, people who felt more anxious about aging and held more negative stereotypes reported greater expectations of social support, suggesting that rather than a sense of security, these expectations reflect concern for the future.

This may be consistent with cultural expectations that family is responsible for taking care of their elders, but also with the absence of better policies to protect them given that until very recently, older adults in Colombia were almost exclusively dependent on themselves or their families (Profamilia, 2010). In fact, it is often the case that younger people depend on older adults pensions, savings or income to improve their life quality (Aging and Old Age Policy 2007–2019, 2007; ENDS, 2010) thus increasing the burden of the aging process. This is consistent with Levy and Macdonald (2016) assertion that older adults represent a valuable resource to our societies offering social and economic support and orientation to younger generations and as such, they are a source of wisdom and experience.

More generally, leadership roles (conflict resolution, cultural, religious and health education) traditionally exercised by older adults have undergone significant changes due to the displacement of communal forms of self-government as a result of changes in the family structure, increasing migration, and the fact that formal education and literacy now occupy a more important place among Latin American cultures. In line with Levy and Macdonald (2016), these leadership roles constitute an important asset for our societies. Accordingly, public policy should consider the important role of the elder not only in the context of their families but more broadly of community and society.

Currently, the Aging and Old Age Policy (2007) states that in developing countries compared to other societies, at 60 years of age people may seem old as a reflection of life conditions that limit their ability to grow old in a healthy manner. Aging in these countries, "takes place along with fundamental structural changes in family composition, work patterns, young population's migration to the cities, deepening urbanization processes, and greater participation in the labor market" (p. 10). As a consequence, older adults frequently turn into caregivers for their children with disabilities and their grandchildren. The ENDS (2010) found evidence that 79% of older adults sampled reported to work in order to help their families, or because of being in charge of one to three persons in their family. When pensioned, they tend to become income providers as well. Yet, as pointed out before, their role as providers doesn't protect them from exclusion which is unfortunate given the importance of their contribution.

Social policy should advance more aggressively addressing the inclusion of older people. Nowadays, older adults have the possibility of joining social support groups allowing them to feel somewhat more integrated; notwithstanding, it should also focus on ways to facilitate their integration in regular social networks. This is often linked to labor inclusion policies. The job market in Colombia is filled with young and inexperienced people dealing with difficult positions while older adults are usually disregarded as overqualified or too expensive (they are thought to be closer to pension or may easily fall sick), thus ignoring their knowledge and experience.

Despite efforts to include and improve the living conditions of older adults it is apparent that "Colombia is not ready to face the changes implied in the population aging" (Nieto & Alonso, 2007, p. 300). The worsening conditions in the social network (labor market, family, and friends), together with ageism seem to negatively affect their life quality during the aging process in several ways. In particular the close dependency between older adults and their families (in either direction) adds to the already urgent need to prepare younger generations for caretaking and support in a context of appreciation and respect, thus preventing discrimination, exploitation and other less desirable paths. It is important to seek out interventions that foster positive relations between older adults and their families (Levy, under review).

Findings from this study suggest the need to continue working in this line of research. As this was an exploratory study, the interpretation of some of the findings should be done with caution. First, the correlational nature of the study allowed us to identify significant relations between positive and negative stereotyping, people's evaluations and expectations of social support, feelings of anxiety towards aging, and reported physical and mental health evaluations and expectations. However, it is impossible to establish with certainty the direction of these relations.

Another important limitation of this study is in relation to the sample size, which may have limited our ability to identify significant correlations and may have affected the strength of our measures. Additionally, a bigger sample may allow us to identify important interactions between our variables that would suggest the need to conduct mediational tests. Finally, our measure of health performance consisted of a self-report measure, and it is thus subject to individual biases. Future work can address these issues by including larger samples that would increase the power of the study and allow for more sophisticated statistical tests. Additionally, further investigation should be done to evaluate the relationship between stereotyping and health performance including other assessments of health such as those collected from physicians or medical records.

Conclusion

Results from this study add to the small literature on aging perceptions and well being of older adults in Latin America. This study found that aging anxiety is predicted by social support and negative stereotyping. Additionally, that aging anxiety (though marginally) and positive stereotyping both independently predict mental health, such that more aging anxiety predicts poorer evaluations of mental health while positive stereotyping predicts the opposite, suggesting that positive stereotyping may play a protective role for the elderly. We also found significant relationships between aging anxiety and stereotyping and people's expectations of health performance. Though not all of these relationships were found in the expected ways, this evidence supports the idea that self-stereotyping and aging anxiety may exert and important influence on health by shaping people's expectations and behaviors as they get closer to the old age.

Finally, significant relationships were found between aging anxiety, negative stereotyping and expectations of social support that may suggest that poorer expectations about the aging process bring about greater concerns with social support in the future. More research is needed to explore the relationship between stereotyping, aging anxiety and social support and their joint effect on older people's well being in Colombia.

References

Aguerre, C., & Bouffard, L. (2008). Envejecimiento exitoso: teorías, investigaciones y aplicaciones clínicas. *Revista de la Asociación Colombiana de Gerontología y Geriatría, 22*(2), 1146–1162. From http://www.acgg.org.co/descargas/revista-22-2.pdf#page=31. Accessed at November 7, 2014.

Bai, X., Lai, D. W. L., & Guo, A. (2016). Ageism and depression: Perceptions of older people as a burden in China. *Journal of Social Issues, 72*(1), 26–46.

Bennett, T., & Gaines, J. (2010). Believing what you hear: The impact of aging stereotypes upon the old. *Educational Gerontology, 36*(5), 435–445. doi: 10.1080/03601270903212336.

Beyene, Y., Becker, G., & Mayen, N. (2002). Perception of aging and sense of well-being among Latino elderly. *Journal of Cross Cultural Gerontology*, *17*(2), 155–172. doi: 10.1023/A:1015886816483.

Berkman, L. F., & Syme, S. L. (1979). Social networks, host resistance, and mortality: A nine-year follow-up study of Alameda county residents. *American Journal of Epidemiology*, *109*(2), 186–204.

Bosma, H., Marmot, M. G., Hemingway, H., Nicholson, A., Brunner, E., & Stansfeld, S. (1997). Low job control and risk of coronary heart disease in Whitehall ii (prospective cohort) study. *British Medical Journal*, *314*(7080), 558–565. doi: http://dx.doi.org/10.1136/bmj.314.7080.558.

Bousfield, C., & Hutchison, P. (2010). Contact, anxiety, and young people's attitude and behavioral intentions towards the elderly. *Educational Gerontology*, *36*(6), 452–466. doi: 10.1080/03601270903324362.

Buchman, A., Boyle, P., Wilson, R., James, B., Leurgans, S., Arnold, S., & Bennett, D. (2010). Loneliness and the rate of motor decline in old age: The rush memory and aging project, a community-based cohort study. *Geriatrics*, *10*(77), 1–8. doi: 10.1186/1471-2318-10-77.

Castellanos, F., & López, A. L. (2010). Mirando pasar la vida desde la ventana: significados de la vejez y la discapacidad de un grupo de ancianos en un contexto de pobreza. *Rev Enfermería*, *12*(2), 37–53. From http://www.redalyc.org/pdf/1452/145217280004.pdf. Accessed at November 7, 2014.

Chrisler, J. C., Barney, A., & Palatino, B. (2016). Ageism can be hazardous to women's health: Ageism, sexism, and stereotypes of older women in the healthcare system. *Journal of Social Issues*, *72*(1), 86–104.

CONPES 2793. (1995). *Envejecimiento y vejez*. Vicepresidencia de la República – DNP: UDS. (Aging and Old Age. Office of the Vice-president of Colombia). From http://fondodesolidaridadpensional.gov.co/prosperargel/sites/default/files/normas/Conpes %202793.pdf. Accessed at October 16, 2014.

Da Silva, M. J., & Peixoto Besa, E. M. E. (2008). Conceitos de saúde e doença segundo a óptica dos idosos de baixa renda. *Ciencia y Enfermería*, *14*(1), 23–31. doi: http://dx. doi.org/10.4067/S0717-95532008000100004.

Departamento Nacional de Estadísticas (DANE). (2010). *Proyecciones nacionales y departamentales de población, 2005–2020* (Population projections for 2005–2020, National Department of Statistics, 2010). From https://www.dane.gov.co/files/investigaciones/ poblacion/conciliacenso/7_Proyecciones_poblacion.pdf. Accessed at October 16, 2014.

Giraldo, C. I., Franco, G. M., Correa, L. S., Salazar, M. O., & Tamayo, A. M. (2005). Cuidadores familiares de ancianos: quiénes son y cómo asumen este rol. *Rev Fac Nac Salud Pública*, *23*(2), 7–15. From http://www.scielo.org.co/scielo. php?script=sci_arttext&pid=S0120-386×2005000200002&lng =en&tlng=es. Accessed at November 7, 2014.

Gonçalves, D. C. (2009). From loving grandma to working with older adults: promoting positive attitudes towards aging. *Educational Gerontology*, *35*(3), 202–225. doi: 10.1080/03601270802466884.

Harris, L. A., & Dollinger, S. (2001). Participation in a course on aging: Knowledge, attitudes, and anxiety about aging in oneself and others. *Educational Gerontology*, *27*(8), 657–667. doi: 10.1080/036012701317117893.

Hausdorff, J. M., Levy B. R., & Wei, J. Y. (1999) The power of ageism on physical function of older persons: Reversibility of age-related gait changes. *Journal of the American Geriatrics Society*, *47*(11), 1346–1349.

Hawkley, L. C., Thisted, R. A., Masi, C. M., & Cacioppo, J. T. (2010). Loneliness predicts increased blood pressure: Five-year cross-lagged analysis in middle-aged and older adults. *Psychology and Aging*, *25*(1), 132–141. doi: 10.1037/a0017805.

Help Age International: Acción Global sobre el Envejecimiento. (2007). *El informe sobre envejecimiento y el desarrollo: un resumen. Pobreza, independencia y las personas mayores en el mundo*. Londres. From http://www.sld.cu/galerias/pdf/ sitios/gericuba/informe_sobre_env_y_desarrollo_1.pdf. Accessed at November 4, 2014.

Hess, T., Auman, C., Colcombe, S., & Rahhal, T. (2003). The impact of stereotype threat on age differences in memory performance. *Journal of Gerontology: Psychological Sciences*, *58*(1), P3–P11.

Hummert, M. L. (2007). As family members age: A research agenda for family communication. *Journal of Family Communication*, *7*(1), 3–21. doi: 10.1080/15267430709336666.

Kite, M. E., Stockdale, G. D., Whitley, B. R., & Johnson, B. T. (2005). Attitudes toward younger and older adults: An updated meta-analytic review. *Journal of Social Issues*, *61*(2), 241–266. doi: 10.1111/j.1540-4560.2005.00404.x.

Kornadt, A., & Rothermund, K. (2015). Views on aging: Domain-specific approaches and implications for developmental regulation. *Annual Review of Gerontology and Geriatrics*, *35*(1), 121–144, doi: 10.1891/0198-8794.35.121.

Krause, N. (2007). Longitudinal study of social support and meaning in life. *Psychology and Aging*, *22*(3), 456–469. doi: 10.1037/0882-7974.22.3.456.

Lakra, D. C., Ng, R., & Levy, B. R. (2012). Increased longevity from viewing retirement positively, *Aging & Society*, *32*(8), 1418–1427. doi: http://dx.doi.org/10.1017/S0144686×11000985.

Lauzen, M. M., & Dozier, D. M. (2005). Maintaining the double standard: Portrayals of age and gender in popular films. *Sex Roles*, *52*(7-8), 437–446. doi: 10.1007/s11199-005-3710-1.

Lasagni, V. X., Bernal, R., del Rosario Tuzzo, M., Rodríguez, M. S., Heredia, D., Muñoz, L. M., Palermo, N., Torrealba, L. M., Crespo, E., Gavira, G., Palacios, M., Villarroel, C. I., Fahmy, W. M., Charamelo, A., & Díaz, P. (2013). Estereotipos negativos hacia la vejez en personas mayores de Latinoamérica. *Revista Kairós Gerontologia*, *16*(4), 9–23.

Levy, B. R. (2009). Stereotype embodiment: A psychosocial approach to aging. *Current Directions in Psychological Science*, *18*(6), 332–336.

Levy, B. R. (2001). Eradication of ageism requires addressing the enemy within. *The Gerontologist*, *41*(5), 578–579. doi: 10.1093/geront/41.5.578.

Levy, B. R., Housdorff, J. M., Hencke, R., & Wei, J. Y. (2000). Reducing cardiovascular stress with positive self-stereotypes of aging. *Journal of Gerontology: Psychological Sciences*, *55*(4), P205–P213. doi: 10.1093/geronb/55.4.P205.

Levy, B. R., Kasl, S. V., & Gill, T. M. (2004). Image of aging scale. *Perceptual and Motor Skills*, *99*(1), 208–210.

Levy, S. R. (under review). Reducing ageism: PEACE (Positive Education about Aging and Contact Experiences) Model.

Levy, S. R., & Macdonald, J. L. (2016). Progress on understanding ageism. *Journal of Social Issues*, *72*(1), 5–25. doi:10.1111/josi.12153.

Levy, B. R., Slade, M. D., & Gill, T. M. (2006). Hearing decline predicted by elders' age stereotypes. *Journal of Gerontology: Psychological Sciences*, *61*(2), 82–87. Retireved from: http://psychsocgerontology.oxfordjournals.org/content/61/2/P82.full.pdf+html

Ley 100. (1993). Congreso de la República de Colombia (Social Security Law of 1993. Colombian National Congress) From http://www.alcaldiabogota.gov.co/sisjur/normas/Norma1.jsp?i = 5248. Accessed at November 7, 2014.

Macdonald, J. L., & Levy, S. R. (2016). Ageism in the workplace: The role of psychosocial factors in predicting job satisfaction, commitment, and engagement. *Journal of Social Issues*, *72*(1), 169–190.

Montero-López Lena, M., & Rivera-Ledesma, A. (2009). Variables con alto valor adaptativo en el desajuste psicológico del adulto mayor del adulto mayor. *Journal of Behavior, Health & Social Issues*, *1*(1), 59–67. doi: http://dx.doi.org/10.5460/jbhsi.v1.1.382.

Nelson, T. (2009). Ageism. In T. Nelson (Ed.), *Handbook of prejudice, stereotyping, and discrimination* (pp. 431–440). New York, NY, US: Psychology Press.

Ng, R., Monin, J. K., Allore, H. G., & Levy, B. R. (2016). Retirement as meaningful: Positive retirement stereotypes associated with longevity. *Journal of Social Issues*, *72*(1), 69–85.

Nieto, M. L., & Alonso, L. M. (2007). ¿Está preparado nuestro país para asumir los retos que plantea el envejecimiento poblacional? *Salud Uninorte*, *23*(2), 292–301. http://rcientificas.uninorte.edu.co/index.php/salud/article/view/4043

Palmore, E. B. (1999). *Ageism: Negative and positive* (2nd ed.). New York: Springer.

Perissinotto, C. M., Stijacic Cenzer, I., Covinsky, K. E. (2012) Loneliness in older persons: A predictor of functional decline and death. *Archives of Internal Medicine, 172*(14), 1078–1084. doi: 10.1001/archinternmed.1993.

Política Nacional de Envejecimiento y Vejez 2007–2019. (2007). Ministerio de la Protección Social. (National Policy on Aging and Old Age. Social Protection –Health- Ministry). From http://www.minsalud.gov.co/Documentos%20y%20Publicaciones/POL%C3%8DTICA %20NACIONAL%20DE%20ENVEJECIMIENTO%20Y%20VEJEZ.pdf. Accessed at November 7, 2014.

Pope, E. H. (2012). A longer life is lived with company. *New York Times.* From http://www.nytimes.com/2012/09/12/business/retirementspecial/for-older-adults-close -connections-are-key-to-healthy-aging.html?module=Search&mabReward=relbias%3Ar. Accessed at November 7, 2014.

Profamilia. (2010). *Encuesta Nacional de Demografía y Salud (ENDS) 2010.* From http://www.profamilia.org.co/encuestas/Profamilia/Profamilia/index.php?option= com_content&view=article&id=62&Itemid=9. Accessed at October 16, 2014.

Shankar, A., McMunn, A., Banks, J., & Steptoe, A. (2011). Loneliness, social isolation, and behavioral and biological health indicators in older adults. *Journal of Health Psychology, 30*(4), 377–385. doi: 10.1037/a0022826.

Travis, C. B., Howerton, D. M., & Szymanski, D. M. (2012). Risk, uncertainty, and gender stereotypes in healthcare decisions. *Women & Therapy, 35*(3-4), 207–220. doi: 10.1080/02703149.2012.684589.

World Health Organization (WHO). (2014). *10 facts on ageing and the life course.* From http://www.who.int/features/factfiles/ageing/ageing_facts/en/. Accessed at November 7, 2014.

LUISA RAMÍREZ is currently a Professor of Psychology at Universidad del Rosario, Colombia. Dr. Ramírez earned an MD in Political Science at Universidad de Los Andes in Colombia in 2001, and her PhD in Social Psychology at Stony Brook University in New York in 2007. Her research interests include beliefs about social categories, prejudice and discrimination and implications for social policy and inclusion.

XIMENA PALACIOS is a Professor of Psychology at Universidad del Rosario, Colombia. Dr. Palacios earned a Master in Clinical and Health Psychology at Universidad de Granada (Spain) in 2000, and her Doctorate in Social Psychology at Università di Bologna in Italy in 2013. Her research interests include psychological and social aspects of physical chronic illness and palliative care.

Journal of Social Issues, Vol. 72, No. 1, 2016, pp. 69–85
doi: 10.1111/josi.12156

Retirement as Meaningful: Positive Retirement Stereotypes Associated with Longevity

Reuben Ng[*]

Yale School of Public Health and Nanyang Technological University

Heather G. Allore

Yale School of Public Health and Yale School of Medicine

Joan K. Monin and Becca R. Levy

Yale School of Public Health

Studies examining the association between retirement and health have produced mixed results. This may be due to previous studies treating retirement as merely a change in job status rather than a transition associated with stereotypes or societal beliefs (e.g., retirement is a time of mental decline or retirement is a time of growth). To examine whether these stereotypes are associated with health, we studied retirement stereotypes and survival over a 23-year period among 1,011 older adults. As predicted by stereotype embodiment theory, it was found that positive stereotypes about physical health during retirement showed a survival advantage of 4.5 years (hazard ratio = 0.88, p = .022) and positive stereotypes about mental health during retirement tended to show a survival advantage of 2.5 years (hazard ratio = 0.87, p = .034). Models adjusted for relevant covariates such as age, gender, race, employment status, functional health, and self-rated health. These results suggest that retirement preparation could benefit from considering retirement stereotypes.

Research studies examining the association between retirement and health have produced mixed results. For example, studies have found that retirement leads to worse health (e.g., Bamia, Trichopoulou, & Trichopoulos, 2007), better health (e.g., Coe & Zamarro, 2011) or has no effect on health (Kasl & Jones, 2000). This may be due to previous studies treating retirement as merely a change in job status rather than a transition associated with stereotypes or societal beliefs (e.g., retirement is a time of mental decline or retirement is a time of growth). Given the social, emotional and cultural complexities of retirement, McVittie

---

*Correspondence concerning this article should be addressed to Reuben Ng [e-mail: reuben.ng@yale.edu; reuben_ng@hotmail.com].

69

and Goodall (2012) challenged researchers to study perception and stereotypes toward retirement. Taking up this challenge, we investigated how stereotypes toward mental and physical health during retirement impact mortality risk in a 23-year prospective cohort study.

Lakra, Ng, and Levy (2012) were the first to conduct such a study, and found that more positive retirement stereotypes were associated with longevity in an American cohort of older adults. In this study, retirement stereotypes were conceptualized as a single variable. In the following study, we built on this previous study by examining whether the multiple meanings individuals attach to retirement may also have a health benefit (Franca, 2004; Sargent, Lee, Martin, & Zikic, 2013). Despite the American context of the aforementioned and present studies, we believe that the focus on the plural meanings of retirement has wider geographical applicability given the cultural universality of retirement as a life milestone (McVittie & Goodall, 2012). These multiple meanings can be grouped as value and theme (Ajzen, 2001; Eagly & Chaiken, 1993).

With regard to value, retirement stereotypes can either be positive or negative. For example, from selling financial plans to travel packages, advertisers typically portray negative images of grumpy and listless elders who could be transformed into beaming "golden agers" basking in the Florida sun by buying their products and services (Ekerdt & Clark, 2001). Similarly, a cross-sectional study among nonacademic employees at an American university found that 65% viewed retirement positively whereas 35% regarded retirement as a negative stage of life. Those with positive retirement stereotypes tended to look forward to retirement as a new phase of life with more time for hobbies and travel while negative thinkers fear the potential loss of the meaning that the work afforded (Fillenbaum, 1971).

Several studies show that stereotypic value is associated with health: Elders with positive perceptions about aging lived 7.5 years longer than peers who think negatively after adjusting for functional health and other covariates (Levy, Slade, Kunkel, & Kasl, 2002); positive age stereotypes have also been associated with better memory (Levy, Zonderman, Slade, & Ferrucci, 2012), and recovery from disability (Levy, Slade, Murphy, & Gill, 2012). Specific to retirement stereotypes, Lakra et al. (2012) found that positive retirement stereotypes were associated with 41% decreased mortality risk.

With respect to theme, retirement stereotypes often center on mental or physical health (Bailey, 1999; Franca, 2004). The former (mental) focus on expectations of one's mental state during retirement, such as living a life full of meaningfulness or loneliness. The latter (physical) focus on expectations of one's physical health, such as living a life full of activity or illness. In the media, images of retirement that are typically used to market services are often thematically driven. Images of glowing physical health that follows retirement are portrayed by fit and active elders who embark on adventures to far-flung destinations as a way to sell travel packages (Savishinsky, 2001), whereas medical companies often show older individuals who suffer from physical problems that need their products (Franca, 2004). On the other hand, dating agencies conjure images of fulfilled elders who found renewed meaning in life through new romantic endeavors whereas television shows often portray older characters who show confusion or forgetfulness (Bailey, 1999; Donlon, Ashman, & Levy, 2005). This dual theme also emerged in Finnish magazines targeted at readers above 50 years (Lumme-Sandt, 2011), and prime time TV in Germany (Kessler, Schwender, & Bowen, 2010). Similar themes have been found in both qualitative studies that interviewed retirees (Pepin & Deutscher, 2011), and quantitative ones, such as the Hartford Retirement Survey (2012).

Research suggests that two themes of retirement stereotypes may affect retirees differently (Franca, 2004). Retirement stereotypes toward mental health are associated with adjustment issues while retirement stereotypes toward physical health are related to health outcomes (Rosenkoetter & Garris, 1998). In a laboratory study, Levy and Leffheit-Limson (2009) found support for the stereotype-matching effect that mental and physical age stereotypes influenced health in different ways. When elders were primed with negative words describing mental states (e.g., dementia, confused), they performed poorer on mental tasks (memory tests) than physical ones (timed chair-stand tests). Likewise, priming elders with negative words on physical states (e.g., feeble, shaky), they performed worse on physical tasks than mental ones. Taken together, it seems useful to examine whether age stereotypes toward mental and physical health impact mortality risk. There are no known studies on how stereotype theme influences mortality.

Our study is the first to investigate how cross categorizations of theme and value for retirement stereotypes influence mortality risk. We draw support from two theoretical frameworks: life course perspective (Settersten, 1998; Wang & Shultz, 2010) and stereotype embodiment theory (Levy, 2009). The life course perspective posits that personal characteristics and situational context influence the experience of life's milestones such as retirement (Wang, Henkens, & van Solinge, 2011). We focus on personal characteristics and argue that retirement stereotypes, heretofore not considered by the life course perspective, play a role in retirement health.

Stereotype embodiment theory (SET; Levy, 2009) proposes that age stereotypes (beliefs about older adults) are internalized across the lifespan, gain relevance as one approaches old age, and ultimately affect one's health. Against this background, SET provides a theoretical basis to explain how retirement stereotypes could exert an effect on mortality risk: internalizing negative retirement stereotypes that become self-relevant as one approaches retirement. These negative age stereotypes may translate into negative health behaviors that further impact mortality risk.

Based on prior evidence, Hypothesis 1 is that participants with more positive stereotypes toward mental health during retirement will have greater longevity, controlling for age, gender, race, marital status, employment, work attitudes, education, self-rated health and functional health. Likewise, Hypothesis 2 states that those with positive stereotypes toward physical health during retirement will have greater longevity, controlling for the same covariates. We controlled for these covariates because they are potential confounders. For example, through a nationally representative cohort study in Poland, Bartoszewska, Tobiasz-Adamczyk, Brzyski, and Kopacz (2007) found that both employment status and work attitudes, defined as how positive one is toward work, are associated with mortality risk. Work attitudes were also found to influence retirement attitudes (Gordon, 1994), and no known studies have investigated the relative influence of both factors on mortality risk. Against this backdrop, we aimed to extend previous research by investigating how different themes of retirement stereotypes relate to survival; cross categorizing the influence of themes (mental, physical) and value (positive, negative); and exploring the impact of retirement stereotypes, adjusting for work attitudes, on survival.

Methods

Participants

The study cohort consisted of participants in the Ohio Longitudinal Study of Aging and Retirement (OLSAR), a prospective study by the Scripps Gerontology Center at Miami University (Atchley, 1999). Retirement stereotypes were measured at baseline and participants were followed for 23 years. Time of death was ascertained through the National Death Index (NDI), and the mean age of death is 79.6 years ($SD = 0.43$). The OLSAR was designed as a longitudinal study of residents of Oxford, Ohio who were over the age of 50 on July 1, 1975 (Atchley, 1999). With the use of voter registration records, welfare records, a postcard census that was mailed to all addresses in the area, and a review of the telephone directory by long-standing members of the community, 1,805 prospective participants were identified. All prospective participants were contacted and data were collected primarily by mail. Participants unable to complete the questionnaire, usually due to visual impairments, were followed-up by telephone and interviewed. For participation in the OLSAR, individuals had to be residents of the community, at least 50 years of age on July 1, 1975 and without cognitive impairment. Of those who met this criterion, 1,018 agreed to participate.

Of the 1018 participants, no vital statistics existed for seven individuals, leaving a usable sample of 1,011. However, 446 participants did not disclose their race and/or employment status but had data on other variables. Rather than exclude them, we included them by creating a category "undisclosed." For race,

Table 1. Description of the Sample According to Participants' Stereotypes toward Physical Health during Retirement

	Retirement stereotypes toward physical health		
	Negative	Positive	
Characteristic	($N = 770$)	($N = 241$)	p^1
Age (years)	64.72	64.09	.379
Sex			.450
Male	327	109	
Female	443	132	
Race			.771
Whites	579	176	
Non-Whites	27	10	
Undisclosed	164	55	
Employment			.084
Retired	266	88	
Employed	254	92	
Housewife	18	8	
Undisclosed	232	53	
Marital status			.146
Single	53	21	
Married	467	151	
Widowed	219	54	
Divorced/separated	31	15	
Self-rated health	4.02	3.96	.288
Work attitude	4.04	4.07	.569
Functional health	1.91	2.00	.265

Note. Table values are mean $\pm$ *SD* for continuous variables and *n* for categorical variables.
[1] The *p* value is for t-test (continuous variables) or χ^2 test (categorical variables).

74.7% self-identified as Whites, 3.7% non-Whites, and 21.7% did not disclose. For employment, 35% self-reported as retired, 34.2% employed, 2.6% housewives, and 28.2% did not disclose. Thereafter, we were concerned whether non-disclosure on race and employment biased their answers on retirement stereotypes. Our concerns were unfounded: there were no significant differences in retirement stereotypes toward mental health across race ($F = 0.71, p = .49$) and employment ($F = 0.81, p = .49$); likewise, no statistical differences for retirement stereotypes toward physical health across race ($F = 0.44, p = .64$) and employment ($F = 0.55, p = .65$). With respect to other demographics, which were representative of the town (see Tables 1 and 2), there were 55.2% female, 74% married, and a mean age of 62.77 ($SD = 9.26$; range: 50–94 years).

Table 2. Description of the Sample According to Participants' Stereotypes toward Mental Health during Retirement

	Retirement stereotypes toward mental health		
	Negative	Positive	
Characteristic	($N = 782$)	($N = 229$)	p[1]
Age (years)	64.49	64.83	.640
Sex			.734
Male	335	101	
Female	447	128	
Race			.077
Whites	596	159	
Non-Whites	29	8	
Undisclosed	157	62	
Employment			.873
Retired	277	77	
Employed	264	82	
Housewife	19	7	
Undisclosed	222	63	
Marital status			.194
Single	51	23	
Married	476	142	
Widowed	220	53	
Divorced/separated	35	11	
Self-rated health	4.01	4.01	.944
Work attitude	4.03	4.08	.422
Functional health	1.92	1.97	.631

Note. Table values are mean $\pm$ *SD* for continuous variables and n for categorical variables.
[1]The *p* value is for t-test (continuous variables) or χ^2 test (categorical variables).

Measures

Retirement Stereotypes

Participants were asked what "best describes what you think about your life in retirement—and how your life is or will be during your retirement" (Atchley, 1999) by rating 14 pairs of adjectives. Two factors emerged from the confirmatory factor analysis (reported below). Ten measured stereotypes toward mental health during retirement (bad–good, inactive–active, sad–happy, uninvolved–involved, hopeless–hopeful, worthless–worthy, dissatisfied–satisfied, empty–full, idle–busy, meaningless–meaningful), while four measured stereotypes toward physical health during retirement (immobile–mobile, sick–healthy, unable–able, dependent–independent). The reliabilities, as measured by Cronbach's α, are 0.79 (95% CI: 0.71, 0.87) and 0.91 (95% CI: 0.87, 0.95), respectively.

For each pair, participants selected a score from one to seven that best reflected their retirement life, such that a higher score indicated a more positive evaluation. For example, the meaningless–meaningful pair would score from 1 (*extremely meaningless*) to 7 (*extremely meaningful*). To facilitate Kaplan–Meier analyses, we created dichotomous versions using a median split as recommended by Chida and Steptoe (2008); scores above the median indicated positive stereotypes. Both dichotomous and continuous versions were used in subsequent analyses. Descriptions of the sample according to both stereotypic themes are presented in Tables 1 and 2.

Covariates

Age, gender, race, marital status, employment status, years of education, work attitudes, functional health, and self-rated health were entered as covariates to adjust for their effects when exploring the stereotype–mortality link. Marital status was classified into two groups (married, not married). Attitude toward work was measured by "how do you feel about work?" from 1 (*strongly dislike work*) to 5 (*strongly enjoy work*). Rosow and Breslau's (1966) six-item Guttmann Health Scale for the Aged measured functional health, defined as the degree to which one can manage adequately or are restricted in their activities because of their physical condition or capacity. Sample items include "able to walk up and down the stairs to the second floor" on a yes/no response format. Self-rated health was answered on a 5-point scale, from 1 (*very poor*) to 5 (*very good*).

Outcome

Survival is the primary outcome of interest. We used the number of days participants survived from baseline interview in 1975 to January 1, 1998, the date for mortality data obtained from the National Death Index (NDI). Consistent with previous studies, death was ascertained through a vital-status protocol based on NDI information that matched the deceased on three criteria: first and last name; date of birth; and state that death happened (Levy, Kunkel, Remmes, & Slade, 2004). To be considered dead, individuals needed to either meet all three or two of the three criteria with added confirmation by an obituary and/or informant. If individuals only tallied with the NDI data by birth date and location of death, to be considered dead they also had to match on first name (some individuals changed their last name with marriage/divorce). On the other hand, to be grouped as living, individuals were (a) verified as alive through January 1, 1998 by participants themselves; (b) verified to be alive through January 1, 1998, by an informant with no record on the NDI; (c) listed in the NDI but sent in a survey response after the

NDI death date. This method was consistent with previous studies (Levy et al., 2002).

Analytic Plan

We followed a three-step plan. First, we conducted a confirmatory factor analysis (CFA) on the retirement stereotypes scale to show factor consistency with previous validations (Lakra, Ng, & Levy, 2012; Ng & Rayner, 2010). Multiple indices are used to evaluate model fit in our CFA. A common evaluation of model fit is to use the Root Mean Square Error Approximation (RMSEA; Steiger & Lind, 1980). The RMSEA measures discrepancy per degree of freedom and imposes a penalty for adding complexity to a model without substantially improving model fit. Smaller RMSEA reflect better model fit, with values less than .05 denoting a "close fit," between .05 and .08 corresponds to an "acceptable" fit, and RMSEA values larger than .10 suggest a "poor fit" (Browne & Cudeck, 1989). The Comparative Fit Index (CFI) and the Tucker–Lewis index (TLI) measure the relative reduction in model misfit when comparing the target model to a baseline (independence) model. CFI and TLI values greater than .90 are an indication of acceptable model fit to the observed data. We reported the χ^2, CFI, TLI, and RMSEA.

Second, we checked the correlation between the two factors of retirement stereotypes: mental and physical health, and expected a moderately-high correlation. To avoid multicollinearity, we ran separate Cox regression models for mental and physical well-being to test each factor's association with all-cause mortality, controlling for covariates. Third, for the two types of retirement stereotypes, we performed Kaplan–Meier analyses to assess differences in survival between positive and negative thinkers. Both curves were compared using the log-rank statistic.

Results

Confirmatory Factor Analysis

Consistent with previous studies, we achieved a good fit for the two-factor structure of retirement stereotypes in our sample, χ^2 (76) = 621.32, CFI = .92, TLI = .89, RMSEA = .07. The two factors are retirement stereotypes toward mental well-being, and retirement stereotypes toward physical well-being. Given that both factors were highly correlated at $r = 0.6, p < .001$, we ran separate Cox regression models to avoid multicollinearity.

Description of Sample by Retirement Stereotypes

When categorizing participants into positive and negative retirement stereotypes, we were surprised that the majority of our sample espoused negative retirement stereotypes: 76% were negative about physical health, and 77% about mental health during retirement. These stereotypes were not different by age, gender, race, marital status, education, work attitudes, functional health, and self-rated health (see Tables 1 and 2). Importantly, we found no bias of employment status on retirement stereotypes, meaning that retirement stereotypes are not significantly different for those before and after retirement. Cox Regression and Kaplan–Meier Analysis

As predicted, Cox regression (Table 3) elucidated that positive retirement stereotypes toward mental health was protective against all-cause mortality (hazard ratio $= 0.87, p = .034$), supporting Hypothesis 1. Every unit increase, that is, more positive stereotypes about mental health, decreased the risk of mortality by 13% after controlling for age, gender, race, marital status, employment, education, work attitudes, functional health, and self-rated health. Other significant predictors of mortality in the sample: older participants evidenced higher risk of mortality (hazard ratio $= 1.07, p = .0001$), females face lower mortality risks than males (hazard ratio $= 0.68, p = .0001$), better self-rated health is associated with lower mortality risk (hazard ratio $= 0.79, p = .0001$), and more positive work attitudes are associated with decreased mortality risk, (hazard ratio $= 0.89, p = .044$). Next, we performed a Kaplan–Meier analysis to examine differences in survival between groups (see Figure 1). At the 52nd percentile, participants with positive stereotypes toward mental health had a survival benefit of 2.5 years relative to those with negative stereotypes (log-rank test: $\chi^2 = 7.28, p = .007$).

With respect to retirement stereotypes toward physical health (Table 4), we found it to be protective against mortality (hazard ratio $= 0.88, p = .022$), supporting Hypothesis 2. Every unit increase, that is, more positive stereotypes about physical health, decreases the risk of mortality by 12% after controlling for gender, age, race, marital status, education, employment, work attitudes, functional health, and self-rated health. Other significant predictors of mortality are similar to those of stereotypes toward mental health (see Table 2). A Kaplan–Meier analysis found that participants with positive stereotypes toward physical health had a survival benefit of 4.5 years relative to those with negative stereotypes (log-rank test: $\chi^2 = 20.16, p < .0001$) at the 54th percentile (see Figure 2).

We repeated both the Cox regression and Kaplan–Meier analyses on the reduced sample ($N = 565$)—deleted list-wise due to missing data on race and employment—and found similar patterns of results. Stereotypes toward physical health during retirement was protective against mortality (hazard ratio $= 0.81, p = .006$); stereotypes toward mental health during retirement was also protective of mortality (hazard ratio $= 0.77, p = .004$), controlling for similar covariates.

Discussion

Unlike previous studies that treated retirement as merely a change in job status, we assessed stereotypes toward this transition, and found a significant

Table 3. Positive Stereotypes toward Mental Health during Retirement is Protective against Mortality Risk

Predictor	Hazard ratio (95% CI[1])	p
Retirement stereotypes toward mental health[2]	0.87 (0.76–0.99)	.034
Age	1.074 (1.06–1.09)	<.001
Gender		
Males	Reference	
Females	0.68 (0.56–0.81)	<.001
Race	1.43 (0.99–2.06)	
Whites	Reference	
Non-Whites	1.43 (0.99–2.06)	.059
Undisclosed[3]	1.27 (1.04–1.55)	.017
Marital status		
Single	Reference	
Married	1.066 (0.77–1.49)	.704
Widowed	0.84 (0.60–1.18)	.311
Divorced/separated	1.25 (0.77–2.01)	.369
Employment status		
Retired	Reference	
Employed	0.78 (0.60–1.01)	.056
Housewife	0.62 (0.30–1.27)	.190
Undisclosed[4]	0.82 (0.64–1.05)	.118
Education[5]	1.01 (0.99–1.05)	.279
Work attitudes[6]	0.89 (0.79–0.997)	.044
Functional health[7]	0.98 (0.88–1.08)	.649
Self-rate health[8]	0.79 (0.71–0.89)	<.001

Note.
[1] Confidence intervals.
[2] Higher scores denote more positive stereotypes.
[3] This category was created to include 22% of the sample missing race information.
[4] This category was created to include 28% of the sample missing employment status.
[5] Number of years of education.
[6] Higher scores represent more positive work attitudes.
[7] Higher scores indicate better functional health.
[8] Higher scores indicate better self-rated health.

association with mortality risk after adjusting for age, gender, race, marital status, employment status, years of education, work attitudes, functional health, and self-rated health. Specifically, we investigated how different themes of retirement stereotypes (mental and physical), and the cross-categorization with stereotypic value (positive and negative) impact mortality. Participants who espoused positive stereotypes about mental and physical health during retirement lived longer than

Table 4. Positive Stereotypes toward Physical Health during Retirement is Protective against Mortality Risk

Predictor	Hazard ratio (95% CI[1])	p
Retirement stereotypes toward physical health[2]	0.88 (0.78–0.98)	.022
Age	1.07 (1.06–1.09)	<.001
Gender		
Males	Reference	
Females	0.68 (0.57–0.82)	<.001
Race		
Whites	Reference	
Non-Whites	1.40 (0.97–2.03)	.071
Undisclosed[3]	1.26 (1.04–1.54)	.021
Marital status		
Single	Reference	
Married	1.07 (0.77–1.50)	.673
Widowed	0.84 (0.60–1.18)	.322
Divorced/separated	1.24 (0.77–2.01)	.373
Employment status		
Retired	Reference	
Employed	0.77 (0.60–0.998)	.048
Housewife	0.61 (0.30–1.25)	.177
Undisclosed[4]	0.80 (0.63–1.03)	.077
Education[5]	1.02 (0.99–1.05)	.272
Work attitudes[6]	0.88 (0.79–0.993)	.038
Functional health[7]	0.98 (0.87–1.07)	.557
Self-rate health[8]	0.80 (0.71–0.90)	<.001

Note.
[1]Confidence intervals.
[2]Higher scores denote more positive stereotypes.
[3]This category was created to include 22% of the sample missing race information.
[4]This category was created to include 28% of the sample missing employment status.
[5]Number of years of education.
[6]Higher scores represent more positive work attitudes.
[7]Higher scores indicate better functional health.
[8]Higher scores indicate better self-rated health.

negative thinkers, 2.5 and 4.5 years respectively. Another novel finding is that positive work attitudes are associated with decreased mortality risk, though its impact is smaller than retirement stereotypes, and retirement stereotypes predicted longevity adjusting for work attitudes.

These findings underscore the importance of studying stereotypes toward major life transitions like retirement, and make two theoretical contributions. First, we contributed to the psychosocial approach to aging by showing that beyond positive age stereotypes (Levy, 2009), positive work attitudes and retirement stereotypes

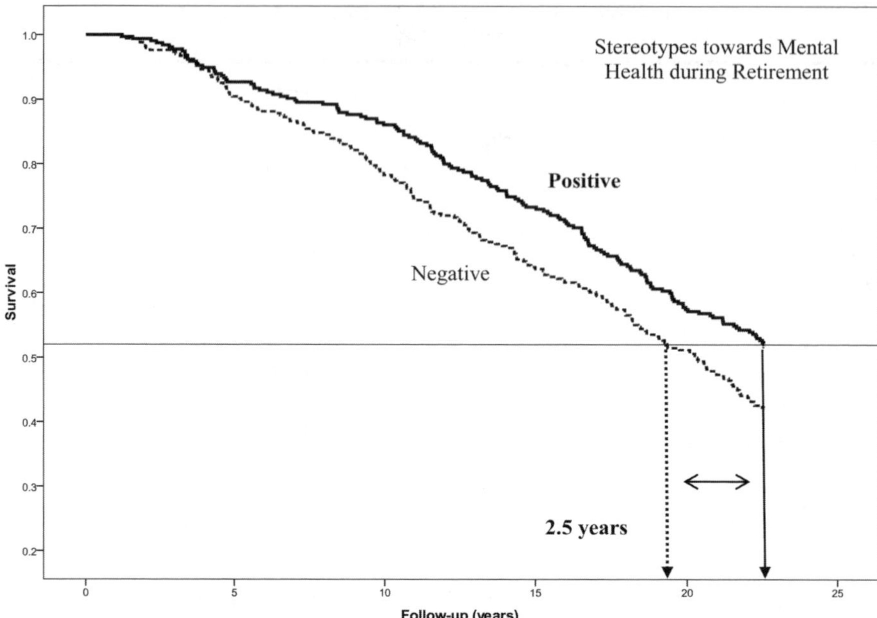

Fig. 1. Influence of positive stereotypes toward mental health during retirement on survival. At the 52nd percentile, survival difference was 2.5 years apart.

toward physical and mental health are also protective against mortality. In essence, the stereotype embodiment theory (SET) provides four tenets to explain our findings: (a) retirement stereotypes are likely part of the many concepts that we take in at a young age and are internalized across the lifespan; (b) operates unconsciously; (c) gain salience from self-relevance especially near retirement; (d) employ multiple mediating pathways to impact mortality. Construed based on age stereotypes, we also show that SET can be extended to explain how retirement stereotypes influence mortality risk.

Our second contribution is showing that retirement stereotypes consist of two components, and both are protective against mortality risk. Previous studies considered retirement stereotypes as a single entity without examining their multifactorial nature (Eagly & Chaiken, 1993; Franca, 2004). It is possible that these different components work via different pathways to impact mortality. Drawing from previous studies, potential mediators include better adjustment (Rosenkoetter & Garris, 1998), greater will to live (Levy et al., 2002), aging anxiety (Ramírez & Palacios-Espinosa, 2016), and depression (Bai, Lai, & Guo, 2016) for the mental health-mortality link. On the other hand, positive health behaviors (Levy, Ng,

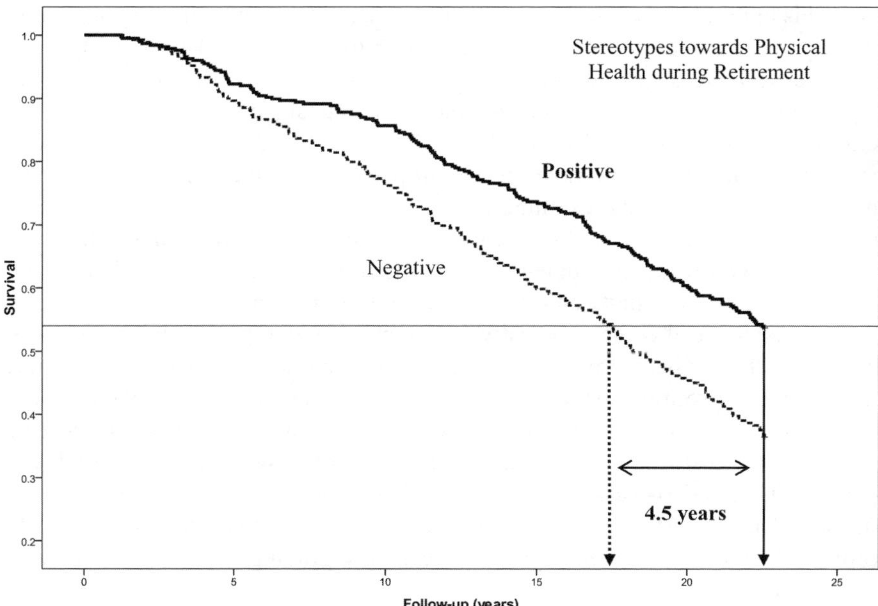

Fig. 2. Influence of positive stereotypes toward physical health during retirement on survival. At the 54th percentile, survival difference was 4.5 years apart.

Myers, & Marottoli, 2004) are potential mediators of the physical health-mortality link. Future studies should test these ideas.

One potential limitation is the (in)stability of retirement stereotypes over time. Goudy, Powers, Keith, and Reger (1980) measured retirement stereotypes of 1,152 participants who were 50 years and employed. Ten years later, they found no significant changes in attitudes. Though retirement stereotypes were shown to be stable, negative stereotypes may be a result of poor health rather than what one thinks about retirement. To reduce this likelihood, we controlled for ratings of functional health, and self-rated health in our model.

Given the harmful effects of negative retirement stereotypes on survival, it is essential to think about changing mindsets. We were somewhat taken aback by the majority of participants expressing negativity toward physical and mental health during retirement. The numbers underscore the state of ageism as perpetuated by the media and society (Dennis & Thomas, 2007; Ng, Allore, Trentalange, Monin, & Levy, 2015). Importantly, the negativity of retirement stereotypes did not differ across age groups in the sample, suggesting that it is not a cohort effect but an entrenched attitude toward retirement.

This highlights an emerging social issue that elders are both psychologically ill-prepared for retirement and generally negative about it. This is worrisome because negative attitudes toward retirement are associated poorer health and higher mortality risk. That baby boomers are retiring in record numbers will only exacerbate this social issue. To manage this social issue, there is a need for social policies that promote retirement preparation, specifically focusing on psychological well-being: examine current retirement stereotypes and promoting the adoption of positive mindsets with regard to mental and physical health during retirement. These social policies lay the ground work for preventive health and resilience against mortality and ill health during retirement.

On the societal front, as negative retirement stereotypes are internalized, in part, from the media, we recommend that guidelines can be drafted to minimize the tendency to portray older adults negatively, especially in a medicalized manner where elders are discussed alongside medical terms and chronic conditions (Ng et al., 2015). Instead, we encourage writing about positive aspects—kindness, perseverance, and successful aging—to balance increases in negative reporting of the elderly. Overtime, these positive age stereotypes could be internalized to promote greater appreciation for an increasingly graying population and better public health.

Despite the American context of the present study, related studies bolster its relevance across cultures. Löckenhoff et al. (2009) found that age stereotypes are mostly negative across 26 countries with striking similarity in content. Moreover, other studies in this issue reported links between negative age stereotypes and psychopathology: aging anxiety (Ramírez & Palacios-Espinosa, 2016) and depression (Ng, Ang, & Ho, 2012; Bai et al., 2016). Taken together, the relevance of retirement, consistent prevalence of age stereotypes and its negative impact, underscore the need to study the stereotypes of retirement, and its impact on health and longevity across cultures. While the impact of negative stereotypes on retirement health is expected, the mediators may differ across cultures. Future studies could expand on this important line of inquiry.

In conclusion, our findings make a case for social policies that promote retirement preparation, specifically focusing on psychological rather than just financial well-being. The former can be easily and realistically implemented in existing programs: help elders plan for activities during retirement that provide meaning, and self-worth. Besides building a nest egg, psychological well-being should feature prominently in recommendations for a good retirement.

References

Ajzen, I. (2001). Nature and operation of attitudes. *Annual Review of Psychology, 52*, 27–58. doi: 10.1146/annurev.psych.52.1.27.

Atchley, R. C. (1999). *Continuity and adaptation in aging: Creating positive experiences.* Baltimore, MD: Johns Hopkins University Press.

Bai, X., Lai, D. W. L., & Guo, A. (2016). Ageism and depression: Perceptions of older people as a burden in China. *Journal of Social Issues, 72(1),* 26–46.

Bailey, B. (1999). Changing images of retirement. *Generations-Journal of the American Society on Aging, 23,* 42–44.

Bamia, C., Trichopoulou, A., & Trichopoulos, D. (2007). Age at retirement and mortality in a general population sample. *American Journal of Epidemiology, 167,* 561–569.

Bartoszewska, E., Tobiasz-Adamczyk, B., Brzyski, P., & Kopacz, M. (2007). Occupational position, working conditions, work-related health attitudes and mortality patterns in older age. An 18 year follow-up study in Krakow, Poland. *European Journal of Public Health, 17,* 87–88.

Browne, M. W., & Cudeck, R. (1989). Single sample cross-validation indices for covariance structures. *Multivariate Behavioral Research, 24,* 445–455.

Chida, Y., & Steptoe, A. (2008). Positive psychological well-being and mortality: A quantitative review of prospective observational studies. *Psychosomatic Medicine, 70,* 741–756.

Coe, N. B., & Zamarro, G. (2011). Retirement effects on health in Europe. *Journal of Health Economics, 30(1),* 77–86. doi: 10.1016/j.jhealeco.2010.11.002.

Dennis, H., & Tbomas, K. (2007). Ageism in the workplace. *Generations-Journal of the American Society on Aging, 31(1),* 84–89.

Denton, F. T., & Spencer, B. G. (2009) What is retirement? A review and assessment of alternative concepts and measures. *Canadian Journal of Aging, 28,* 63–76.

Donlon, M. M., Ashman, O., & Levy, B. R. (2005). Re-Vision of older television characters: A stereotype-awareness intervention, *Journal of Social Issues, 61,* 307–319. doi: 10.1111/j.1540-4560.2005.00407.x.

Eagly & Chaiken. (1993). *The psychology of attitudes,* Fort Worth, TX: Harcourt Brace Jovanovich.

Ekerdt, D. J., & Clark, E. (2001). Selling retirement in financial planning advertisements. *Journal of Aging Studies, 15,* 55–68. doi: 10.1016/S0890-4065(00)00016-5.

Fillenbaum, G. G. (1971). Relation between attitude of work and attitude to retirement. *Journals of Gerontology, 26,* 244–259.

Franca, L. (2004). Attitudes towards retirement: A cross-cultural study between New Zealand and Brazilian executives. PhD Thesis. 456 p, *Department of Psychology,* New Zealand: The University of Auckland.

Gordon, E. (1994). The relationship of attitudes toward work and toward retirement—A female perspective. *Affilia-Journal of Women and Social Work, 9,* 269–287. doi: 10.1177/088610999400900303.

Goudy, W. J., Powers, E. A., Keith, P. M., & Reger, R. A. (1980). Changes in attitudes toward retirement—Evidence from a panel study of older males. *Journal of Gerontology, 35(6),* 942–948.

The Hartford (2012). Pre-retirees and retirees happy and optimistic. Retrieved from http://newsroom. thehartford.com/releases/pre-retirees-and-retirees-happy-optimistic-new-study-from-the-hartford-mit-agelab-finds. Accessed at July 20, 2015.

Kasl, S. V., & Jones, B. A. (2000). The impact of job loss and retirement on health. In L. F. Berkman & I. Kawachi (Eds.), *Social epidemiology.* Oxford, UK: Oxford University Press, pp. 118–136.

Kessler, E.-M., Schwender, C., & Bowen, C. E. (2010). The portrayal of older people's social participation on German prime-time TV advertisements. *Journals of Gerontology Series B-Psychological Sciences and Social Sciences, 65(1),* 97–106. doi: 10.1093/geronb/gbp084.

Lakra, D. C., Ng, R., & Levy, B. R. (2012). Increased longevity from viewing retirement positively. *Ageing & Society, 32,* 1418–1427.

Levy, B. (2009). Stereotype embodiment: A psychosocial approach to aging. *Current Directions in Psychological Science, 18(6),* 332–336.

Levy, B. R., Ng, R., Myers, L. M., & Marottoli, R. A. (2013). A psychological predictor of elders' driving performance: Social-comparisons on the road. *Journal of Applied Social Psychology, 43(3),* 556–561. doi: 10.1111/j.1559-1816.2013.01035.x.

Levy, B. R., Kunkel, S., Remmes, K., & Slade, M. (2004). Wanted dead or alive - Implication of death classification on longevity. *Research on Aging*, *26*(3), 317–329. doi: 10.1177/0164027503262478.

Levy, B. R., Slade, M. D., Murphy, T. E., & Gill, T. M. (2012). Association between positive age stereotypes and recovery from disability in older persons. *Journal of the American Medical Association*, *308*(19), 1972–1973.

Levy, B. R., Slade, M. D., Kunkel, S. R., & Kasl, S. V. (2002). Longevity increased by positive self-perceptions of aging. *Journal of Personality and Social Psychology*, *83*(2), 261–270.

Levy, B. R., Zonderman, A. B., Slade, M. D., & Ferrucci, L. (2012). Memory shaped by age stereotypes over time. *Journals of Gerontology Series B-Psychological Sciences and Social Sciences*, *67*(4), 432–436. doi: 10.1093/geronb/gbr120.

Levy, B. R., & Leffheit-Limson, E. (2009). The stereotype-matching effect: Greater influence on functioning when age stereotypes correspond to outcomes. *Psychology and Aging*, *24*(1), 230–233. doi: 10.1037/a0014563.

Löckenhoff, C. E., De Fruyt, F., Terracciano, A., McCrae, R. R., De Bolle, M., Costa, P. T., Aguilar-Vafaie ME, Ahn CK, Ahn HN, Alcalay L, Allik J, Avdeyeva TV, Barbaranelli C, Benet-Martinez V, Blatný M, Bratko D, Brunner-Sciarra M, Cain TR, Crawford JT, Lima MP, Ficková E, Gheorghiu M, Halberstadt J, Hrebíčková M, Jussim L, Klinkosz W, Knezevic G, de Figueroa NL, Martin TA, Marusic I, Mastor KA, Miramontez DR, Nakazato K, Nansubuga F, Pramila VS, Puric D, Realo A, Reátegui N, Rolland JP, Rossier J, Schmidt V, Sekowski A, Shakespeare-Finch J, Shimonaka Y, Simonetti F, Siuta J, Smith PB, Szmigielska B, Wang L, Yamaguchi M, & Yik, M. (2009). Perceptions of aging across 26 cultures and their culture-level associates. *Psychology and Aging*, *24*(4), 941–954. doi: 10.1037/a0016901.

Lumme-Sandt, K. (2011). Images of ageing in a 50+ magazine. *Journal of Aging Studies*, *25*(1), 45–51. doi: 10.1016/j.jaging.2010.08.013.

McVittie, C., & Goodall, K. (2012). The ever-changing meanings of retirement. *American Psychologist*, *67*, 75–76.

Ng, R., Ang, R.P., & Ho, M.H.R. (2012). Coping with anxiety, depression, anger and aggression: The mediational role of resilience in adolescents. *Child and Youth Care Forum*, *41*, 529–546. doi: 10.1007/s10566-012-9182-x.

Ng, R., Allore, H. G., Trentalange, M., Monin, J. K., & Levy, B. R. (2015). Increasing negativity of age stereotypes across 200 years: Evidence from a database of 400 million words. *PLoS ONE*, *10*, e0117086. doi: 10.1371/journal.pone.0117086.

Ng, R., & Rayner, S. (2010). Integrating psychometric and cultural theory approaches to formulate an alternative measure of risk perception. *Innovation: The European Journal of Social Science Research*, *23*, 85–100. doi: 10.1080/13511610.2010.512439.

Nusbaum, N. J. (2003). Preparation for healthy retirement. *Journal of the American Geriatrics Society*, *51*(3), 429–429. doi: 10.1046/j.1532-5415.2003.51122.

Ong, A. D. (2010). Pathways linking positive emotion and health in later life. *Current Directions in Psychological Science*, *19*(6), 358–362. doi: 10.1177/0963721410388805.

Pepin, G., & Deutscher, B. (2011). The lived experience of Australian retirees: 'I'm retired, what do I do now'? *British Journal of Occupational Therapy*, *74*(9), 419–426. doi: 10.4276/030802211×13153015305556.

Ramírez, L. F., & Palacios-Espinosa, X. (2016). Stereotypes about old age, social support, aging anxiety and evaluations of one's own health. *Journal of Social Issues*, *72*(1), 47–68.

Rosenkoetter, M. M. & Garris, J. M. (1998). Psychosocial changes following retirement. *Journal of Advanced Nursing*, *27*, 966–976. doi: 10.1046/j.1365-2648.1998.00569.x.

Rosow, I., & Breslau, N. (1966). A Guttman health scale for aged. *Journals of Gerontology*, *21*(4), 556–559.

Sargent, L. D., Lee, M. D., Martin, B., & Zikic, J. (2013). Reinventing retirement: New pathways, new arrangements, new meanings. *Human Relations*, *66*(1), 3–21. doi: 10.1177/0018726712465658.

Savishinsky, J. (2001). Images of retirement: Finding the purpose and the passion. *Generations-Journal of the American Society on Aging*, *25*(3), 52–56.

Settersten, R. A. Jr. (1998). Time, age, and the transition to retirement: New evidence on life-course flexibility. *International Journal of Aging and Human Development, 47*, 177–203.

Steiger, J. H., & Lind, J. C. (1980). Statistically based tests for the number of factors. Paper presented at the annual spring meeting of the Psychometric Society, Iowa City, IA.

Wang, M., & Shultz, K. S. (2010). Employee retirement: A review and recommendations for future investigation. *Journal of Management, 36*(1), 172–206. doi: 10.1177/0149206309347957.

Wang, M., Henkens, K., & van Solinge, H. (2011). Retirement adjustment: A review of theoretical and empirical advancements. *American Psychologist, 66*(3), 204–213. doi: 10.1037/a0022414.

REUBEN NG is a Visiting Research Scientist at the Yale School of Public Health and adjunct Senior Research Fellow at the Nanyang Technological University. He received a PhD in Epidemiology & Public Health with a Gerontology focus from Yale University as an International Fulbright Science and Technology Scholar, and a MSc (Distinction) in Management Research from Oxford University. His research interests are in aging, resilience, culture, and Psychomics—the study of societal stereotypes via high throughput semantic data.

HEATHER ALLORE is an Associate Professor of Medicine (Geriatrics), of Public Health (Biostatistics), and Director of the Biostatistics Core at the Yale Program on Aging. She received a PhD from Cornell University. Allore's research is focused on issues related to the design and analysis of studies of multicomponent interventions and the design and analysis of observational studies of multifactorial geriatric health conditions. She developed a subdiscipline of biostatistics within the American Statistical Association that focuses on training and methodological development in Aging Research called "Gerontologic Biostatistics."

JOAN K. MONIN is an Assistant Professor of Epidemiology (Chronic Diseases) at the Yale School of Public Health. She received a PhD in Psychology from the Carnegie Mellon University. Professor Monin's research examines how emotional processes affect health in older adult relationships.

BECCA R. LEVY is an Associate Professor at the Yale School of Public Health. She has a joint appointment with the Department of Psychology. She received her PhD in Psychology from Harvard University and held a National Institute on Aging postdoctoral fellowship at the Division of Aging and Department of Social Medicine at Harvard Medical School. Levy's research explores psychosocial factors that influence elders' cognitive and physical functioning, as well as their longevity. She is credited with creating a field of study that focuses on how positive and negative age stereotypes, which are assimilated from the culture, can have beneficial and adverse effects, respectively, on the health of older individuals.

Journal of Social Issues, Vol. 72, No. 1, 2016, pp. 86–104
doi: 10.1111/josi.12157

Ageism can be Hazardous to Women's Health: Ageism, Sexism, and Stereotypes of Older Women in the Healthcare System

Joan C. Chrisler[*]**, Angela Barney, and Brigida Palatino**
Connecticut College

Women tend to live longer than men, and thus typically have more interactions with the healthcare system in old age than men do. Ageism and stereotypes of older people in general can have an important impact on elders' physical and mental health and well-being. For example, internalized negative stereotypes can produce self-fulfilling prophecies through stereotype embodiment and contribute to weakness and dependency. Ageist beliefs and stereotypes can interfere with health care seeking as well as with diagnosis and treatment recommendations; they can, for example, contribute to gender disparities in the health care of older adults if older women are perceived as too frail to undergo aggressive treatments. Ageism also results in disrespectful treatment of older patients, which is communicated through baby talk and other forms of infantilization or the shrugging off of patients' complaints and concerns as "just old age." Intersectional identities can result in a cumulative burden for older women patients who may have a history of disrespectful treatment for other reasons (e.g., sexism, racism, bias against lesbians). Reduction of ageism and sexism and promotion of more realistic and diverse views of older women could improve doctor–patient relationships, facilitate adherence to treatment regimens, and reduce disparities in health and health care.

Women make up the majority of elders, and their percentage of that population group increases with age. There are 82 men for every 100 women in the "young-old" group (ages 65–74), 65 men for every 100 women in the "old" group (ages 75–84), and 41 men for every 100 women in the "old-old" group (ages 85 and over) (http://transgenerational.org/aging/demographics.htm). Yet, despite the

---

[*]Correspondence concerning this article should be addressed to Joan C. Chrisler, Department of Psychology, Connecticut College, New London, CT 06320. Tel.: 1-860-439-2336 [e-mail: jcchr@conncoll.edu].

numerical prominence of older women, there has been little interaction between the fields of women's studies and gerontology (Bookwala, 2015; Calasanti & Slevin, 2001, 2006); social and health psychologists also have paid less attention than is needed to older women's issues (Freixas, Luque, & Reina, 2012; Sugar, Anstee, Desrochers, & Jambor, 2002), despite the potential for ageism and sexism to intertwine and impact older women's health and well-being. Because of the paucity of literature concerning ageism, sexism, and women's health, we discuss research and theory about elders in general and speculate about its impact on women, and we discuss the available research about older women and subgroups of older women (e.g., women of color, lesbians). We conclude with a call for additional research on older women's health and suggest policy recommendations to improve older women's health and well-being.

Ageism and the Double Standard of Aging

Evidence of ageism is all around us in popular culture, public policy debates, and both popular and professional discourse. For example, public policy debates about (and media coverage of) the increasing numbers of elders frame living longer as a social problem; comments are made about deadwood, "old farts," the "burden" of aging, and "greedy geezers," as younger people see elders as an "unproductive" drain on resources (Gullette, 2004). Politicians have attempted to turn young adults against elders by warning about "the gray tsunami" that will deplete funding for pensions and programs such as Social Security and Medicare in the United States, leaving nothing behind for generations that follow. Jokes about "old timer's disease" and "senior moments" suggest that all elders have cognitive deficits. The medicalization of aging (aka "longevity medicine"; Calasanti & Slevin, 2001, 2006) has produced "antiaging" products and cosmetic procedures and surgeries designed to erase evidence of age so that people can "pass" as younger than they are (Ostenson, 2008). Euphemisms for elders are also common; "senior citizens," "golden agers," and "pensioners" are used by many, and elders are typically referred to as "aging" or "older" rather than "old." Of course, everyone alive is aging, and we are all older than we were yesterday, yet those terms, although not appropriately descriptive, are preferred to the more accurate term "old," which too clearly denotes a stigmatized condition. Further evidence of ageism is distancing from elders (North & Fiske, 2012), as younger people prefer to avoid too much physical and social contact with elders and often emphasize differences between themselves and elders. Public policy that encourages the development of special social spaces (e.g., "senior centers") and housing (e.g., "senior living") facilitates distancing. Internalized ageism may also be reflected in distancing behaviors (e.g., attempts to pass as younger). Consider the first author's 89-year-old mother, who regularly refers to an acquaintance of her same age, as "the old man," whereas she does not think of herself as an "old woman." She also firmly believes that "a lady never tells her age."

Why should a lady avoid revealing her age? A double standard of aging (Deutsch, Zalenski, & Clark, 1986; Sontag, 1979) has been described in which signs of aging (e.g., gray hair, facial lines) are seen as making men look distinguished, wise, and experienced, whereas they merely make women look "old." Studies done in the United States show that women are perceived as old at earlier ages than men are (Hummert, Gartska, & Shaner, 1997; Kite & Wagner, 2002). Ageism and sexism join hands as midlife and older women are judged more harshly than men of the same age for their looks and behavior (e.g., refusal to "act their age"). Hollywood actresses age out of lead roles decades earlier than actors do (Lemish & Muhlbauer, 2012), and even powerful politicians are judged more or less negatively depending on their gender. Hillary Clinton is a case in point. In 2007, radio commentator Rush Limbaugh predicted that then U.S. Senator Clinton would not win the presidency because people would not want to "watch a woman get older before their eyes" (Dowd, 2007). In 2014 her critics said that she is too old to run again for the presidency, although those same critics had no concerns about Ronald Reagan's or John McCain's age when they ran for president (Tomasky, 2013). The more negative portrayal of older women than older men in popular culture (including the greater number of jokes about old women; Crawford & Unger, 2004; Lemish & Muhlbauer, 2012) and the greater pressure on women than on men to hide signs of aging (Dingman, Otte, & Foster, 2012; e.g., hair dye, "antiaging" skin cream, botox) may result in older women being ashamed of their age (Holstein, 2006) and more sensitive to age-related microaggressions (i.e., brief, sometimes ambiguous actions that communicate a derogatory view of a particular social group and make the individual targets of the action feel inferior; Heintz, DeMucha, Deguzman, & Softa, 2013).

Frequent exposure to ageist prejudice and discrimination can constitute a form of minority stress. Elders are not often classified as "minorities," perhaps because there has been a great deal of emphasis in recent years on their growing numbers in the population. However, the marginalization and degradation that elders as a group experience in youth-oriented countries (e.g., the United States and other Western or Westernized nations) suggests that the concept of minority stress may be relevant to them and deserves investigation by researchers. This is important because stress reduces immune system functioning and is known to be a contributor to the onset (and the worsening) of some chronic illnesses (Taylor, 2012); public health experts are especially concerned about stress effects on the health of vulnerable people (e.g., children, elders, low-income individuals). The majority of elders are women, and the older the population segment, the greater the gender imbalance (Gullette, 2004). Although stress related to ageism usually does not start before age 50, older women have a lifetime of exposure to stress related to frequent (or occasional) sexism. Older women of color have a lifetime of experience with racism, older sexual minority women have long experience with homophobia, and transgender elders have experience with transphobia. A recent study (Sabik, 2013) of African American and European American women in their 60s showed that subjective ratings of their health were related to their perceptions of age discrimination; the more discrimination they perceived, the lower their ratings of both their physical health and their psychological well-being. Interviews with older lesbians indicate frequent experiences of homophobia, heterosexism, and ageism (Averett, Yoon, & Jenkins, 2013) in the healthcare system and elsewhere.

The perceived unfairness model (Jackson, Kubzansky, & Wright, 2006, p. 21) proposes that experiencing discrimination or prejudice oneself, or observing it directed at a member of a group to whom one has an emotional attachment, sets off "a cascade of psychological and physiological processes" that, with repeated episodes, can produce or contribute to negative health outcomes. Unfairness arouses hostility, and research has shown direct effects of hostility on cardiovascular and pulmonary functioning (Jackson, Kubzansky, Cohen, Jacobs, & Wright, 2007; Kubzansky et al., 2006). More frequent experiences of sexism and racism have been shown to predict more health problems (Kloniff & Landrine, 1995; Landrine & Klonoff, 1996; Moody, Brown, Matthews, & Bromberger, 2014), and a recent study (Page-Gould, Mendoza-Denton, & Mendes, 2014) showed that the more sensitive people of color are to race-based rejection, the more stress-related symptoms they report. It is likely that perceived unfairness related to ageism would have similar effects. Of course, older women, especially older ethnic or sexual minority women, have more and different kinds of opportunities to experience bias; thus, they may face a greater cumulative burden of the stress effects of unfairness.

Stereotypes of Elders

Ageism is based in part on stereotypes about elders, which contain both positive (e.g., wise, sage, experienced) and negative (e.g., grumpy, lonely, senile) aspects (Kite & Johnson, 1988). Stereotypes of elders are pervasive in popular culture and in professional literature, including medical and gerontology textbooks (Robinson, Briggs, & O'Neill, 2012). In youth-oriented cultures, the negative aspects are emphasized, perhaps as a way of distancing younger from older people. Many negative aspects are related to changes in the body that render it unattractive (e.g., wrinkled, gray-haired, ugly) or incompetent (e.g., forgetful, passive, weak, feeble, frail, debilitated, disabled, dependent, ill). Weakness, frailty, passivity, and dependence are also the aspects of the feminine gender role stereotype, another point of intersection between ageism and sexism, which might make it easier for people to perceive older women than older men as incompetent. The stereotype content model places elders in the pitied group—warm but incompetent ("doddering but dear"; Cuddy & Fiske, 2004, p. 3), a pattern that is found across cultural groups and that persists even when attention is drawn to counterexamples (Cuddy,

Norton, & Fiske, 2005). Housewives (Eckes, 2002) and pregnant women (Masser, Grass, & Nesic, 2007) are also rated warm but incompetent by participants in social psychology studies, which may make being pitied when they age a more common experience for women than for men.

Ageist stereotypes can produce negative halo effects (North & Fiske, 2012); when people are seen as old and unattractive, they may be expected to exhibit other negative aspects as well (e.g., ill health, inability to understand technology, depression, anxiety). For example, younger adults who think that it must be awful to be old expect older adults to be depressed and anxious about aging (Gullette, 2004). As a result, depression is undertreated in elders (Van Egeren, 2004), who are less likely than younger people to be referred for psychotherapy. Those who believe that old age and illness are firmly linked (including many elders themselves) may also be likely to dismiss the complaints and symptoms of elders as "just old age" rather than schedule a thorough medical examination (Calasanti & Slevin, 2006; Stewart, Chipperfield, Perry, & Weiner, 2012).

Internalized ageist stereotypes can become self-fulfilling prophecies (Stewart et al., 2012) and lead to learned helplessness (Cousins, 2000). For example, stereotypical beliefs applied to the self can serve as a barrier to health promotion (Yeom, 2013) if elders believe they are not capable of adherence to exercise or dietary regimens, or are too forgetful to follow complicated medication regimens, or believe that their aches and pains or depression are "just old age." Public policies that require elders to exhibit "frailty" in order to receive services influence the way that social workers, medical personnel, and other gatekeepers see elders (perhaps especially women, as frailty is a better fit with the feminine gender role), and also the way that elders who want the services see (and portray) themselves (Grenier & Hanley, 2007). In addition, self-stereotyping lowers people's self-esteem and self-efficacy; it also causes stress, which depletes psychological resources needed to engage in self-care and adhere to medical regimens (Rivera & Paredez, 2014).

Stereotype embodiment theory (Levy, 2009) suggests that when internalized ageist stereotypes are activated through stereotype threat (e.g., a healthcare professional commenting on a person's frailty), a microaggression (e.g., an ageist remark or joke), or other route (e.g., aches and pains, looking at a photograph of a younger self) people act out (or embody) those stereotypes in self-definitional and self-fulfilling ways. Laboratory studies have shown that elders primed with positive (e.g., wise, spry) or negative (e.g., senile, shaky) aspects of the stereotype match their performance to the prime (Levy, 2000). For example, negative priming has been shown to lead to worse handwriting (Levy, 2000), poorer performance on a memory (Desrichard & Kopetz, 2005; Hess, Auman, Colcombe, & Rahhal, 2003) or math (Abrams, Eller, & Bryant, 2006) test, stronger cardiovascular response (an indication of stress) when asked to solve verbal puzzles or do arithmetic (Levy, Hausdorff, Henche, & Wei, 2000), lower willingness to take a risk, lower scores on a measure of perceived health, higher scores on a measure of loneliness, and more frequent requests for help (Coudin & Alexopoulos, 2010). Elders with a stronger internalization of negative stereotypes also report more frequent hospitalizations (Levy, Slade, Chung, & Gill, 2014) and a more negative assessment of their own physical health (Ramírez & Palacios-Espinosa, 2016) than do those whose view of aging is more positive. Furthermore, elders who endorsed positive stereotypes lived longer than their more negative peers (Lev, Slade, Kunkel, & Kasl, 2002; Ng, Levy, Allore, & Monin, 2016). The results of these studies indicate that negative stereotypes can actually contribute to dependency, weakness, inability (Coudin & Alexopoulos, 2010), and perceived ill health in elders (Ramírez & Palacios-Espinosa, 2016), and thereby reinforce those stereotypes and undermine elders' physical and mental health.

Negative Attitudes toward Elders among Healthcare Professionals

Given that ageism and negative stereotypes of elders are ubiquitous, it is not surprising that healthcare professionals also exhibit them. Studies of physicians show that their attitudes are "complex and mixed" (Meisner, 2012, p. 61). That is, they may express both positive and negative aspects of stereotypes of elders, and their reasons for not liking to work with elders are also complex. Those reasons might have to do with distancing, perhaps as a terror management strategy (Martens, Goldenberg, & Greenberg, 2005), or, in the United States, they might have more do with economics, given that Medicare reimbursement is less than physicians get from private insurance for the same services (Meisner, 2012). Furthermore, physicians are trained to "cure," and, in general, they prefer to work with patients who have acute illnesses that can be cured, rather than with patients who have chronic illnesses that can only be managed (often with mixed success) (Taylor, 2012). Chronic illnesses are more common among older than younger people (Taylor, 2012), and elders may have more than one type of chronic illness, which can make their cases more difficult to manage. Regardless of the reasons for healthcare professionals' attitudes and decisions about which patients to welcome to their practices, elders may be aware (or suspect) that their doctors do not like to work with older people or are disrespectful or impatient with them. "Leaky" ageist attitudes can be experienced as microaggresssions, and physicians' negative attitudes might make elders hesitate to seek or follow medical advice or even cause them to cancel appointments.

Physicians' and medical students' thoughts about elders are primarily related to death, disease, and decline in functionality (Chodosh et al., 2000). Their stereotypes of elders include rigid, religious, irritable, boring, lonely, isolated, asexual, easily confused, depressed and depressing, needy, frustrating, and nonproductive (Green, Adelman, Charon, & Hoffman, 1986; Higashi, Tillack, Steinman, Harper, & Johnston, 2012; Michielutte & Diseker, 1985; Reyes-Ortiz, 1997). There is some evidence that physicians are more cynical about working with, and more distrustful of, elders than other types of health professionals are (Montplaisir & Dufour, 1982 as cited by Meisner, 2012), perhaps because they doubt elders' willingness or ability to follow "doctor's orders." Given a choice, physicians say they would rather work with younger patients than with older ones (Helton & Pathman, 2008), and they are most unwilling to work with "old-old" (age 85+) and frail patients (Chodosh et al., 2000). When physicians do report a mix of both positive and negative aspects of the stereotype of elders, their responses support the stereotype content model: Elders are warm and likable, yet frustrating and difficult because of their incompetence (Higashi et al., 2012). Medical students seem to like "old people" better than "old patients" (Liu, While, Norman, & Ye, 2012).

Nurses tend to have more positive attitudes toward working with elders than physicians do (Fisher & Peterson, 1993; Liu et al., 2012). This may be because the mission of nursing is to "care," rather than to cure (Bristow, 2012). Therefore, patients who need (or are believed to need) the most care may be the most rewarding to nurses. However, a recent study (McKenzie & Brown, 2014) of nursing students' interest in working with dementia patients revealed low intention to choose that path. Reasons why the students did not want to work with dementia patients include a mix of negative attitudes (e.g., boring, repetitive, inability to "relate" to the patients) and economics (e.g., lower pay than other specialty areas). The researchers speculated that terror management theory might also explain the students' reluctance to nurse dementia patients, the majority of whom are women (Vina & Lloret, 2010).

There have been a number of studies of implicit and explicit attitudes toward other marginalized groups, which, of course, intersect with age, although intersectionality was not considered in the studies. Healthcare professionals have been shown, for example, to exhibit race bias (e.g., Sabin, Nosek, Greenwald, & Rivara, 2009; Sabin, Rivara, & Greenwald, 2008), antifat bias (e.g., Sabin, Marini, & Nosek, 2012; Schwartz, Chambliss, Brownell, Blair, & Billington, 2003), and bias against sexual minorities (e.g., Lim, Brown, & Kim, 2014; Stevens, 1998). For example, healthcare professionals endorsed the stereotypes that heavy weight people are lazy, stupid, and worthless (Schwartz et al., 2003) and that European Americans are more compliant than African Americans (Sabin et al., 2008); "lazy" and noncompliant people are less likely to adhere to medical regimens, and thus are likely to be perceived as less rewarding patients. In a study of elders' attitudes toward and experiences with physicians (George & Jackson, 1998), European Americans were significantly more likely than African Americans to agree that doctors do their best to allay patients' worries and always treat them respectfully. The researchers also reported that well-educated and urban people have the most positive attitudes toward physicians and that Black and poor people receive the worst care in hospitals. Women of color make up the largest proportion of low-income elders in the United States (Gullette, 2004), thus they are among the most vulnerable patients.

Results of qualitative research demonstrate that some healthcare professionals treat elders disrespectfully in ways that suggest that older patients are unworthy of care. For example, a 39-year-old diabetes patient asked to comment about clinic staff told Marris (1996): "I'm horrified at the way they speak to older people, the lack of respect shown . . . You hear somebody yelling at them, 'You've been eating!'" (p. 162). In a study (Fisher & Peterson, 1993) of surgeons' attitudes toward elders, participants said they had heard colleagues refer to old patients as "goners" (p. 175) and joke about finishing the surgery quickly before the patient dies. In a particularly egregious example, two surgeons who were about to do a hip replacement on an older woman realized that the prosthesis they had been given was not the right size for the patient. They decided to go ahead and insert it, and one commented, "Well, I don't think she is going to be doing much dancing anyway" (p. 178). In an ethnographic study, the researchers (Higashi et al., 2012) observed a professor and several residents discuss two patients of different ages who had equally poor prognoses. The physicians expressed sympathy for the 42-year-old patient in visible ways and used the word "tragic" repeatedly (p. 478). No such concern was expressed for the 84-year-old patient. As one older woman told researchers, "Sometimes you get the feeling that the doctor is thinking I am 75 and don't have much time left anyways, so why worry about her — I don't know if they really think that, but you certainly get that impression" (Tannebaum, Nasmith, & Mayo, 2003; p. 8). Another form of disrespectful behavior is depersonalization, for example, discussing a patient's case in front of the patient without addressing the patient. This might happen more often to elders if they are assumed to have cognitive deficits (Higashi et al., 2012).

Stereotypic assumptions about cognitive deficits and functional decline may explain elders' frequent experience of infantilization in medical settings. Elders may be given assistance they do not need or experience others making decisions that they could make for themselves. Healthcare professionals may not explain as much to elders as they do to younger adults, perhaps because they think elders would not understand; instead they focus more on reassuring elders that they will be okay (Higashi et al., 2012). Use of simple sentences and elementary vocabulary with elders is also common, as is baby talk (Taylor, 2012). Baby talk refers to the use of simple sentences with childish vocabulary, which are spoken in a higher pitch and brighter tone than usual; adults use this form of language primarily with very young children and pets. For example, an older patient might be told to "pop up on the table" so that the doctor can "take a look at your tummy." Older women have complained that healthcare professionals treat them as though they were children by addressing them as "sweetie," "dearie," and "young lady" and by referring to a cooperative or compliant patient as a "good girl" (Cruikshank, 2008; Heintz et al., 2013; Leland, 2008). Some elders might be comforted by baby talk (Cruikshank, 2008; Nelson, 2005), perhaps especially when they are feeling anxious or are in pain, however others resent being "talked down to" and dislike people who address them that way (Ryan, Hamilton, & See, 1994). In a national survey in the United States (Commission on Women's Health, 2003), women of all ages were significantly more likely than men to report dissatisfaction with their doctors, including that their doctors talked down to them or dismissed their complaints. Elders who are assumed to have functional deficits might also be spoken to more slowly and in a loud voice, a form of overaccommodation that might not be necessary (Nelson, 2005; Van Egern, 2004). Infantilization and overaccommodation can be experienced by elders as microaggressions that communicate their low status, which allows others to treat them disrespectfully and impolitely (Williams, Herman, Gajweski, & Wilson, 2009). A tendency to infantilize elders might also result in healthcare professionals not taking elders and their complaints and questions seriously, which could compromise the care they receive.

North and Fiske (2012) suggested that the mix of attitudes toward and stereotypes about elders constitute ambivalent ageism, akin to ambivalent sexism. Ageism might be hostile (e.g., beliefs that elders are incompetent, frustrating, and use too many societal resources) or benevolent (e.g., beliefs that elders are warm, frail, and need to be cared for gently). Infantilization and baby talk could be expressions of benevolent ageism. Given that women so often experience benevolent sexism and that women are the majority of elders, older women may be especially likely to be perceived by younger male physicians in a paternalistic manner. Benevolent sexism (in this case, a desire to protect) has been suggested as a reason why older women receive less aggressive medical treatment than older men with similar conditions (Travis, Howerton, & Szymanski, 2012).

Age- and Gender-related Healthcare Disparities

Ageist beliefs (e.g., the growing number of elders is a burden on society) and stereotypes that all elders are frail, depressed, and cognitively compromised fuel debates about rationing health care. In an appearance on the U.S. television program *Morning Joe* on September 22, 2014, Ezekiel Emanuel, MD, PhD, Chair of the Department of Medical Ethics and Health Policy at the University of Pennsylvania's Perelman School of Medicine, defended his belief that age 75 is the "perfect age to die." The well-known bioethicist Daniel Callahan, PhD, a founder of the Hastings Center and a Senior Scholar at Yale University, has said that everyone over age 80 should voluntarily refuse medical treatment or be denied it (Gullette, 2004). Such pronouncements from respected experts constitute hostile ageism; the statements suggest that all people over 75 or 80 have ill health that requires expensive treatments or that their cognitive and functional decline produces such a low quality of life that it would not be worth living. That, of course, is not true, as elders are a diverse group in many ways; for example, Sister Madonna Buder, known as "the Iron Nun," who finished the Ironman triathlon at age 82, and the South African grandmothers' soccer league are examples of healthy, active elders (Chrisler & Palatino, in press). Gullette (2004, p. 95) considers discussion of the expense of medical care for elders "without sympathy for the sufferers" to be hate speech.

Hostile ageism could result in denial of health care to elders, especially if the care is expensive, and it could result in coercion of elders into signing do not resuscitate (DNR) orders (Gullette, 2004). On the other hand, benevolent ageism (in this case, that elders do not know what is best for them) could result in refusal to honor DNR requests and coercion of elders to agree to intensive treatment (e.g., another round of chemotherapy) that they do not want. These matters are difficult to study, but there is some evidence that White people's DNR requests, as well as their requests for intensive medical care, are more likely than Black people's requests to be honored (Loggers et al., 2009) and that men's decisional capacity and DNR requests are honored more often than women's (Parks, 2000). There is also evidence that elders are more likely than other patients to be under- or overmedicated, especially in regard to pain management (Correa-de-Araujo, 2006; Gullette, 2004).

Just as there are health-related problems that elders are "expected" to have (e.g., hearing deficits, depression), there are problems that they are not expected to have. For example, elders are not expected to be alcohol or drug abusers, and so they are not typically screened for those problems (Van Egeren, 2004). Many younger adults assume that elders are not sexually active, so they are not likely to suggest screening for sexually transmitted infections, nor are elders (especially women) likely to request such screening (Durvasula, 2014). However, among the most common reasons older women give for low sexual activity is partner's health or lack of a partner (McHugh & Interligi, 2015). After the death of a partner, or after moving into senior housing where potential partners are available, sexual activity may increase. Older women who are no longer concerned about avoiding pregnancy may not think about safe sex practices unless they have been educated by a healthcare professional. Elder abuse is another problem that may go undetected by healthcare providers who expect elders to be weak and unsteady on their feet, and thus readily accept explanations that injuries have resulted from falls (Davidson, DiGiacomo, & McGrath, 2011; De Four, 2012). Older women may not be asked about caregiving roles they play in their families, which can be stressful and impact their physical and mental health (Rondon, 2010). Thus, stereotypic beliefs about elders can result in lack of education, treatment, or prevention of health problems.

Older patients may receive less aggressive treatment than younger patients do; for example, they are less likely to be placed on organ transplant lists and less likely to be enrolled (or even discouraged from enrolling) in clinical trials of new medications (Ageism in the health care system, 2003; Bowling, 1999; Correa-de-Araujo, 2006; Gullette, 2004; Wenger, 2012). Furthermore, a number of gender disparities among elders have been documented by researchers, and these differences in treatment could be hazardous to older women's health. Men receive more thorough medical examinations, more follow-up (Travis et al., 2012), and more evidence-based medical care (Gochfeld, 2010) than women do, and they are more likely to receive preventive care (Cameron, Song, Manheim, & Dunlop, 2010). For example, older women are less likely than older men to get flu shots, cholesterol screenings, colonoscopies, and carotid endarterectomy for stroke prevention (Cameron et al., 2010; Correa-de-Araujo, 2006; Donovan & Syngal, 1998). Although women have higher prevalence of knee and hip arthritis and other forms of joint disease and disability, they are less likely than men to undergo joint replacement surgery, and they receive replacements later in the disease process than men do, which means that they suffer longer (Knee joint replacement, n.d.; Fitzgerald et al., 2004).

Perhaps the greatest gender disparity occurs in the treatment of various forms of cardiac disease, which is the most common cause of death among both women and men over the age of 80 (Centers for Disease Control and Prevention, 2011). Women are less likely than men to receive heart bypass surgery (Travis, 2005; Travis, Meltzer, & Howerton, 2009 as cited by Travis et al., 2012), cardiac resynchronization therapy, atrial fibrillation ablation (Wenger, 2012), and cardiac catheterization (Correa-de-Araujo, 2006) even when their conditions are similar. Women are also less likely than men to be prescribed beta-blockers, anticoagulants, and daily aspirin (Correa-de-Araujo, 2006), and they are less likely than men to be referred to a rehabilitation program after a heart attack (Keefe, 2004; Wegner, 2012). Women may also be disadvantaged in the diagnosis of heart attacks because their symptoms may vary from the prototypical profile of a heart attack, which is based on men's symptoms (Travis et al., 2012). Women also tend to be older than men when they are diagnosed with cardiac disease, thus age and gender stereotypes may combine to suggest that women are too weak or frail to withstand the procedures mentioned above (Travis et al., 2012), yet the available evidence does not support greater risk or less success in women (Wegner, 2012). Race disparities have also been noted for some of these procedures (e.g., bypass surgery); European Americans are more likely than African Americans with the same condition to receive them (Travis, 2005).

Policies and Practices to Reduce Ageism and Improve Women's Health

Research is needed on age, gender, and other disparities in health and health care, with attention to intersectionalities. Additional research is also needed on biases in healthcare decision making, including qualitative studies that ask healthcare professionals to think about how and why they make the decisions they do about what kinds of treatment their patients should have. Until people realize that their decisions might be influenced by ageist, sexist, racist, and homophobic beliefs and stereotypes, they are unlikely to recognize and challenge their own and their colleagues biases.

Education is needed for both healthcare professionals and older patients. More extensive and better quality education in gerontology for all healthcare professionals is necessary. That education should include exposure to healthy older adults (Stewart et al., 2012) and emphasize positive aspects of aging. Students should be taught that "aging" means both growth and loss for all age groups (Robinson et al., 2012). Cohort effects on health behavior should also be taught; the young–old are different from the old–old in many ways, and those differences should be recognized, as should other forms of diversity (e.g., gender, race/ethnicity, sexual orientation, social class) that impact the experience of aging. Ageism cannot be reduced until it is made visible (Sabik, 2013), so it must be included in curricula. Healthcare providers and students need to be taught about ageism, sexism, and stereotypes of elders and understand their role in reducing bias and stereotyping of all kinds (Nemmers, 2004). They should be taught that ageism is unethical and unacceptable (Bowling, 1999). Better communication skills should also be taught (Pfeifer, 2014), including respectful ways to interact with people with actual (or suspected) disabilities (Van Engeren, 2004).

Older people also need education about ageism and stereotypes so that they can recognize and resist them. Positive self-perceptions can benefit physical health and well-being (North & Fiske, 2012) and reduce the likelihood of negative stereotype embodiment. Older women might be especially likely to benefit from assertiveness training (Adler, McGraw, & McKinlay, 1998) and other forms of empowerment (e.g., exercise; Chrisler & Palatino, in press). If older women are unafraid to tell their doctors about their symptoms (Holstein, 2006; Marris, 1996) and able to insist upon getting the information they want (Tannebaum et al., 2003), the quality of their healthcare might improve. Elders should be taught to distinguish between chronic illness and "old age" to avoid self-fulfilling prophecies and so that they know when to seek medical care. Older women's health might benefit if they are taught stress management techniques. Assertiveness and stress management training could be taught by nurses, health educators, social workers, or psychologists (O'Brien & Whitbourne, 2015). Professionals might find fruitful educational partnerships with activists in the Women's Health Movement (e.g., National Women's Health Network, Black Women's Health Imperative; Dan, Jonikas, & Ford, 1994).

Older patients (especially older women) should be included in clinical trials unless there is a nonage-related reason for exclusion (Bowling, 1999). Clinical guidelines should be developed for screening older patients (including questions about elder abuse, alcohol and drug use, sexual health, and caregiver stress) and for evidence-based treatment of various forms of cardiac disease. Current guidelines might not be applied to older women because of their frequent exclusion from clinical trials. Older women are particularly susceptible to medication side effects ("appropriate" doses are usually determined by studies of men) so careful monitoring is needed (Gatz, Harris, & Turk-Charles, 1995); cognitive side effects (e.g., confusion, fuzzy thinking) can be misdiagnosed as dementia in women given their increased risk for Alzheimer's disease. Health promotion campaigns should explicitly include elders (Levy, 2009), as both physical and mental health can be improved at any age.

Access to healthcare services and the quality of services available are always political and influenced by policy makers' priorities and biases (Travis, Gressley, & Adams, 1995). Public policy initiatives are needed to reduce barriers to healthcare access for low-income rural and inner city dwelling older women, such as transportation services and home care visits (Dan et al., 1994; Fitzpatrick, Powe, Cooper, Ives, & Robbin, 2014); these barriers are more often reported in the United States by older women of color (Fitzpatrick et al., 2014). Given that the best predictor of older women's health is how healthy they were when they were younger (Gatz et al., 1995), it is important to work to reduce health disparities among people at all ages (e.g., by ensuring access to immunizations, preventative care, healthy food, safe places to exercise, reproductive health services). Community-based caregiver respite programs, opportunities to socialize (not just with other elders, but with people of all ages), and bereavement counseling might be especially helpful to older women's mental health and well-being. Many older women are afraid of falling; both the results of falls and the fear of falling result in compromised independence (Chrisler, Rossini, & Newton, 2015). Programs that provide low-cost mobility aids (e.g., walkers, canes, scooters) and teach tai chi (or other activities that improve balance) will produce changes in older women's quality of life (Chrisler et al., 2015). Public policy will always be more effective if older women are consulted about what services they need and involved in the design of programs and interventions (Dan et al., 1994).

Advocacy will be necessary to teach policy makers at all levels (from hospital administrators and insurance company executives to local and national government agencies) about the needs of elders and to assist in the development of policies that take the diversity of elders into account (Cummings, 2002). Pensions or social security benefits sufficient to keep elders out of poverty and healthcare plans that reduce or eliminate out-of-pocket costs for low-income elders are especially important to older women (Fitzpatrick et al., 2014). Social justice cannot be achieved without the efforts of both activists and experts. However, if we commit to work together on initiatives such as those described here, perhaps ageism will become less hazardous to women's health.

References

Abrams, D., Eller, A., & Bryant, J. (2006). An age apart: The effects of intergenerational contact and stereotype threat on performance and intergroup bias. *Psychology and Aging, 21,* 691–702. doi: 10.1037/0882-7974.21.1.691.

Adler, S. R., McGraw, S. A., & McKinlay, J. B. (1998). Patient assertiveness in ethnically diverse older women with breast cancer: Challenging stereotypes of the elderly. *Journal of Aging Studies, 12*, 331–350. doi: 10.1016/S0890-4065(98)90023-8.

Ageism in the health care system: Short shrifting seniors? (2003). *Hearing before the Special Committee on Aging of the United States Senate [Serial No. 108-10].* Washington, DC: U.S. Government Printing Office.

Averett, P., Yoon, I., & Jenkins, C. L. (2013). Older lesbian experiences of homophobia and ageism. *Journal of Social Service Research, 39*, 3–15. doi: 10.1080/01488376.2012.727671.

Bookwala, J. (2015). Foreword. In V. Muhlbauer, J. C. Chrisler, & F. L. Denmark (Eds.), *Women and aging: An international, intersectional, power perspective* (pp. v–vii). New York: Springer.

Bowling, A. (1999). Ageism in cardiology. *British Medical Journal, 319*, 1353–1355.

Bristow, N. K. (2012). *American pandemic: The lost worlds of the 1918 influenza epidemic.* New York: Oxford University Press.

Calasanti, T. M., & Slevin, K. F. (2001). *Gender, social inequalities, and aging.* Walnut Creek, CA: AltaMira Press.

Calasanti, T. M., & Slevin, K. F. (2006). Introduction: Age matters. In T. M. Calasanti & K F. Slevin (Eds.), *Age matters: Realigning feminist thinking* (pp. 1–17). New York: Routledge.

Cameron, K. A., Song, J., Manheim, L. M., & Dunlop, D. D. (2010). Gender disparities in health and healthcare use among older adults. *Journal of Women's Health, 19*, 1643–1649. doi: 10.1089/jwh.2009.1701.

Centers for Disease Control and Prevention. (2011). *Deaths, percent of total deaths, and death rates for the 15 leading causes of death in 5-year age groups, by race and sex: United States, 2011.* From http://www.cdc.gov/nchs/data/dvs/LCWK1_2011.pdf. Accessed at September 1, 2014.

Chodosh, J., Tulsky, A., Naumberg, E., Braca, L., Frankel, R. M., McCann, R. M., Katz, P. R., & Hall, W. J. (2000). What residents want to know about geriatrics. *Gerontology and Geriatrics Education, 20*(2), 19–35. doi: 10.1300/J021v20n02_03.

Chrisler, J. C., & Palatino, B. (in press). Stronger than you think: Older women and physical activity. *Women & Therapy.*

Chrisler, J. C., Rossini, M., & Newton, J. R. (2015). Older women, power, and the body. In V. Muhlbauer, J. C. Chrisler, & F. L. Denmark (Eds.), *Women and aging: An international, intersectional, power perspective* (pp. 9–30). New York: Springer.

Commission on Women's Health. (2003). *The Commonwealth Fund survey of women's health.* New York: Commonwealth Fund.

Correa-de-Araujo, R. (2006). Serious gaps: How the lack of sex/gender-based research impairs health. *Journal of Women's Health, 15*, 1116–1122.

Coudin, G., & Alexopoulos, T. (2010). "Help me! I'm old!": How negative aging stereotypes create despondency among older adults. *Aging & Mental Health, 14*, 516–523. doi: 10.1080/13607861003713182.

Cousins, S. O. (2000). "My heart couldn't take it": Older women's beliefs about exercise benefits and risks. *Journal of Gerontology, 55*, 243–294. doi: 10.1093/geronb/55.5.P283.

Crawford, M., & Unger, R. (2004). *Women and gender: A feminist psychology* (4th ed.). New York: McGraw-Hill.

Cruikshank, M. (2008). Aging and identity politics. *Journal of Aging Studies, 22*, 147–151. doi: 10.1016/j.jaging.2007.12.011.

Cuddy, A. J. C., & Fiske, S. T. (2004). Doddering but dear: Process, content, and function in stereotyping of older persons. In T. D. Nelson (Ed.), *Ageism: Stereotyping and prejudice against older persons* (pp. 3–26). Cambridge, MA: MIT Press.

Cuddy, A. J. C., Norton, M. I., & Fiske, S. T. (2005). This old stereotype: The pervasiveness and persistence of the elderly stereotype. *Journal of Social Issues, 61*, 267–285. doi: 10.1111/j.1540-4560.2005.00405x.

Cummings, S. M. (2002). Predictors of psychological well-being among assisted-living residents. *Health & Social Work, 27*, 293–302. doi: 10.1093/hsw/27.4.293.

Dan, A. J., Jonikas, J. A., & Ford, Z. L. (1994). Epilogues: An invitation. In A. J. Dan (Ed.), *Reframing women's health: Multidisciplinary research and practice* (pp. 386–392). Thousand Oaks, CA: Sage.

Davidson, P. M., DiGiacomo, M., & McGrath, S. J. (2011). The feminization of aging: How will this impact on health outcomes and services. *Health Care for Women International, 32*, 1031–1045. doi: 10.1080/07399332.2011.610539.

DeFour, D. (2012). "The test of a civilization is the way it cares for its helpless members": Violence against older women. *Women & Therapy, 35*, 248–260. doi: 10.1080/02703149.2012.684587.

Desrichard, O., & Kopetz, C. (2005). A threat in the elder: The impact of task instructions, self-efficacy, and performance expectations on memory performance in the elderly. *European Journal of Social Psychology, 35*, 537–552. doi: 10.1002/ejsp.249.

Deutsch, F. M., Zalenski, C. M., & Clark, M. E. (1986). Is there a double standard of aging? *Journal of Applied Social Psychology, 16*, 771–785. doi: 10.1111/j.1559-1816.1986.tb01167.x.

Dingman, S., Otte, M. E. M., & Foster, C. (2012). Cosmetic surgery: Feminist perspectives. *Women & Therapy, 35*, 181–192. doi: 10.1080/02703149.2012.684536.

Donovan, J. M., & Syngal, S. (1998). Colorectal cancer in women: An underappreciated but preventable risk. *Journal of Women's Health, 7*, 45–48. doi: 10.1089/jwh.1998.7.45.

Dowd, M. (2007). Rush to judgment. *New York Times.* From http://www.nytimes.com/2007/12/19/opinion/19dowd.html?pagewanted=print&_r=0. Accessed at September 1, 2014.

Durvasula, R. (2014). HIV/AIDS in older women: Unique challenges, unmet needs. *Behavioral Medicine, 40*, 85–98. doi: 10.1080/08964289.2014.893983.

Eckes, T. (2002). Paternalistic and envious gender stereotypes: Testing predictions from the stereotype content model. *Sex Roles, 47*, 99–114. doi: 10.1023/A:1021020920715.

Fisher, B. J., & Peterson, C. (1993). She won't be dancing much anyway: A study of surgeons, surgical nurses, and elderly patients. *Qualitative Health Research, 3*, 165–183. doi: 10.1177/104973239300300203.

Fitzgerald, J. D., Orav, E. J., Lee, T. H., Marcantonio, E. R., Poss, R., Goldman, L., & Mangione, C. M. (2004). Patient quality of life during the 12 months following joint replacement surgery. *Arthritis Care & Research, 51*, 100–109. doi: 10.1002/art.20090.

Fitzpatrick, A. L., Powe, N. R., Cooper, L. S., Ives, D. G., & Robbin, J. A. (2014). Barriers to health care access among the elderly and who perceives them. *American Journal of Public Health, 94*, 1788–1794. doi: 10.2105/AJPH.94.10.1788.

Freixas, A., Luque, B., & Reina, A. (2012). Ceitical feminist gerontology: In the back room of research. *Journal of Women & Aging, 24*, 44–58. doi: 10.1080/08952841.2012.638891.

Gatz, M., Harries, J. R., & Turk-Charles, S. (1995). The meaning of health for older women. In A. L. Stanton & S. J. Gallant (Eds.), *The psychology of women's health: Progress and challenges in research and application* (pp. 491–529). Washington, DC: American Psychological Association.

George, L. K., & Jackson, P. B. (1998). Racial differences in satisfaction with physicians: A study of older adults. *Research on Aging, 20*, 298–316. doi: 10.1177/0164027598203002.

Gochfeld, M. (2010). Sex-gender research sensitivity and healthcare disparities. *Journal of Women's Health, 19*, 189–193. doi: 10.1089/jwh.2009.1632.

Green, M. G., Adelman, R., Charon, R., & Hoffman, S. (1986). Ageism in the medical encounter: An exploratory study of the doctor-elderly patient relationship. *Language & Communication, 6*, 113–124. doi: 10.1016/0271-5309(86)90010-8.

Grenier, A., & Hanley, J. (2007). Older women and "frailty": Aged, gendered, and embodies resistance. *Current Sociology, 55*, 211–228. doi: 10.1177/0011392107073303.

Gullette, M. M. (2004). *Age wise: Fighting the new ageism in America.* Chicago: University of Chicago Press.

Heintz, P. A., DeMucha, C. M., Degrezman, M. M., & Softa, R. (2013). Stigma and microaggressions experienced by older women with urinary incontinence: A literature review. *Urologic Nursing, 33*, 299–305. doi: 10.7257/1053-816X.2013.33.6.299.

Helton, M. R., & Pathman, D. E. (2008). Caring for older patients: Current attitudes and future plans of family medicine residents. *Family Medicine, 40*, 707–714.

Hess, T. M., Auman, C., Colombe, S. J., & Rahhal, T. A. (2003). The impact of stereotype threat on age differences in memory performance. *Journal of Gerontology: Psychological Sciences, 58B*, 3–11. doi: 10.1093/geronb/58.1.P3.

Higashi, R. T., Tillack, A. A., Steinman, M., Harper, M., & Johnston, C. B. (2012). Elder care as "frustrating" and "boring": Understanding the persistence of negative attitudes toward older patients among physicians-in-training. *Journal of Aging Studies, 26*, 476–483. doi: 10.1016/j.jaging.2012.06.007.

Holstein, M. B. (2006). On being an aging woman. In T. M. Calasanti & K. F. Slevin (Eds.), *Age matters: Realigning feminist thinking* (pp. 313–334). New York: Routledge.

Hummert, M. L., Gartska, T. A., & Shaner, J. (1997). Stereotyping of older adults: The role of target facial cues and perceived characteristics. *Psychology and Aging, 12*, 107–114. doi: 10.1037/0882-7974.12.1.107.

Jackson, B., Kubzansky, L. D., Cohen, S., Jacobs Jr., D. R., & Wright, R. J. (2007). Does harboring hostility hurt? Associations between hostility and pulmonary function in the coronary artery risk development in (young) adults (CARDIA) study. *Health Psychology, 26*, 333–340. doi: 10.1037/0278-6133.26.3.333.

Jackson, B., Kubzansky, L. D., & Wright, R. J. (2006). Linking perceived unfairness to physical health: The perceived unfairness model. *Review of General Psychology, 10*, 21–40. doi: 10.1037/1089-2680.10.1.21.

Keefe, S. (2004). Women and cardiac rehab. *Advanced Healthcare Network*. From http://physical-therapy.advanceweb.com/Article/Women-and-Cardiac-Rehab-1.aspx. Accessed at September 1, 2014.

Kite, M. E., & Johnson, B. T. (1988). Attitudes toward older and younger adults: A meta-analysis. *Psychology and Aging, 3*, 232–234. doi: 10.1037/0882-7974.3.3.233.

Kite, M. E., & Wagner, L. S. (2002). Attitudes toward older adults. In T. D. Nelson (Ed.), *Ageism: Stereotyping and prejudice against older persons* (pp. 129–161). Cambridge, MA: MIT Press.

Klonoff, E. A., & Landrine, H. (1995). The schedule of sexist events: A measure of lifetime and recent sexist discrimination in women's lives. *Psychology of Women Quarterly, 19*, 439–472. doi: 10.111/j.1471-6402.1995.tb00086x.

Knee joint *replacement*. (n.d.) From the Kadhiwala Orthopaedic Hospital website. http://www.arthritisa2z.co.in/joint_replacement.html. Accessed at September 1, 2014.

Kubzansky, L. D., Sparrow, D., Jackson, B., Cohen, S., Weiss, S. T., & Wright, R. J. (2006). Angry breathing: A prospective study of hostility and lung function in a normative aging study. *Thorax, 61*, 863–868. doi: 10.1136/thx.2005.050971.

Landrine, H., & Klonoff, E. A. (1996). The Schedule of Racist vents: A measure of racial discrimination and a study of its negative physical and mental health consequences. *Journal of Black Psychology, 22*, 144–168. doi: 10.1177/00957984960222002.

Leland, J. (2008). In 'sweetie" and "dear," a hurt for the elderly. *New York Times*. From www.nytimes.com/2008/10/07aging.html?=todayspaper&pagewanted+print. Accessed at September 1, 2014.

Lemish, D., & Muhlbauer, V. (2012). "Can't have it all": Representations of older women in popular culture. *Women & Therapy, 35*, 165–180. doi: 10.1080/02703149.2012.68541.

Levy, B. R. (2000). Handwriting as a reflection of aging self-stereotypes. *Journal of Geriatric Psychiatry, 33*, 81–94.

Levy, B. R. (2009). Stereotype embodiment: A psychological approach to aging. *Current Directions in Psychological Science, 18*, 332–336. doi: 10.1111/j.1467-8721.2009.01662.x.

Levy, B. R., Hausdorff, J., Henche, R., & Wei, J. Y. (2000). Reducing cardiovascular stress with positive stereotypes of aging. *Journal of Gerontology: Psychological Sciences, 55*, 202–213. doi: 10.1093/geronb/55.4.P205.

Levy, B. R., Slade, M. D., Chung, P., & Gill, T. (2014). Resiliency over time of elders' age stereotypes after encountering stressful events. *Journals of Gerontology, Series B: Psychological and Social Sciences*. Advanced online publication. doi: 10.1093/geronb/gbu082.

Levy, B. R., Slade, M. D., Kunkel, S. R., & Kasl, S. V. (2002). Longevity increased by positive self-perceptions of aging. *Journal of Personality and Social Psychology, 83*, 261–170. doi: 10.1037/0022-3514.83.2.261.

Lim, F. A., Brown, D. V., & Kim, S. M. J. (2014). Addressing health care disparities in lesbian, gay, bisexual, and transgender populations: A review of best practices. *American Journal of Nursing, 114*, 24–34.

Liu, Y., While, A. E., Norman, I. J., & Ye, W. (2012). Health professionals' attitudes toward older people and older patients: A systematic review. *Journal of Interprofessional Care, 26*, 397–409. doi: 10.3109/13561820.2012.702146.

Loggers, E. T., Maciejewski, P. K., Paulk, E., DeSanto-Madeya, S., Nilsson, M., Viswanath, V., Wright, A. A., Balboni, T. A., Temel, J., Stieglitz, H., Block, S., & Prigerson, H. G. (2009). Racial differences in predictors of intensive end-of-life care in advanced cancer patients. *Journal of Clinical Oncology, 27*, 5559–5564. doi: 10.1200/JCO.2009.22.4733.

Marris, V. (1996). *Lives worth living: Women's experiences of chronic illness.* San Francisco: Pandora Books.

Martens, A., Goldenberg, J. L., & Greenberg, J. (2005). A terror management perspective on ageism. *Journal of Social Issues, 61*, 223–239. doi: 10.1111/j.1540-4560.2005.00403.x.

Masser, B., Grass, K., & Nesic, M. (2007). We like you, but we don't want you: The impact of pregnancy in the workplace. *Sex Roles, 57*, 703–712.

McHugh, M. C., & Interligi, C. (2015). Sexuality and older women: Desirability and desire. In V. Muhlbauer, J. C. Chrisler, & F. L. Denmark (Eds.), *Women and aging: An international, intersectional, power perspective* (pp. 89–116). New York: Springer.

McKenzie, E. L., & Brown, P. M. (2014). Nursing students' intentions to work in dementia care: Influence of age, ageism, and perceived barriers. *Educational Gerontology, 40*, 618–633. doi: 10.1080/03601277.2013.863545.

Meisner, B. A. (2012). Physicians' attitudes toward aging, the aged, and the provision of geriatric care: A systematic narrative review. *Critical Public Health, 22*, 61–72. doi: 10.1080/09581596.2010.539592.

Michielutte, R., & Diseker, R. A. (1985). Health care providers' perceptions of the elderly and level of interest in geriatrics as a specialty. *Gerontology and Geriatrics Education, 5*(2), 65–85.

Moody, D. L. B., Brown, C., Matthews, K. A., & Bromberger, J. T. (2014). Everyday discrimination prospectively predicts inflammation across 7-years in racially diverse midlife women: Study of women's health across the nation. *Journal of Social Issues, 70*, 298–314. doi: 10.1111/josi.12061.

Nelson, T. D. (2005). Ageism: Prejudice against our feared future self. *Journal of Social Issues, 61*, 207–221. doi: 10.1111/j.1540-4560.2005.00402.x.

Nemmers, T. (2004). The influence of ageism and ageist stereotypes on the elderly. *Physical & Occupational Therapy in Geriatrics, 22*(4), 11–20. doi: 10.1023/A:1013013322947.

Ng, R., Levy, B. R., Allore, H. G., & Monin, J. K. (2016). Retirement as meaningful: Positive retirement stereotypes associated with longevity. *Journal of Social issues, 72*(1), 69–85.

North, M. S., & Fiske, S. T. (2012). An inconvenienced youth? Ageism and its potential intergenerational roots. *Psychological Bulletin, 138*, 982–997. doi: 10.1037/a0027843.

O'Brien, J. L., & Whitbourne, S. K. (2015). Clinical interventions to empower older women. In V. Muhlbauer, J. C. Chrisler, & F. L. Denmark (Eds.), *Women and aging: An international, intersectional, power perspective* (pp. 147–167). New York: Springer.

Ostenson, R. S. (2008). Who's in and who's out? The results of oppression. In J. C. Chrisler, C. Golden, & P. D. Rozee (Eds.), *Lectures on the psychology of women* (4th ed., pp. 16–25). New York: McGraw-Hill.

Page-Gould, E., Mendoza-Denton, R., & Mendes, W. B. (2014). Stress and coping in interracial contexts: Influence of race-based rejection sensitivity and cross-group friendship in daily experiences of health. *Journal of Social Issues, 70*, 256–278. doi: 10.1111/josi.12059.

Parks, J. A. (2000). Why gender matters to the euthanasia debate: On decisional capacity and the rejection of women's death requests. *Hastings Center Report, 30*(1), 30–36.

Pfeifer, G. M. (2014). More work needed to equalize U.S. health care. *American Journal of Nursing, 114*(3), 15.

Ramírez, L., & Palacios-Espinoza, X. (2016). Stereotypes about old age, social support, aging anxiety, and evaluations of one's own health. *Journal of Social Issues, 72*(1), 47–68.

Reyes-Ortiz, C. (1997). Physicians must confront ageism. *Academic Medicine, 72*, 831.

Rivera, L. M., & Paredez, S. M. (2014). Stereotypes can "get under the skin": Testing a self-stereotyping and psychological resource model of overweight and obesity. *Journal of Social Issues, 70*, 226–240. doi: 10.1111/josi.12057.

Robinson, S., Briggs, R., & O'Neill, D. (2012). Cognitive aging, geriatric textbooks, and unintentional ageism. *Journal of the American Geriatric Society, 60,* 2183–2185.

Rondon, M. B. (2010). A gender perspective is fundamental to improve women's health. *Journal of Women's Health, 19,* 1949–1950. doi: 10.1089/jwh.2010.2402.

Ryan, E. B., Hamilton, J. M., & See, S. K. (1994). Patronizing the old: How do younger and older adults respond to baby talk in the nursing home? *International Journal of Aging and Human Development, 39,* 21–32.

Sabik, N. J. (2013). Ageism and body esteem: Associations with psychological well-being among late middle-aged African American and European American women. *Journals of Gerontology (Series B): Psychological and Social Sciences, 68,* 1–11. doi: 10.1093/geronb/gbt080.

Sabin, J. A., Marini, M., & Nosek, B. A. (2012). Implicit and explicit anti-fat bias among a large sample of medical doctors by BMI, race/ethnicity, and gender. *PLoS ONE, 7*(11), e48448. doi: 10.1371/journal.pone.0048448.

Sabin, J. A., Nosek, B. A., Greenwald, A. G., & Rivara, F. P. (2009). Physicians' implicit and explicit attitudes about race by MD race, ethnicity, and gender. *Journal of Health Care or the Poor and Underserved, 20,* 896–913. doi: 10.1353/hpu.0.0185.

Sabin, J. A., Rivara, F. P., & Greenwald, A. G. (2008). Physician implicit attitudes and stereotypes about race and quality of medical care. *Medical Care, 46,* 678–685. doi: 10.1097/MLR.06013e3181653d58.

Schwartz, M. B., Chambliss, H. O., Brownell, K. D., Blair, S. N., & Billington, C. (2003). Weight bias among health professionals specializing in obesity. *Obesity Research, 11,* 1033–1039. doi: 10.1038/064.2003.142.

Sontag, S. (1979). The double standard of aging. In J. H. Williams (Ed.), *The psychology of women: Selected readings* (pp. 462–478). New York: W.W. Norton.

Stevens, P. E. (1992). The experiences of lesbians of color in health care encounters: Narrative insights for improving access and quality. *Journal of Lesbian Studies, 2,* 77–94.

Stewart, T. L., Chipperfield, J. G., Perry, R. P., & Weiner, B. (2012). Attributing illness to "old age": Consequences of a self-directed stereotype for health and mortality. *Psychology and Health, 27,* 881–897. doi: 10.1080/08870446.2011.630735.

Sugar, J. A., Anstee, J. L. K., Desrochers, S., & Jambor, E. E. (2002). Gender biases in gerontological education: The status of older women. *Gerontology & Geriatrics Education, 22*(4), 43–55. doi: 10.1300/J021v22n04_04.

Tannebaum, C. B., Nasmith, L., & Mayo, N. (2003). Understanding older women's health concerns: A qualitative study. *Journal of Women & Aging, 15,* 3–15. doi: 10.1300/J074v15n04_09.

Taylor, S. E. (2012). *Health psychology* (8th ed.). New York: McGraw-Hill.

Tomasky, M. (2013). The ageist attack on Hillary. *Daily Beast.* From http://www.thedailybeast.com/articles/2013/07/01/the-ageist-attack-on-hillary.html. Accessed at September 1, 2014.

Travis, C. B. (2005). Heart disease and gender inequality. *Psychology of Women Quarterly, 29,* 15–23. doi: 10.1111/j.1471-6402.2005.00163.x.

Travis, C. B., Gressley, D. L., & Adams, P. L. (1995). Health care policy and practice for women's health. In A. L. Stanton & S. J. Gallant (Eds.), *The psychology of women's health: Progress and challenges in research and application* (pp. 531–565). Washington, DC: American Psychological Association.

Travis, C. B., Howerton, D. M., & Szymanski, D. M. (2012). Risk, uncertainty, and gender stereotypes in healthcare decisions. *Women & Therapy, 35,* 207–220. doi: 10.1111/j.1471-6402.2005.00163.x.

Van Egeren, L. (2004). Assessment approaches in health psychology: Issues and practical considerations. In P. M. Camic & S. J. Knight (Eds.), *Clinical handbook of health psychology* (2nd ed., pp. 11–26). Cambridge, MA: Hogrefe & Huber.

Vina, J., & Lloret, A. (2010). Why women have more Alzheimer's disease than men: Gender and mitochondrial toxicity of amyloid-beta peptide. *Journal of Alzheimer's Disease, 20,* S527–533. doi: 10.3233/JAD-201-100501.

Wenger, N. K. (2012). Gender disparity in cardiovascular disease: Bias or biology? *Expert Review of Cardiovascular Therapy, 10,* 1401–1411.

Williams, K. N., Herman, R., Gajweski, B., & Wilson, K. (2009). Elderspeak communication: Impact of dementia care. *American Journal of Alzheimer's Disease & Other Dementias, 24*, 11–20. doi: 10.1177/1533317508318472.

Yeom, H-E. (2013). Symptoms, aging-stereotyped beliefs, and health-promoting behaviors of older women with and without osteoarthritis. *Geriatric Nursing, 34*, 307–313. doi: 10.1016/j.gerinurse.2013.05.002002.

JOAN C. CHRISLER, PhD, is The Class of 1943 Professor of Psychology at Connecticut College, where she teaches courses on health psychology, social psychology, and the psychology of women. She has published extensively on the psychology of women and gender roles, and is especially known for her work on women's health, menstruation, weight, and body image. She is a former editor of *Sex Roles* and the current editor of *Women's Reproductive Health*.

ANGELA BARNEY is an MA candidate in Psychology at Connecticut College. Her research interests are in personality, social psychology, and women's health. She earned a BA in psychology and women's studies at the State University of New York, College at Fredonia.

BRIGIDA PALATINO is an MA candidate in Psychology at Connecticut College, where she also serves as assistant coach of the women's soccer team. Her research interests are in gender roles and health behavior. She earned a BA in psychology and environmental studies at Connecticut College.

Journal of Social Issues, Vol. 72, No. 1, 2016, pp. 105–121
doi: 10.1111/josi.12158

Old and Unemployable? How Age-Based Stereotypes Affect Willingness to Hire Job Candidates

Dominic Abrams*, Hannah J. Swift, and Lisbeth Drury
University of Kent

Across the world, people are required, or want, to work until an increasingly old age. But how might prospective employers view job applicants who have skills and qualities that they associate with older adults? This article draws on social role theory, age stereotypes and research on hiring biases, and reports three studies using age-diverse North American participants. These studies reveal that: (1) positive older age stereotype characteristics are viewed less favorably as criteria for job hire, (2) even when the job role is low-status, a younger stereotype profile tends to be preferred, and (3) an older stereotype profile is only considered hirable when the role is explicitly cast as subordinate to that of a candidate with a younger age profile. Implications for age-positive selection procedures and ways to reduce the impact of implicit age biases are discussed.

Global population aging means that between 2000 and 2050 the percentage of the world's population aged over 60 years will double from 11% to 22% (WHO, 2014). In many industrialized nations, this may create an unavoidable obligation to work longer (Feyrer, 2007). However, extending working life means older people may face age stereotypes, resulting in discrimination and exclusion from the labor market (McCann & Giles, 2002). Negative stereotypes that surround older people and older workers (Ng & Feldman, 2012) can harm their performance (Lamont, Swift, & Abrams, 2015) and influence employers' hiring decisions (Gringart, Helmes, & Speelman, 2005). However, research has yet to examine whether people's *assumptions* about a candidate's age may affect hiring decisions even

---

*Correspondence concerning this article should be addressed to Dominic Abrams, Centre for the Study of Group Processes, School of Psychology, University of Kent, Canterbury CT2 7NP, UK. Tel: 0044-1227-827475 [e-mail: D.Abrams@kent.ac.uk].

All authors are members of the EURAGE research team. The last author was supported by a grant from the Economic and Social Research Council ES/J500148/1 and by AgeUK. We are grateful to Giovanni A. Travaglino for support in setting up the experiments and to members of EURAGE and GroupLab for their comments and suggestions as the research progressed.

when there is no disclosure of actual age. In this article, drawing on theories of age stereotypes, social roles and hiring bias, we report a series of studies that investigate how age-stereotypical characteristics are used as criteria for job hire.

Many countries legislate against age discrimination in the workplace, preventing employers from limiting positions to particular ages (unless objectively justified), and entitling applicants to omit their age from their resumés (Age Discrimination and Employment Act, 1967; Equality Act, 2010). However, information included in job applications and resumés (e.g., including dated qualifications) often enable employers to discern an applicant's age. This could consciously or unconsciously lead to discrimination.

The present studies build on previous research on hiring biases but which has typically varied applicants' gender or their gender-stereotypic characteristics to see how this affects judges' preferences or hiring decisions (Eagly & Karau, 2002). For example, in a series of studies expanding on the "Think Manager— Think Male" effect, Ryan, Haslam, Hersby, and Bongiorno (2011) established a series of traits that are judged to characterize either men or women and discovered that people associate managers of successful companies with masculine traits and managers of unsuccessful companies with feminine traits.

To date, it appears that little research has explored how age-stereotypic characteristics rather than explicit age may affect judgments of hirability. Indeed, the one study that has examined explicit age-based candidate preference for an age-neutral job revealed that younger workers were rated slightly higher on their relevant job qualifications (Cleveland & Landy, 1983). The present work therefore sought to establish characteristics stereotypically associated with younger and older workers and then test whether profiles of candidates possessing these traits influence perceivers' willingness to hire them.

Based on theories of ageism, which demonstrate that people have implicit preferences for young over old (Levy & Banaji, 2002), and on evidence that youth is more often associated with competence and relatively higher status (Abrams, Russell, Vauclair, & Swift, 2011; Cuddy, Norton, & Fiske, 2005; Fiske, Cuddy, Glick, & Xu, 2002), we expect people to be more willing to hire a candidate with a relatively younger stereotypic profile even though there is no explicit information about that candidate's age. However, given the multidimensional nature of old-age workplace stereotypes (Dordoni & Argentero, 2015; Swift, Abrams, & Marques, 2012), we assume there may be circumstances that might moderate bias based on tenure (Postuma & Campion, 2008) and status of the position (Abrams et al., 2011).

Moderators of Age Discrimination in the Workplace

Short- and Long-Term Goals

One reason why employers may avoid hiring older people for a new position is that older people may provide fewer years of return on any training and investment

(Finkelstein & Burke, 1998). Hirers may therefore have greater preference for stereotypically younger candidates if the investment is viewed as long- rather than short-term. In contrast, a review of moderators of workplace age discrimination research revealed evidence for the opposing hypothesis—that older workers are a better long-term investment because they are less likely to quit (Postuma & Campion, 2008). Study 2 in this research tests these and a third (null) prediction that, because age is not explicit, judges cannot make a rational calculation based on age, and therefore implicit preferences for stereotypically younger candidates would arise regardless of the time frame.

Role Fit

Social role theory holds that discrimination may occur when there is a mismatch between a person's (gender) stereotypical characteristics and the requirements of the position for which they are applying (Eagly, 1987; Eagly & Karau, 2002). Translated to the age context, older workers are more likely to be discriminated against when there is a stereotypical mismatch between the worker's perceived age and characteristics of a particular position or profession (Postuma & Campion, 2008). Based on societal perceptions that older adults hold lower status than younger adults (Abrams et al., 2011), we expect that stereotypically older candidates will be more likely to be hired if the job itself is lower-status.

We report pilot work and three empirical studies to test these predictions In each study, people judge two candidates whose ages are not specified but who differ in their age-stereotypic characteristics. Study 1 examines hiring preferences for these candidates. Study 2 explores whether preferences are affected by the time frame for potential benefit for the employer, and Study 3 examines the effect of job status that is focal for the hiring decision.

Pilot Studies

Pilot work established two skill sets that would be viewed as stereotypically "young" and "old" by U.S. participants by adapting and adding to the attributes identified originally in U.K. research (Ray, Sharp, & Abrams, 2006; Swift et al., 2013). Participants were recruited and paid to complete the questions via Amazon's Mechanical Turk. The questionnaire presented a set of 20 skills and abilities. Participants were asked to choose whether each ability was "more typical of people in their 20s" (scored 1), "more typical of people in their 60s" (scored 3), or "equally typical of both" (scored 2).

The age stereotypicality of each ability was evaluated by 60 participants (ranging from 18 to 72 years, $M = 35.1$, $SD = 12.93$, 57% Male). Attributes were designated as stereotypical if they were distinctively typical of one group (half

Table 1. Age-Stereotypic Ability Profiles and Hiring Preferences across Studies

	Person A	Person B
	Settling arguments	Learning new skills
	Understanding other's views	Being creative
	Dealing with people politely	Using new computer technology (e.g., Smartphones)
	Solving crosswords	Rapid decision making
	Being an effective complainer	Being open to new ideas/experiences
	Using a library	Communicativeness
	Carefulness	Using social media (e.g., Facebook)
Pilot M (SD)		
Age categorization	2.42 (0.30)	1.46 (0.31)
Valence	5.39 (0.47)	5.55 (0.50)
Study 1 hiring preference for Person B (%)		80
Study 2 hiring preference		
Long-term		85
Short-term		81
Study 3 hiring preference		
Control		73
Supervised		72
Subordinate		50

Note. Age categorization ranges from 1 = *typical of a person in their 20s* to 3 = *typical of a person in their 60s*. Valence ratings can range from 1 = *very negative* to 7 = *very positive*.

or more of respondents assigned it to one age group and fewer than a quarter of respondents assigned it to the other or both age groups). Abilities were defined as neutral if at least half the respondents judged that it applied to both age categories, and no more than 30% selected either age group.

A separate sample of 25 participants (ranging from 18 to 66 years, $M = 32.9$, $SD = 13.1$, 56% Male) rated each attribute on a 7-point scale (1 = *very negative*, 7 = *very positive*). We then compiled two age-stereotypic profiles that were matched in terms of mean valence and then added a neutral item to each profile (carefulness and communicativeness).

The two profiles are shown in Table 1. The age categorization of the abilities in the two profiles differed significantly, $t(59) = 16.12$, $p < .001$ and both differed significantly from the scale-neutral point (2). The mean valence of the two profiles did not differ significantly, $t(24) = 1.61$, $p = .121$. We therefore used these profiles, which are equivalent in valence but differ in age stereotypicality, as the stimuli in the studies that followed.

Study 1

Study 1 tested preferences for these two positive profiles when participants considered each as a candidate for a job. We explicitly stated that the candidates had similar qualifications and neither had previous experience of the job. We expected that the "younger" profile (Candidate B) would be more likely to be selected as a potential job hire.

Method

Participants. Participants were 40 MTURK workers (ranging from 21 to 62 years, $M = 36.9$, $SD = 11.9$, 54% Male). No constraints were placed on participants. The data stopping rule was 40 cases because, from lecture demonstrations that had used a similar stimulus set, we anticipated a large effect size.

Procedure and measures. Participants were instructed: "In this study we are asking you to imagine that you are an employer who is looking at applications from two different people that are applying for the same job. As the employer, your goal is to hire someone who will maximize the profits of your company. Your task is quite difficult because there are a lot of candidates who have similar qualifications and none have any previous experience in this kind of job. Each candidate also completed a psychometric questionnaire about their interests, skills and abilities, and this has given you a profile of ways in which each candidate is distinctive from the other candidates. Using this information your task is to select the person that you wish to employ to maximize the profits of your company. To keep these names anonymous, we have labelled these candidates with letters A and B rather than providing their actual names."

Hiring decision. Participants then viewed the two profiles simultaneously before responding to the question: "Who would you hire?" They were asked to select a button to show if they would hire Person A, Person B, or were unsure.

Age estimates. On the next screen, participants were then asked to estimate the age of each candidate using a slider scale (from 19 to 81).

Results

Hiring decision. Eighty percent (32) of the participants chose to hire Candidate B (the younger profile). Fifteen percent selected Candidate A and 5% (2) were unsure, $\chi^2 = 14.40$, $p < .001$ (see Table 1).

Point biserial correlation analyses showed that participants' age and gender were not significantly related to their candidate choice ($ps > .70$).

Age estimates.   A repeated measure ANOVA showed that Candidate A was judged to be older ($M = 36.53$, $SD = 9.76$) than Candidate B ($M = 32.10$, $SD = 9.65$), $F(1, 39) = 4.56$, $p = .039$, $\eta_p^2 = .105$. Moreover, the participants who chose Candidate B estimated Candidate B's age to be lower than did participants who did not choose Candidate B (point biserial $r = -.39$, $p = .012$). Finally, multiple regression analysis showed that when participants' own age and gender and their estimates of Candidate A's age were included as covariates, the relationship between estimates of Candidate B's age and hiring choice remained significant ($\beta = -.36$, $t = 2.16$, $p = .038$).

In summary, only a minority of participants chose to hire the stereotypically older age profile (A). Participants' assumed Candidate B was younger and the more they did so, the more they preferred to hire Candidate B, consistent with the idea that implicit age stereotypes affected hiring decisions.

Study 2

Given the goal of "maximizing profits," a plausible explanation for hiring a stereotypically younger candidate is based on "rational" cost-benefit calculations. If participants had long-term profits in mind in Study 1, the "younger" candidate could work for longer before reaching retirement and provide greater total profit for the company. Alternatively, if participants had short-term profits in mind, their preference for the younger profile may be because they discounted the stereotypically older candidate's potentially greater long-term value due to their lower turnover intention (Posthuma & Campion, 2008). To test these possibilities, Study 2 examined whether the selection chances of the stereotypically older profile (Candidate A) would depend on whether the employer's goal was short-, rather than long-term profits. However, we noted from Study 1 that the age-stereotype link generated quite a small explicit difference in age estimates for the two candidates. This makes it less likely that it is the specific age of candidates that affects decisions but rather perceptions of relative age and implicit ageism. In that case, the preference for the "younger" profile may persist regardless of time perspective.

Method

Participants and design.   Eighty MTURK workers (ranging from 19 to 70 years, $M = 35.3$, $SD = 11.7$, 60% Male) were recruited as participants. Using random assignment to condition (via Qualtrics software), we presented the profiles for Candidates A and B and defined either short- or long-term objectives.

Procedure and measures.   In the short- and long-term conditions (respective differences shown in parentheses), participants were instructed as Study 1. However, "maximize the profits of your company" was replaced with "be an ideal worker for the [short term/long term] benefit of your company over [the next financial year/ a number of financial years]." Participants then completed the job hire and age estimation measures as in Study 1.

Results

Hiring decision. Eighty-three percent of participants selected Candidate B ($\chi^2 = 37.33, p < .001$). Moreover, time frame condition made no difference to the selection of candidates, $\chi^2 = 0.34$. Eighty-one percent and 85% chose Candidate B in the short- and long-term conditions, respectively (see Table 1).

Age estimations. Candidate B was judged to be significantly younger than Candidate A, repeating the finding from Study 1, $F(1, 79) = 20.58$, $\eta_p^2 = .207$.

In summary, regardless of whether they were considering hiring for a short-term or long-term position, participants strongly preferred a stereotypically younger age profile.

Study 3

We extended our consideration of the stereotypical status differences between older and younger people. Based on Eagly's Role Theory (1987) and the stereotype content model (Fiske et al., 2002), we considered that the warm/less competent older stereotype would be more compatible with a low-status role. Therefore, in Study 3, we compared whether specifying a position as low-status would increase the probability that the stereotypically older candidate (A) would be hired.

Given that Studies 1 and 2 revealed a strong preference for hiring Candidate B, and based on role theory, we wondered if low status per se would be sufficient to make Candidate A attractive. Specifically, whereas stereotype-based models of ageism have identified that being older (in general) is associated with lower societal status (Abrams et al., 2011; Cuddy et al., 2005), a role-based interpretation might assume that the low status might only affect a hiring decision if there is certainty that the job position would be subordinate to someone who should have higher status, thereby assuring role fit.

To test this idea, we compared the baseline condition of Study 1 (Control condition) against two alternative scenarios involving a low-status criterion for hiring. We either specified that the task was to hire a person to occupy a supervisee role (Supervisee condition), or we specified that participants should select which of the two candidates should be supervised by (subordinate to) the other (Subordinate condition). The Supervisee and Subordinate conditions both required participants to select a person to be supervised, but the Subordinate condition involved explicit subordination of one candidate to the other, thus ensuring fulfillment of a comparatively lower-status role. To explore how participants were thinking about the different roles, we also investigated perceptions of the candidates. If hiring decisions are driven by implicit ageism and only one candidate can be hired, participants should still favor the "younger profile," even as a supervisee. But this "younger" preference should reduce if the selected candidate will be subordinate to the other because of the less close role fit between being stereotypically younger and a relatively lower status position.

Method

Participants and design.   One hundred and fifty MTURK participants (ranging from 19 to 67 years, $M = 35.6$, $SD = 12.4$, 55% Female) were randomly assigned to condition (Control, Supervisee, Subordinate).

Procedure and measures.   The Control condition instructed participants to hire a candidate to maximize profits, exactly as in Study 1. The Supervisee condition and Subordinate condition instructions (distinguished by a slash in parentheses) were as follows: "In this study we are asking people to imagine that they are an employer who is looking at applications from two different people who are applying for [a job/two jobs]. You will hire [one person/both people] so you must decide which one should be hired to be [supervised /supervised by the other]. As the employer, your goal is to choose which one should be [supervised/the subordinate (supervised)]. The other one [will not be hired/will be the supervisor]. Your task is quite difficult because these have similar qualifications and neither has any previous experience in this kind of job. But both people completed a psychometric questionnaire about their interests, skills and abilities, and this has given you a profile of ways in which each candidate is distinctive from the other. Using this information your task is to select which person should hired to be [supervised/subordinate (supervised)]. The other one will [not be hired/ be the supervisor]. To keep these names anonymous, we have labeled candidates with letters (Person A, and Person B) rather than providing actual names. Your task is to decide whether Person A or Person B should be the one who should be [hired to be supervised /subordinate (supervised)]. Click next to view the profile of each candidate."

Participants then completed the hiring decision and age estimation measures. In order to understand reasons for hiring decisions, we asked participants to judge how important each attribute was for the job, to evaluate the profiles of the two candidates, and to infer demographic characteristics for the two profiles.

Job-related importance of attributes.   Participants were asked how important each of the following attributes was for the job ($1 = $ *not at all important*, $7 = $ *extremely important*): settling arguments, understanding others' views, dealing with people politely, solving crosswords, being an effective complainer, using a library, carefulness, learning new skills, being creative, using new computer technology (e.g., smartphones), rapid decision making, openness to new ideas and experiences, communicativeness, using social media (e.g., Facebook), and other (free response). Presentation of all but the last item was randomized.

Trait inferences. Participants were asked to rate (1 = *very unlikely*, 5 = *very likely*) whether Person A and Person B were gentle, intelligent, warm, moral, exciting, interesting, admirable, perform well at tasks, have a lot of potential, are resourceful, reliable, loyal, open, efficient, motivated, experienced, needy, financially smart, risk takers, and natural leaders. The presentation order of these characteristics was randomized.

Demographic inferences. Participants were asked to indicate whether they thought Person A and/or Person B were male/female, White/Black/Hispanic/Asian, heterosexual/gay or bisexual, religious/nonreligious, American. Order of presentation was randomized.

Results

Hiring decision. Overall, 64.8% selected Candidate B ($\chi^2 = 12.75$, $p < .001$). However, this proportion varied as a function of condition, χ^2 (2 df) $= 7.38$, $p = .029$). Specifically, whereas 73.3% chose Candidate B in the control condition, and 72% in the supervisee condition, this reduced to 50% in the subordinate condition (see Table 1).

Age estimates. Candidate B ($M = 32.42$, $SD = 8.66$) was judged as significantly younger than Candidate A ($M = 37.92$, $SD = 9.66$), repeating the findings from Studies 1 and 2, $F(1,138) = 23.26$, $p < .001$, $\eta_p^2 = .144$. Moreover, estimates of candidates' ages did not vary by condition, suggesting that differences in hiring decisions were not because the subordinate condition had altered the perceived age difference between the candidates.

Inspection of correlations within conditions indicated that participants in the Control condition who selected Person B were significantly more likely to estimate Person B's age as younger ($r = -.40$, $p = .009$). In contrast, participants in the Subordinate condition who selected Candidate B were significantly more likely to estimate Candidate B's age as being older ($r = .38$, $p = .007$). In the Supervisee condition, there was no significant correlation ($r = .04$, $p = .790$). This suggested an interactive effect of condition and perceived age on hiring decisions. To test this possibility, we dummy coded conditions and created interaction terms between the Control condition and estimates of Candidate B's age, and between the Subordinate condition and Candidate B's estimated age. We then conducted a regression analysis to test the effects of participants' age and gender, Control condition and Subordinate condition, age estimate of Candidate B, and the two interaction terms on whether participants selected Candidate B.

The analysis confirmed that there were no significant effects of participants' age or gender (βs = -.09, -.15) or their estimates of Candidate A's age (β = -.05). Both the Control condition and the Subordinate condition differed from the means of the alternative conditions (βs = .65, -1.04, ps = .01, < .001, respectively). More interesting were the Control x estimated age of Candidate B interaction, β = -.65, t = -2.62, p = .01, and the Subordinate x age of Candidate B interaction, β = .86, t = 3.21, p = .002. The addition of these interaction terms increased the R^2 from .08 to .18, and F for the final equation was F (7,132) = 4.24, p < .001. To summarize this finding, when participants simply had the goal of selecting the best candidate, the younger they estimated Candidate B's age, the more likely they were to select Candidate B. When participants had the goal of selecting which candidate should be subordinate, the older they perceived Candidate B to be the more likely they were to select Candidate B.

We repeated these analyses but with the estimated age of Candidate A as the independent variable, whether Candidate A was chosen as the dependent variable, and estimated age of Candidate B as a covariate. This revealed no effects except a significant Subordinate condition versus other conditions effect (β = .23, t = 2.44, p = .028), all other ps > .10. This simply reflects that finding that Candidate A was more likely to be selected in the Subordinate condition than in other conditions.

Job-related importance of attributes.   The job characteristics were averaged into two scores, one for the importance of the characteristics presented in the profile of Candidate A (the older profile) and one for Candidate B (the younger profile.). We conducted a repeated measure ANCOVA (Condition x Profile), with Condition as a between participants factor and Profile (older, younger) as a within participants factor. Participant age and gender were covariates. This revealed no significant effects of the covariates, but a significant effect of Condition, F (2,135) = 4.50, p = .013, η_p^2 = .062, a significant effect of Profile, F (1,135) = 8.18, p = .005, η_p^2 = .057, and a significant Condition x Profile interaction, F (2,135) = 5.94, p = .003, η_p^2 = .081.

Attributes were regarded as less important when no role was specified (M = 4.88, SD = 0.72), than when the role was either supervised (M = 5.18, SD = 0.61) or subordinate (M = 5.26, SD = 0.53). The older profile attributes were regarded as less important (M = 4.58, SD = 0.87), than the younger profile attributes (M = 5.64, SD = 0.76). Simple effects tests showed that whereas the importance of the young profile attributes did not differ between conditions, F (2,135) = 0.79, p = .457, η_p^2 = .012, the importance of the older profile attributes did differ, F (2,135) = 8.87, p < .001, η_p^2 = .116. Pairwise comparisons showed that the attributes were accorded less importance in the Control condition (M = 4.18, SD = 1.05) than in either the Supervisee (M = 4.64, SD = 0.81) or Subordinate (M = 4.92,

$SD = 0.58$) conditions ($ps = .017$, $< .001$, respectively) and that the importance was greater in the Subordinate than in the Supervisee condition ($p = .062$).

Trait inferences. The items were averaged into mean positivity ratings for each candidate (alphas $> .7$) and these were subjected to analysis by ANCOVA. This revealed a significant main effect of Condition, $F (1,134) = 10.59, p < .001$, $\eta_p^2 = .137$, and a marginal interaction, $F (2,134) = 2.58, p = .08, \eta_p^2 = .037$). However, the simple effect of Condition was significant only for Candidate A, $F (1,134) = 10.89, p < .001, \eta_p^2 = .140$. Candidate A was rated less positively in the Control condition ($M = 3.25, SD = 0.67$) than in either the Supervisee condition ($M - 3.52, SD = 0.51, p = .02$) or the Subordinate condition ($M = 3.78$, $SD = 0.42, p < .001$), and less favorably in the Supervisee condition than the Subordinate condition ($p = .017$). In contrast, the simple effect of Condition was nonsignificant for Candidate B, $F (1,134) = 1.58, p = .209, \eta_p^2 = .023$, as this candidate was rated equally positively in all conditions ($Ms = 3.71, 3.82, 3.89$, $SDs = 0.53, 0.50, 0.45$, respectively, all pairwise $ps > .07$). Moreover, whereas ratings of A and B differed significantly in both the Control, $F (1,134) = 16.02$, $p < .001, \eta_p^2 = .107$, and the Supervisee condition, $F (1,134) = 8.87, p = .003$, $\eta_p^2 = .062$, they did not differ significantly in the Subordinate condition, $F (1,134) = 1.33, p = .250, \eta_p^2 = .01$.

Demographic inferences. These data were coded first according to whether or not the candidate was judged to have a majority group characteristic (White, male, American, religious, heterosexual). Repeated measure MANCOVA revealed no significant differences due to Condition, Candidate, or participant gender or age. These scores were factor analyzed for each candidate. Because they all loaded significantly on the first principle component, an average "majority" score was created for each candidate. This score could range from 0 (no majority characteristics) to 1 (entirely majority characteristics). Overall, participants judged that at least half of the candidates' characteristics were majority memberships ($M = 0.58, SD = 0.28$). A repeated measure ANCOVA on this score confirmed the MANCOVA findings and revealed no significant differences due to Condition, candidate, or participant gender or age. These analyses confirm that the profiles differed only in terms of their stereotypical age and were not associated with other major demographic characteristic.

Mediation analyses. Because hiring choices differed between the Subordinate and other conditions, we sought to explain why preferences shifted in the Subordinate condition. To simplify analyses, we constructed a difference score for the relative importance of the profile characteristics for the job (Candidate B minus Candidate A), and a difference score for the relative positivity ratings of Candidate

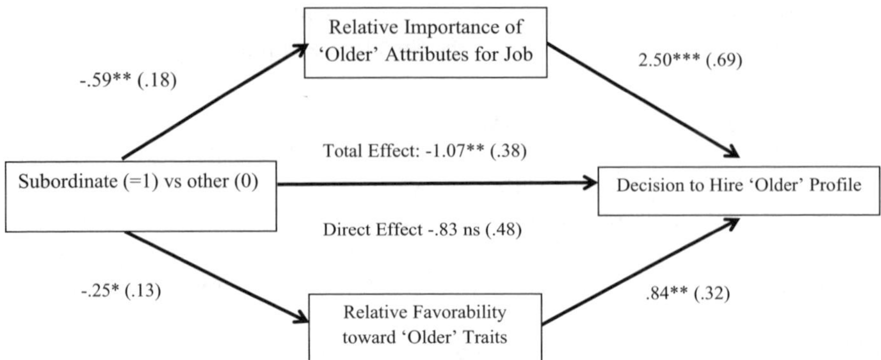

Fig. 1. Effect of condition on hiring decisions, mediated by attribute importance and favorability ratings.
Note. Indirect effects via relative importance, $B = -.501$, $SE = .25$, 95% CI [-1.11, -0.14] and relative favorability, $B = -.633$, $SE = .37$, 95% CI [-1.46, -0.07], do not differ from one another, $B = .132$, $SE = .43$, 95% CI [-1.12, 0.56].

B minus the positivity ratings of Candidate A. ANCOVAs showed that these two scores differed significantly between the Subordinate and other conditions.

The relative importance and relative favorability measures were significantly correlated with one another ($r = .49$, $p < .001$), and each was significantly correlated with hiring choice (point biserial $r = .48$, .49, respectively). Given that both could potentially mediate between conditions and hiring decisions, we conducted a parallel mediation analysis using Hayes' (2013) Process SPSS Macro (model 4 with 5,000 bootstraps), including participant age and gender as covariates.

The covariates were nonsignificant and the total effect of Subordinate condition was significant, $B = -1.07$, $SE = .38$, 95% CI [-1.81, -0.33]. There were significant indirect effects of both job importance $B = -.50$, $SE = .25$, 95% CI [-1.11, -0.14], and profile ratings, $B = -.63$, $SE = .70$, 95% CI [-1.46, -0.07], and the direct effect of Subordinate condition was not significant, $B = -.83$, $SE = .48$, 95% CI [-1.77, 0.11] (see Figure 1).

In summary, the subordinate condition increased participants' relative favorability toward Candidate A's characteristics, and also their judgments of whether those characteristics were relatively important for the job. These two effects accounted for increased selection of Candidate A.

Discussion

This research is the first, to our knowledge, to have systematically tested whether exhibiting age-stereotypic characteristics *per se* may affect a candidate's chances of being hired. We established profiles of age-stereotyped job characteristics that are more stereotypical of a person in their 20s or in their 60s, respectively. We established that the characteristics, judged without reference to the job context, are judged equally positively. In the studies that followed, we ascribed the profiles to Candidate A (older profile) and Candidate B (younger profile), respectively. Across three studies, these profiles led participants to assume Candidate B was younger than Candidate A. In Study 1, 80% of participants selected the younger profile (B) to maximize their company's profits. Study 2 established that this preference could not be attributed to judges' adoption of a long- or short-term time frame. Therefore, decisions were unlikely to be rationally based on candidates' likely cumulative contribution or turnover intention. Candidate B was strongly preferred, regardless of whether the goal was to maximize short- or long-term profits.

Study 3 tested whether role fit accounted for whether the older age profile would be "hirable." Even when the role involved being supervised, selection of Candidate A only increased when the role was explicitly subordinate to that of the younger profile (B).

Study 3 also examined the perceptions and inferences that participants made about the attributes of the two candidates and what would be necessary for the job. Overall, participants rated Candidate B's characteristics as more important for the job and rated them more positively. Note that the latter finding appears to contradict the idea that the two profiles shared a similar valence. However, whereas the pilot research showed that the characteristics themselves had similar valence, these evaluations were clearly altered when participants considered them as being relevant to a job rather than in a context-free manner. Importantly, we found that the differences in the job relevance and ratings of the two sets of attributes were significantly lower when participants were considering them for the subordinate role. Moreover, this reduced differentiation also explained, statistically, why participants were willing to select Candidate A, the older profile, when considering a subordinate role.

Taken together, these findings are in line with a social role account (Eagly, 1987) and strongly indicate that job applicants may well be vulnerable to implicit age stereotyping and ageist assumptions that older workers belong in low-status roles. Ironically, even when an applicant highlights positively valued traits and skills, if mentioning these skills invokes old-age stereotypes, they could well create implicit beliefs that the candidate is "older" than others, and this could place them at a disadvantage relative to applicants who only highlight their "young" stereotypical attributes.

Limitations, Future Directions, and Implications for Policy and Practice

These studies are novel and we acknowledge several limitations. International generalizability of the findings has yet to be established because, whilst drawing

initially from U.K. evidence, the studies all involve only North American participants. Nor is it known whether the requirement to "maximize profits" affected the
level of bias. Many organizations define profit as their primary objective but the
salience of other goals (e.g., providing excellent services) might tilt biases in other
directions (cf. Finkelstein & Burke, 1998). The decisions of actual managers and
recruitment staff may differ if they are motivated to avoid stereotype-based bias
(Singer & Sewell, 1989). More generally, making judges feel more accountable
for their decisions (Gordon, Rozelle, & Baxter, 1988), reducing their cognitive
busyness (Perry, Kulik, & Bourhis, 1996), or reducing intergenerational resource
scarcity (North & Fiske, 2016) may moderate their reliance on stereotypes for
hiring decisions.

Based on role theory (Eagly, 1987), we argued that older = lower status.
Even if this is not always true for high levels of certain occupations (e.g., judges,
surgeons, politicians, CEOs), these older high-status roles may still involve significant "younger" stereotypic attributes. Thus, even for these roles there may be
an advantage in highlighting a higher proportion of such attributes at the selection
stages. These are all questions for future research.

Implicit age bias in hiring has policy relevance for individuals, organizations,
and society. For individuals, exclusion from the labor market can increase the
likelihood of depression and mental health problems for older adults (Aquino,
Russell, Cutrona, & Altmaier, 1996; Gallo et al., 2006) whereas there are significant psychological benefits for older people that remain in the workforce (Schooler,
Mulatu, & Oates, 1999). If job candidates who present or reveal older-stereotypic
abilities and skills activate recruiters' implicitly ageist hiring preferences, this suggests that both applicants and recruiters should be made aware of these potential
biases in order to avoid or challenge them directly. Strategically, candidates could
tailor their resumés to display only competence and other stereotypically "young"
traits that organizations have preferences for, such as learning new skills, creativ-
ity, and competence using technology to mitigate the application of old stereotypes. Although this may actually increase resentment toward older workers in
conditions where resources are scarce and if older workers are perceived to violate prescriptive norms (North & Fiske, 2016). Ideally, however, employers would
learn to recognize the actual advantages and strengths of both older and younger
stereotypical qualities rather than to assume one set is inevitably better.

Even for objectively or stereotypically younger people these findings are
troubling. Younger people eventually become older, so the perpetual application
of ageist hiring assumptions means that people may approach aging with growing
anxiety and dread of age discrimination. This not only poses a stereotype threat that
could well harm their actual capacity to perform well at work (Lamont et al., 2015),
but has potential to decrease job satisfaction and job commitment (Macdonald &
Levy, 2016).

The implication of these findings is that implicit age bias could lead organizations to fail to select the best candidates because of unacknowledged assumptions about candidates' age. Thus, organizations may well underperform because age inferences are drawn that downplay the strengths of candidates who show relatively more "older" characteristics.

At a societal level, the need to retain people in the workforce longer and to sustain incomes and resources into later old age all mean that biases against "older" abilities and skills will lead to reduced opportunities, greater impoverishment, and ultimately more dependency among the oldest members of society. This research shows that even positive age stereotypes may be a substantial driver of age discrimination in employment.

References

Abrams, D., Russell, P. S., Vauclair, C.-M., & Swift, H. (2011). *Ageism in Europe, findings from the European Social Survey*. London: Age UK. Retrieved from http://www.ageuk.org.uk/documents/en-gb/id10704%20ageism%20across%20europe%20report%20interactive.pdf?dtrk=true

Age Discrimination and Employment Act. (1967). Pub. L., No. 90–202, 81 Stat 602. 1967. (coded as amended at 29 U.S.C.A) §§ 621–634. West, 2000.

Aquino, J. A., Russell, D. W., Cutrona, C. E., & Altmaier, E. M. (1996). Employment status, social support, and life satisfaction among the elderly. *Journal of Counseling Psychology*, *43*, 480. doi: org/10.1037/0022-0167.43.4.480.

Cleveland, J. N., & Landy, F. J. (1983). The effects of person and job stereotypes on two personnel decisions. *Journal of Applied Psychology*, *68*, 609–619. doi: org/10.1037/0021-9010.68.4.609.

Cuddy, A. J. C., Norton, M. I., & Fiske, S. T. (2005). This old stereotype: The pervasiveness and persistence of the elderly stereotype. *Journal of Social Issues*, *61*, 267–285. doi: 10.1111/j/1540-4560.2005.00405.x.

Dordoni, P., & Argentero, P. (2015). When age stereotypes are employment barriers: A conceptual analysis and a literature review on older workers stereotypes. *Ageing International*. doi: 10.2466/pr0.1960.7.2.203.

Eagly, A. H. (1987). *Sex differences in social behavior: A social role interpretation*. Hillsdale, NJ: Lawrence Erlbaum.

Eagly, A. H., & Karau, S. J. (2002). Role congruity theory of prejudice towards female leaders, *Psychological Review*, *109*, 573–598. doi: 10.1037/0033-295X.109.3.573.

Equality Act. (2010). Available online at http://www.legislation.gov.uk/ukpga/2010/15. Accessed at October 1, 2015.

Feyrer, J. (2007). Demographics and productivity. *The Review of Economics and Statistics*, *89*, 100–109. doi: org/10.1162/rest.89.1.100

Finkelstein, L. M., & Burke, M. J. (1998). Age stereotyping at work: The role of rater and contextual factors on evaluations of job applicants. *Journal of General Psychology*, *125*, 317–345. doi: 10.1080/00221309809595341.

Fiske, S. T., Cuddy, A. J. C., Glick, P., & Xu, J. (2002). A model of (often mixed) stereotype content: Competence and warmth respectively follow from perceived status and competition. *Journal of Personality and Social Psychology*, *82*, 878–902. doi: 10.1037/0022-3514.82.6.878.

Gallo, W. T., Bradley, E. H., Dubin, J. A., Jones, R. N., Falba, T. A., Teng, H. M., & Kasl, S. V. (2006). The persistence of depressive symptoms in older workers who experience involuntary job loss: Results from the health and retirement survey. *Journals of Gerontology Series B*, *61*, S221–S228. doi: 10.1093/geronb/61.4.S221.

Gordon, R. A., Rozelle, R. M., & Baxter, J. C. (1988). The effect of applicant age, job level, and accountability on the evaluation of job applicants. *Organizational Behavior and Human Decision Processes*, *41*, 20–33. doi: 10.1016/0749-5978(88)90044-1.

Gringart, E., Helmes, E., & Speelman, C. P. (2005). Exploring attitudes toward older workers among Australian employers: An empirical study. *Journal of Aging & Social Policy, 17*, 85–103. doi: org/10.1300/J031v17n03_05

Hayes, A. F. (2013). *Introduction to mediation, moderation and conditional process analysis: A regression-based approach.* NY: Guilford Press.

Lamont, R.A., Swift, H. J., & Abrams, D. (2015). A review and meta-analysis of age-based stereotype threat: Negative stereotypes, not facts, do the damage. *Psychology and Aging, 30*, 180–193. doi: 10.1037/a0038586.

Levy, B., & Banaji, M. R. (2002). Implicit ageism. In T. D. Nelson (Ed.), *Ageism, stereotyping and prejudice against older persons* (pp. 163–199). Cambridge, MA: MIT Press.

Macdonald, J. L., & Levy, S. R. (2016). Ageism in the workplace: The role of psychosocial factors in predicting job satisfaction, commitment, and engagement. *Journal of Social Issues, 72*(1), 169–190.

McCann, R., & Giles, H. (2002). Ageism in the workplace: A communication perspective. In T. D. Nelson (Ed.), *Ageism, stereotyping and prejudice against older persons* (pp. 163–199). Cambridge, MA: MIT Press.

Ng, T. W. H., & Feldman, D. C. (2012). Evaluating six common stereotypes about older workers with meta-analytical data. *Personnel Psychology, 65*, 821–858. doi: 10.1111/peps.12003.

North, M. S., & Fiske, S. T. (2016). Resource scarcity and prescriptive attitudes generate subtle, intergenerational older-worker exclusion. *Journal of Social Issues, 72*(1), 122–145.

Perry, E. L., Kulik, C. T., & Bourhis, A. C. (1996). Moderating effects of personal and contextual factors in age discrimination. *Journal of Applied Psychology, 81*, 628. doi: 10.1037/0021-9010.81.6.628.

Posthuma, R. A., & Campion, M. A. (2008). Age stereotypes in the workplace: Common stereotypes, moderators, and future research directions. *Journal of Management, 35*, 158–188. doi: 10.1177/0149206308318617.

Ray, S., Sharp, E., & Abrams, D. (2006). *Age discrimination 2006: A benchmark for public attitudes.* London: Age Concern England, Policy Unit. Retrieved from http://www.ageuk.org.uk/documents/en-gb/for-professionals/equality-and-human-rights/ageism%20%20-%20a%20benchmark%20of%20public%20ageist%20attitudes_pro.pdf

Ryan, M. K., Haslam, S. A., Hersby, M. D., & Bongiorno, R. (2011). Think crisis–think female: The glass cliff and contextual variation in the think manager–think male stereotype. *Journal of Applied Psychology, 96*, 470. doi: 10.1037/a0022133.

Schooler, C., Mulatu, M. S., & Oates, G. (1999). The continuing effects of substantively complex work on the intellectual functioning of older workers. *Psychology and Aging, 14*, 483–506. doi: 10.1037/0882-7974.14.3.483.

Singer, M. S., & Sewell, C. (1989). Applicant age and selection interview decisions: Effect of information exposure on age discrimination in personnel selection. *Personnel Psychology, 42*, 135–154. doi: 10.1111/j.1744-6570.1989.tb01554.x.

Swift, H. J., Abrams, D., & Marques, S. (2013). Threat or boost: Social comparison affects older people's performance differently depending on task domain. *Journals of Gerontology, Series B, 68*, 23–30. doi:10.1093/geronb/gbs044.

World Health Organisation (WHO). (2014). Ageing and the life course: Facts about ageing. Retrieved from http://www.who.int/ageing/about/facts/en. Accessed at October 1, 2015.

DOMINIC ABRAMS is Professor of Social Psychology and Director of the Centre for the Study of Group Processes at the University of Kent. His research focuses on the psychological dynamics of social exclusion and inclusion within and between groups. He is codirector and founder of the European Research Group on Attitudes to Age, which designed the European Social Survey Round 4 module on experiences and expressions of ageism, (http://www.eurage.com). He is coeditor with Michael A. Hogg of the journal *Group Processes and Intergroup*

Relations, and recently (with Melanie Killen) of a JSI issue on social exclusion and children. He is a past president of SPSSI, and Fellow of the British Academy and the Academy of Social Sciences.

HANNAH J. SWIFT is Eastern ARC Research Fellow at the Centre for the Study of Group Processes at the University of Kent, from where she also completed her PhD (2012) as an ESRC-CASE grant holder in conjunction with AgeUK. Her research focuses on attitudes to aging, ageism, stereotype threat, well-being and factors that contribute to loneliness in later life as well as active, healthy aging. As well as contributing to U.K. government reports and European Social Survey and Gerontological Society of America policy briefings, her work has been published in journals including *Psychology and Aging, Journal of Gerontology, BMJ-Open, Addiction,* and *Journal of Applied Social Psychology.*

LISBETH DRURY is currently an ESRC-AgeUK CASE award holder completing her PhD in Social Psychology at the University of Kent. Her interests include intergenerational contact, age stereotypes, and the intersection of ageism and sexism. Her research includes reports for the U.K. Government's Foresight project on enablers of positive attitudes to age. She is Managing Editor of *Group Processes and Intergroup Relations.*

Journal of Social Issues, Vol. 72, No. 1, 2016, pp. 122–145
doi: 10.1111/josi.12159

Resource Scarcity and Prescriptive Attitudes Generate Subtle, Intergenerational Older-Worker Exclusion

Michael S. North[*]
New York University

Susan T. Fiske
Princeton University

Prior work describes specific, prescriptive resource tensions between generations, comprising active Succession, passive Consumption, and symbolic Identity (SCI; North and Fiske). The current paper focuses on how these domains potentially drive intergenerational exclusion in work-related networking and training spheres. Studies 1a–c—each focusing on a different SCI domain—manipulated perceived resource availability between generations, then introduced a professional networking opportunity. Across studies, scarcity reduced the likelihood of young participants' networking engagement with older workers who violated SCI resource expectations. Study 2 impelled participants to allocate scarce training resources among three similarly qualified but different-aged employees (younger, middle-aged, and older). Older workers received the lowest such investment, particularly among younger participants—an effect driven by Succession beliefs, per mediation analyses. Overall, the findings emphasize resource tensions in driving older workers' subtle exclusion by younger generations; minimizing such tensions will be critical for aging, increasingly intergenerational workplaces.

The global older population is growing at an unprecedented rate, generating concerns about whether societies worldwide can accommodate all generations (Nelson, 2004; North & Fiske, 2012; Olshansky et al., 2011). In the United States specifically, generational equity challenges affect a variety of domains, including Social Security, health care, employment, and taxation (North & Fiske, 2013c). Given the hot-button nature of these issues, especially in austere times, and genuine

---

[*]Correspondence concerning this article should be addressed to Michael S. North, Management & Organizations Department, New York University Stern School of Business, 40 West 4th Street, Tisch 713, New York, NY 10012. Tel: (212) 998-0429; [e-mail: mnorth@stern.nyu.edu.Abstract].

122

fears over whether an aging society can adequately manage the needs of multiple cohorts, increasingly common beliefs emphasize intergenerational warfare over scarce resources—pitting "Boomers versus Millennials," or "canes versus kids" (Minkler, 2006; Winerip, 2012).

Such zero-sum concerns are perhaps nowhere more salient than in employment contexts, where recent demographic trends have strained both ends of the age spectrum. On the older side, rising rates of delayed retirement have corresponded with a significant rise in age discrimination charges, and disproportionately long unemployment duration (Kreamer, 2012; Macdonald & Levy, 2016; Tugend, 2013). Meanwhile, younger workers currently face the highest unemployment rates overall (U.S. Bureau of Labor Statistics, 2013). Balancing the needs of these two large generations has thus become a labor priority, but not one that is easy to solve.

Despite apparent employment barriers, the modern workplace is nevertheless more intergenerational than ever. This unprecedented age diversity presents its own set of challenges. For instance, as older workers more commonly hold on to enviable positions of employment, younger generations may come to resent what they perceive as obstruction of their own outcomes, both practical (e.g., employment, health care, and Social Security dollars) and figurative (e.g., what is mainstream or popular; see North & Fiske, 2012, for a review). Exacerbating these step-aside expectations are outdated social policies, such as traditional retirement age, which do not adequately comprehend demographic realities of people working longer than ever (North & Fiske, 2013c). Moreover, the inexperience of workplaces needing to consider accommodating multiple generations has coincided with a relative lack of scholarly knowledge of the subject, in organizational behavior and other management disciplines (Joshi, Dencker, & Franz, 2011). The psychological sciences, too, despite a history of resource-driven perspectives on prejudice (e.g., Realistic Group Conflict Theory; Sherif, Harvey, White, Hood, & Sherif, 1961), rarely cover intergenerational resource tensions (Levy & Macdonald, 2016; North & Fiske, 2012).

An Uncharted Policy Issue: Intergenerational Workplace Interaction

The potential for intergenerational tension poses a significant problem for organizations, where generations coexist more frequently than ever before. It is indeed not uncommon for modern workplaces to comprise four generations: The Silent Generation/Traditionalists (born roughly in 1925–1945), Baby Boomers (roughly in 1946–1964), Generation X (roughly in 1965–1981), and Generation Y/Millennials (roughly after 1981) (Lieber, 2010; Twenge, 2010). As such, understanding the different work outlooks of multiple labor generations is a pressing issue, one that extends even to attitudes toward the nature of work and career per se (Dries, Pepermans, & De Kerpel, 2008).

Although research within this domain is as nascent as recent demographic trends would dictate, there is reason to believe that, like other forms of workplace diversity, the presence of different age groups is potentially beneficial. For instance, mixed-age teams maximize older workers' duration of employment, and at least one audit study has found that lower levels of an organization's age-discriminatory hiring practices correlate with higher levels of its overall success (Bendick, Jackson, & Romer, 1997; Centre for European Economic Research/ZEW, 2013). Nevertheless, approximately 60% of workplaces report intergenerational conflict (per a recent survey; Murphy, 2007), presenting managerial challenges for those attempting to reap the benefits of multiple-aged workplaces.

The current paper focuses on two specific domains of such potential benefits. The first is *professional networking,* the importance of which is well known (e.g., in occupational attainment, where some estimate as many as 80% of jobs are found through unpublished means; Kaufman, 2011). From an intergenerational perspective in particular, older workers have larger established professional networks than younger workers, and thus present a great deal of value (Pitt-Castouphes, Smyer, Matz-Costa, & Kane, 2007). Moreover, older adults (compared with younger ones) possess the kind of interpersonal skills that facilitate the creation of valuable interpersonal connections, including enhanced agreeableness, conscientiousness, and perspective taking (Grossmann et al., 2010; Helson, Kwan, John, & Jones, 2002). Naturally, inherent benefits of working a long time (particularly experience and savings) also render older workers excellent sources of intergenerational utility. However, factors such as the pervasive social separation of old and young may preclude younger workers from seeking such guidance (Hagestad & Uhlenberg, 2005), as well as the high potential for viewing older workers as competitors with younger workers, instead of allies (North & Fiske, 2013a).

A second domain with possible intergenerational boons is that of *older worker training.* Generally speaking, the growing number of people prolonging retirement is necessitating organizations to adapt and retrain older workers (Kooji & Zacher, 2016; North & Hershfield, 2014). From an intergenerational perspective in particular, training between generations can minimize negative stereotypes and promote learning that is both reproductive (dealing with routine problems) and expansive (creative, knowledge-based problem solving; Ropes, 2013). Nevertheless, achieving a productive, mixed-age workplace is difficult if employers or other-aged coworkers exhibit covert bias toward older employees in hiring decisions, resource distribution, or training opportunities, (Abrams, Swift, & Drury, 2016; Kooji & Zacher, 2016; Maurer & Rafuse, 2001). Young workers may be particularly reluctant to help older generations if they perceive their own outcomes as potentially obstructed, as discussed next.

Succession, Consumption, and Identity: Domains of Intergenerational Resource Tension

One recent perspective, central to the current paper, identifies specific types of resource tensions between generations (North & Fiske, 2013a,b). This frame identifies prescriptive expectations ("shoulds"), through which younger generations seek to limit resource use by older generations. Resembling other types of prescriptive stereotypes (most notably, gender; Fiske & Stevens, 1993; Prentice & Carranza, 2002; Rudman & Glick, 2001), the desire to control resource use by competitive outgroups (i.e., social groups with which one does not identify but may present some sort of obstructive threat) stems from a motivation to maximize benefits for the ingroup (i.e., the social group in which one does claim membership). However, age prescriptions are unique in deriving from an expected, turn-taking progression, dictating that old make way for new, largely sparing the middle (North & Fiske, 2012).

This standpoint on intergenerational relations identifies three specific domains of prescriptive age stereotypes: Succession, Consumption, and Identity (SCI). Prior work (North & Fiske, 2013a,b) identifies each as uniquely intergenerational: That is, these expectations are harbored most strongly by younger generations—as measured by regression analyses treating rater age as a continuous variable, showing that rater age diminishes these expectations—and targeted most directly at older generations (as measured by targets concretely near or past retirement age, or in the general statement of "older people").

Succession: Step aside and pass along.   Succession encompasses attitudes toward active passing along of enviable resources. In a work context, Succession-based attitudes most notably concern the expectation that older generations should step aside and retire, thereby making way for younger generations. Sample Succession items, from a recent scale of prescriptive age-based resource beliefs, include: "Most older workers don't know when it's time to make way for the younger generation" and "Younger people are usually more productive than older people at their jobs" (North & Fiske, 2013b).

Consumption: Don't be a passive burden.   Unlike Succession's emphasis on actively ceding enviable assets, Consumption prescribes avoiding passive overuse of shared resources. Because Consumption prescriptions concern overdepletion of the shared resource pool, such beliefs most notably manifest in the domain of health care, but really may involve any type of shared, allotted societal space, including highway driving. Sample Consumption scale items describing these passive, presumed inconveniences include: "Older people are too big a burden on the healthcare system" and "AARP (American Association of Retired Persons) wastes charity money" (North & Fiske, 2013b).

Identity: Act your own (old) age.   In contrast to Succession and Consumption's focus on practical assets, Identity prescribes avoidance of territory that is more symbolic in nature. This domain thus comprises expectations for older generations to avoid invading the figurative turf of younger generations. Sample scale items for Identity include: "Older people shouldn't even try to act cool" and "Older people probably shouldn't use Facebook" (North & Fiske, 2013b). However, other youth-centric activities, such as popular music, can also be implicated (North & Fiske, 2013a).

Prior SCI findings and the current research.   In contrast to various studies failing to find consistent age differences in endorsing ageism (e.g., some find older people themselves to be the strongest ageists; Kite, Stockdale, Whitley, & Johnson, 2005), prior SCI-based results find that younger generations are the greatest endorsers of such expectations, and older generations are the most targeted. For instance, the noted individual difference measure, comprising prescriptive, older age-focused statements, robustly yields the highest agreement scores from younger generations (North & Fiske, 2013b). Likewise, when confronted with targets of varying ages, younger (more than other-aged) participants are the most polarized toward older (more than other-aged) targets, resenting them the most for prescription violations, but holding the greatest positive regard for prescription adherence (North & Fiske, 2013a).

Nevertheless, whether these patterns hold up in a work context per se is an open question. This might be the case, as each SCI domain reflects contemporary, intergenerational workforce tensions. For instance, as older workers stave off retirement at unprecedented rates, younger generations consequently worry about both the active (Succession) obstruction of potential job and promotion opportunities, as well as the passive (Consumption) cost that might use up pooled resources (Pew Charitable Trust, 2012; Sedensky, 2014). Moreover, as technology advances at break-neck pace, youth-driven, tech-related sectors appear to be excluding older generations entirely (Scheiber, 2014). If violations of SCI expectations provoke penalties in ordinary person perception, as the already noted prior research indicates, then such violations might likewise foster work-related demerits from younger generations.

Finally, the current research also explores whether perceived availability of resources between generations impacts intergenerational workplace inclusion. From a theoretical standpoint, although the SCI framework posits that resource tension underlies age-based prescriptions, direct empirical evidence of resource salience moderating these biases does not yet exist. The effect of resource perceptions on ageism is also worth addressing from a prejudice-reduction standpoint—an area on which researchers have called for more focused attention, and in which zero-sum competition continues to be implicated (Norton & Sommers, 2011; Paluck & Green, 2009). Understanding the impact of zero-sum narratives on intergenerational perceptions also has real-world relevance, as noted, because such messages have grown more frequent in the real world.

Research overview.   Four experiments investigated the impact of resource scarcity on intergenerational exclusion of older workers. Three studies (Studies 1a–c), focusing respectively on key domains of Succession, Consumption, and Identity, manipulated broad, macro-level resource scarcity between generations, then examined the impact of prescriptive biases within a professional networking context. Exploring the potential for perceived competition to undermine intergenerational networking and mentoring is a relevant context, given well-documented organizational benefits of each (Wilson & Elman, 1990) and the already-cited, increasingly intergenerational nature of modern workplaces. In all three of these first studies, we hypothesized that resource scarcity (respectively S, C, and I) would result in negative intergenerational views of older workers who violate prescriptive expectations—but that perceived resource abundance would mitigate this prescriptive bias.

Meanwhile, a fourth study (Study 2) incorporated the three SCI domains simultaneously in a specific scarce-resource context pertaining to worker skills training. Participants were given the task of distributing limited training resources among three interested employees of varying ages. Skills training is another salient domain in which to examine the current subject matter, as older workers face frequent obstacles in receiving necessary such training, stemming from managers' direct (often negative) comparisons with younger workers (Lee, Czaja, & Sharit, 2008). Similar to Study 1, we hypothesized that conditions of resource scarcity should result in the greatest withholding toward older workers, which, in this study, we operationalized as the amount of new skills training investment allotted.

Notably, although participants across studies comprised both genders, all studies utilized an experimentally manipulated male *target* only, across conditions. Although age–gender intersectionality is an understudied topic in social psychology (and an increasingly relevant one, given the aging population), the current research stuck with the default of older male targets, per prior work (North & Fiske, 2013b).

Study 1a: Intergenerational Succession Attitudes toward Older-Worker Networking

Method

Participants.   Responding to explicit requests for under-30 participants, a USA-only, young sample ($N = 60$; age $= 18$–30; mean age $= 23.03$, $SD = 3.72$, median $= 22$; 47 female) participated via Amazon Mechanical Turk (Mturk) and a university-wide paid-experiments website. The ethnic distribution of the participants was 68.3% White/European American, 13.3% East Asian/East Asian American, 5.0% Latino/Hispanic American, 1.7% Black/African American, 1.7% South Asian/South Asian American, and 10.0% identified as "Other" or mixed ethnicity.

Procedure. Participants agreed to participate in a "current events and professional profile study." Participants first read a brief newspaper article concerning the growing older population in the United States and resulting implications for available jobs and assets. One of two possible frames appeared (see Appendix): In the *scarce* condition, the article emphasized how the enlarged older population signifies that "there simply won't be as much to go around" between generations. In the *abundant* condition, the article put a more positive spin on shifting age dynamics, stating that "there should be plenty to go around" even with a greater number of older people. After reading the article, as a manipulation check, participants summarized the article in a few sentences to ensure that they understood it and read it carefully. In order to motivate participants to read the article as carefully as possible, they were also told that a quiz on the article would appear at the end of the survey.

Afterward, participants completed an ostensibly separate part of the study, reading a "network member's profile" from a professional database. The profile always concerned a 71-year-old man named "Max," who acknowledges that his continued employment is preventing younger employees from getting hired, but two distinct conditions manipulated Max's behavior concerning succession of enviable resources: In the *violating* condition, Max states that he's "not retiring anytime soon" and is "not ready to step aside yet"; in the *adhering* condition, Max concedes that "it's probably time to step aside." Thus, the overall 2 × 2 design of the experiment manipulated resource salience via the newspaper article (scarce, abundant) and Succession-based behavior via the networking target (violating or adhering to Succession of enviable employment).

A 6-item behavioroid variable gauged participants' desire to get in touch with Max in the context of the professional networking profile ($\alpha = .86$): "Would you be willing to interact further with Max after the study is over?"; "Would you be willing to write and send Max a supportive message?"; "Would you prefer to ignore Max altogether?" (reverse-scored); "If you were to interact further, how likely would you be to say mean things to Max?" (reverse-scored); "Would you recommend other participants in this survey to interact with Max?"; "Would you suggest to other participants in this survey that they ignore Max" (reverse-scored). Participants responded using a 5-point Likert scale (1 = *very unlikely;* 5 = *very likely*). Participants were thoroughly debriefed, informed that the article had been edited and that no quiz would occur, and provided a payment code for compensation for an amount commensurate with typical MTurk standards.

Results

No significant main effect emerged for adhering/violating to Succession-based behavior on the dependent variable of networking appeal, $F < 1$. Additionally, no main effect of resource scarcity framing emerged, $F < 1$.

However, a significant 2 (scarcity) x 2 (behavior) interaction emerged, $F(1, 60) = 4.79$, $p = .033$, $\eta_p^2 = .08$ (see Figure 1). When resources appeared scarce, participants' desire to network with refusing-to-retire Max was considerably lower ($M = 2.61$, $SD = 0.67$), compared with planning-to-retire Max ($M = 3.33$, $SD = 0.52$), $t(32) = 3.43$, $p = .002$. By contrast, resource abundance appeared to mitigate this difference, such that nonretiring Max ($M = 3.64$, $SD = 1.04$) did not differ from retiring Max ($M = 3.49$, $SD = 0.81$) in networking appeal, $t(24) < 1$.

Study 1b: Intergenerational Consumption Attitudes toward Older-Worker Networking

Method

Participants.   A young-only sample from the United States ($N = 62$; age = 18–31, mean age = 25.21, $SD = 3.85$, median = 25.50; 29 female) again participated via either MTurk or an undergraduate participant pool. The ethnic distribution of the participants was 79.0% White/European American, 6.5% Black/African American, 3.2% East Asian/East Asian American, 3.2% Latino/Hispanic American, 3.2% Native American/American Indian, and 4.8% identified themselves as "Other" or of mixed ethnicity.

Procedure.   The procedure was identical to the prior study, but concerning Consumption of shared resources. First, a brief newspaper article created a "scarce" versus an "abundant" condition (Appendix). Then, as before, participants read a professional profile depicting Max, this time 74 years old and having come down with a "pretty serious illness" requiring a resource-intensive treatment. In the Consumption-violating condition, Max decides to go through with the burdensome, resource-consuming procedure anyway; in the adhering version, he decides it is best for everyone if he does not go through with the procedure.

Based upon this brief depiction, participants rated their networking inclination using the same 6-item variable ($\alpha = .90$ for this dataset) on a 5-point Likert scale as in Study 1a. At the end, participants were debriefed, thanked, and provided a payment code for compensation.

Results

As in Study 1a, no significant main effects emerged for prescription-based behavior or scarcity (both Fs < 1) on the dependent variable of networking appeal.

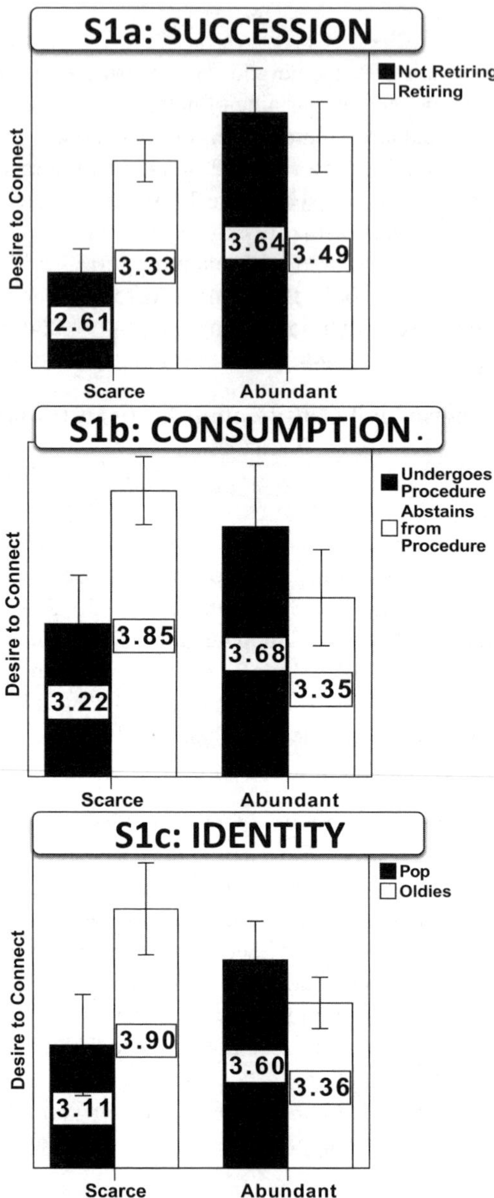

Fig. 1. Willingness to connect with older members of a professional network database as a function of SCI adherence and macro-level resource framing (Studies 1a–c).

However, a significant 2 (scarcity) x 2 (behavior) interaction emerged, $F(1, 62)$ = 4.48, $p = .039$, $\eta_p^2 = .07$ (see Figure 1). Under resource scarcity, participants' desire to network with Consumption-violating Max ($M = 3.22$, $SD = 0.97$) was lower than their desire to network with Consumption-adhering Max ($M = 3.85$, SD = 0.70), $t(34) = 2.27$, $p = .029$. However, under conditions of resource abundance, participants did not differ in their desire to network with violating Max ($M = 3.68$, $SD = 1.04$) versus adhering Max ($M = 3.35$, $SD = 0.82$), $t(23) < 1$.

Study 1c: Intergenerational Identity Attitudes toward Older-Worker Networking

Method

Participants.   As with Studies 1a and 1b, younger participants located in the United States ($N = 53$; age = 19–30, mean age = 23.19, $SD = 3.60$, median = 22; 33 female) were recruited from Amazon Mechanical Turk and a university-wide paid experiments website. The ethnic distribution of the participants was 71.7% White/European American, 7.5% East Asian/East Asian American, 5.7% Black/African American, 3.8% Latino/Hispanic American, 3.8% Middle Eastern, and 7.5% identified as "Other" or mixed ethnicity.

Procedure.   The procedure of Study 1c mirrored that of Studies 1a and 1b, ostensibly asking participants to complete an online "current events and professional profile study," which randomly assigned participants to a scarce resource versus abundant resource condition, via the same newspaper article (Appendix).

The main difference was Max's profile, which focused on symbolic, Identity resources (rather than enviable Succession-based ones or shared Consumption ones). In the *violating* condition, Max conspicuously declared his affinity for the latest pop music, a threat to symbolic young territory. By contrast, the *adhering* version demonstrated his affinity for oldies music. Thus, like Studies 1a and 1b, Study 1c comprised a 2 (scarce versus abundant availability of Resources) × 2 (target violation versus adherence to Identity) design.

Dependent measures were also the same as those in Studies 1a and 1b. Participants rated their desire to network with Max using the same 6-item variable ($\alpha = .86$ for this dataset) on the same 5-point Likert scale. At the study's conclusion, participants were debriefed, thanked, and provided a payment code for compensation.

Results

As in Studies 1a and 1b, no significant main effects emerged for SCI-based behavior ($F(1, 53) = 1.32$, $p = .26$) or scarcity ($F < 1$) on the dependent variable of networking appeal.

However, a significant 2 (scarcity) × 2 (behavior) interaction again emerged, $F(1, 53) = 4.88, p = .03$, partial $\eta^2 = .09$ (see Figure 1). Facing resource scarcity, participants' desire to network with Identity-violating, pop-music Max ($M = 3.11$, $SD = 1.02$) was marginally lower than that concerning Identity-adhering, oldies-music Max ($M = 3.90, SD = 0.84$), $t(19.99) = 1.99, p = .06$. In contrast, under conditions of resource abundance, participants did not differ in their desire to network with pop-music Max ($M = 3.60, SD = 0.90$) versus oldies-music Max ($M = 3.36, SD = 0.57$), $t(29) < 1$.

Study 2: Intergenerational Resource Attitudes toward Older-Worker Training

Although Studies 1a–c consistently demonstrated resource scarcity's influence on younger resentment toward older violators of SCI resource expectations, Study 2 built upon these findings in two major ways. First, we widened the age range of both participants and targets, aiming to more closely show that these prescriptive biases uniquely exist between young and old, and to be able to conduct more sensitive age-based regressions. Both of these adjustments closely follow prior paradigms (North & Fiske, 2013a,b). Second, this study created a more hands-on paradigm, in which participants actively controlled the allotment of scarce resources to older (and other-aged) workers.

Method

Participants.   Study 2's wider age range of the U.S. participants also composed a larger sample than Studies 1a–c ($N = 392$; age = 18–75, mean age = 33.97, $SD = 11.84$, median = 30; 166 female). Recruited from MTurk, participants were 77.3% White/European American, 6.1% Black/African American, 4.6% East Asian/East Asian American, 4.1% Latino/Hispanic American, and 2.3% South Asian/South Asian American, whereas 5.6% identified as "Other" or mixed ethnicity.

Materials.   In addition to the main measures (see Procedure), participants completed the noted individual-difference measure of resource-focused, prescriptive ageism (North & Fiske, 2013b). As indicated, the scale comprises 20 items centering on "should"-based beliefs about distribution of resources to older people, which together form the three distinct SCI prescriptive domains.

Procedure.   Participants entered a two-part "Social Survey." The first part of the study mirrored that of Studies 1a–c, ostensibly asking participants to complete an online "current events task," randomly assigning participants to a scarce-resource versus abundant-resource condition, via a newspaper article (see Appendix).

Next, in an ostensibly separate task, participants were asked to assume the role of Manager of Training and Development at a small company, in charge of distributing company funds toward new skills training for current employees. Here, two further manipulations arose. First, a within-subjects variable manipulated the age of three employees interested in training: In each case, these employees were 24, 43, and 64, respectively, all having 2 years' tenure with the company and similar educational backgrounds. Second, a between-subjects variable manipulated the industry in question: Participants were either managers at a small *tech company*, funding skills related to "coding, web design, [and] social media," or else at a small *insurance company*, funding skills pertaining to "public speaking, persuasion, [and] effective presentations." (A priori, we expected any ageism effects to be stronger in youth-centered tech than insurance.) Notably, a Latin Square design ensured that the repeated-measures order and combinations, of three employee ages and three individual names and credentials, was counterbalanced across conditions.

In order to manipulate resource scarcity in a manner pertinent to the current paradigm, participants had only \$2,800 to spend on three interested employees, despite the full skill set's training cost of \$1,200 for each individual. Thus, the overall $2 \times 2 \times 3$ mixed-factorial study design manipulated macro-level scarcity (scarce vs. abundant news frame, between-subjects), company industry (tech vs. insurance, between-subjects), and employee age (young, middle-aged, older, within-subjects)—all within a scarce-resource, workplace context.

After learning about the study task, participants used slider buttons to allocate training dollars among the three interested employees. After this, participants completed the resource-focused SCI Scale of Ageism. Finally, participants were debriefed and provided a payment code for compensation.

Results

Mixed-model $2 \times 2 \times 3$ ANOVA.   A $2 \times 2 \times 3$ mixed-factorial ANOVA found a significant main effect of target age on training dollars invested. Collapsing across between-subjects conditions, older workers received significantly lower training investment ($M = 749.07$, $SD = 221.04$) than did the other-aged workers (middle-aged $M = 1005.79$, $SD = 130.90$; younger $M = 1045.14$, $SD = 177.46$), $F(2, 762) = 202.56$, $p < .001$, $\eta_p^2 = .35$; see Figure 2. However, no significant interaction emerged between target age and industry, target age and scarcity, nor among all three variables, all $Fs < 2$, all $ps > .14$. Given these initial results, further analyses unpacked the older-target resource-denial effect only.

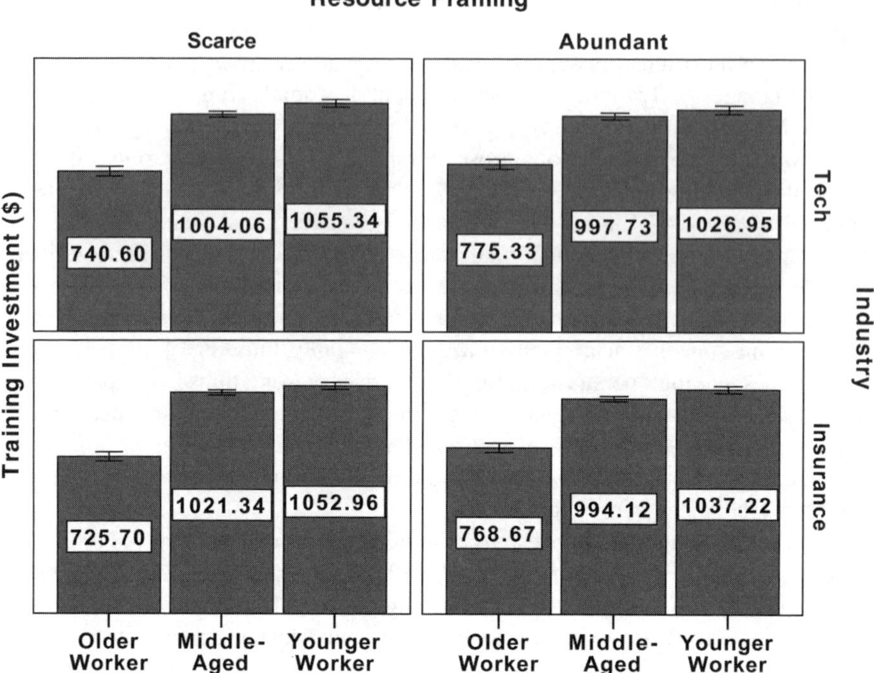

Fig. 2. Training investment as a function of worker age, industry, and macro-level resource framing (Study 2).

Between-subjects 2 × 2 ANOVA. Taking older-worker investment as the dependent variable, a univariate 2 (scarce/abundant frame) × 2 (tech/insurance industry) ANOVA found a marginally significant main effect of scarcity on funds invested in older-worker training, such that older workers received less investment under scarce circumstances (scarce $M = 733.08$, $SD = 219.47$; abundant $M = 771.83$, $SD = 220.64$), $F(1, 392) = 3.04$, $p = .08$, $\eta_p^2 = .01$. The main effect of industry was nonsignificant, as was the scarcity × industry interaction, both $Fs < 1$, $ps > .62$.

Participant age. Given results of prior work implicating younger people as resentful of older resource use (North & Fiske, 2013a,b; Studies 1a–c from the current paper), we then explored whether participant age predicted resource allocation toward the older target. Indeed, rater age predicted the amount of training dollars participants allotted the older target, $\beta = .11$, $t = 2.15$, $p = .03$. Moreover, when entering participant age as a covariate in the mixed-factorial, 3 × 2 × 2

ANOVA specified above, participant age emerged as a significant covariate, $F(2, 760) = 45.61, p < .001$ (all other effects remained the same).

Individual Differences in Resource-based Prescriptive Ageism

Using the North-Fiske (2013b) SCI ageism scale, we explored the potential role of individual differences in resource attitudes. First, 2 × 2 ANOVAs confirmed that each SCI subscale did not differ by between-subjects condition (all $Fs < 1$, all $ps > .41$), thereby justifying the scale's treatment as an individual difference variable, rather than a dependent variable.

In line with prior findings (North & Fiske, 2013b), participant age significantly predicted people's level of prescriptive resource attitudes, such that younger people most strongly endorsed SCI statements (Succession $\beta = -.39, t = -8.15, p < .001$; Consumption $\beta = -.17, t = -3.27, p = .001$; total SCI $\beta = -.27, t = -5.45, p < .001$). Unexpectedly, participant age only trended toward predicting Identity subscale score ($\beta = -.08, t = -1.48, p = .14$), but perhaps taste in youth-centric activities is less relevant in this workplace context.

Using the current study's main DV of older-worker training investment, we found that Succession subscale score ($\beta = -.31, t = -6.27, p < .001$) and Consumption subscale score ($\beta = -.15, t = -2.87, p = .004$) both predicted money invested in older-worker training, whereas symbolic Identity subscale again did so only marginally ($\beta = -.08, t = -1.65, p = .10$). However, in a multiple regression entering all three subscales simultaneously, only the Succession subscale (controlling for the other two subscales) predicted money invested in older-worker training ($\beta = -.38, t = -5.80, p < .001$). This was not the case for other two subscales, each controlling for the others (both βs $< .07, ps > .26$).

Mediation Model

With participant age and Succession attitudes both emerging as the strongest predictors of older-worker resource allocation, we then tested a mediation model, incorporating these variables and the DV of resources allocated to the older target.

A multiple regression including both predictor variables found that Succession subscale score, controlling for participant age, significantly predicted older-worker investment, $\beta = -.31, t = -5.93, p < .001$. By contrast, participant age no longer predicted older-worker investment when accounting for Succession attitudes, $\beta = -.01, t = -.17, p = .87$. Thus, mediation analyses first tested to see whether Succession attitude was a significant mediator between the participant-age → money-to-older-worker relationship.

Mediation analyses utilized a bootstrapping method with bias-corrected confidence estimates (MacKinnon, Lockwood, & Williams, 2004; Preacher & Hayes, 2004). This procedure obtained a 95% confidence interval of the indirect (mediat-

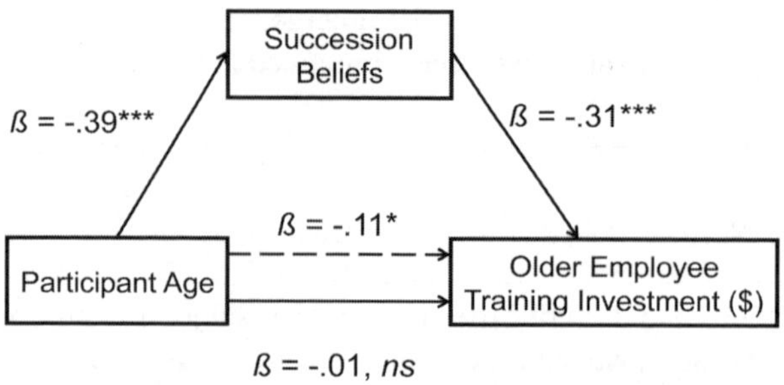

Fig. 3. Prescriptive Succession attitudes mediate the relationship between participants' age and money allotted to older worker skills training (Study 2). ***p < .001, **p < .01 *p < .05, ns = nonsignificant.

ing) effect with 5,000 bootstrap resamples (Preacher & Hayes, 2008). Results of the analysis confirmed the mediating role of Succession beliefs in the relationship between participant age and training money allotted to older participants, as the confidence interval for the intervening variable effect (the path through the mediator) fell outside of zero (CI = 1.40, 3.27); see Figure 3. Bootstrap-based tests of the alternate indirect effect model—that is, participant age mediating the relationship between Succession beliefs and money allotted to older workers—resulted in a zero-inclusive confidence interval (-8.83, 10.08), indicating participant age to be a nonsignificant mediator.

General Discussion

Four studies demonstrated the impact of resource scarcity and prescriptive resource attitudes in fostering intergenerational exclusion of older workers. The same general pattern emerged across studies: Conditions of resource scarcity exacerbated the tendency of younger participants to subtly disregard older workers, but particularly when prescriptive, resource-based attitudes were salient.

Recruiting younger participants only, Studies 1a–c confirmed hypotheses that resource scarcity would exacerbate resentment toward older workers who violated prescriptive stereotypes, finding a polarized effect concerning willingness to connect professionally with them. Under a macro-level, intergenerational scarcity frame, older workers were avoided to a significantly greater extent when acting in ways contrary to prescriptive expectations (violating Succession by staving off retirement, violating Consumption by undergoing a resource-intensive healthcare procedure, and violating Identity by enjoying popular music) than when adhering to such prescriptions. However, macro-level resource abundance between generations mitigated this polarization effect. These results replicate prior findings that older people face the most extreme reactions for their prescription-based behaviors (North & Fiske, 2013a), but also suggest that resource abundance attenuates this bias.

Study 2's hypotheses were also supported. Indeed, under circumstances in which the very resources to be allocated were presented as scarce, Study 2 also found scarcity to drive subtle, punitive exclusion from young toward old. With a limited amount of worker training funds, older (compared with middle-aged and younger) workers received the lowest investment. Moreover, older-worker investment per se was marginally exacerbated by macro-level resource scarcity, similar to Study 1's findings. Resembling prior research (North & Fiske, 2013a,b), the subtle exclusion of older workers was most strongly driven by younger participants. Nevertheless, mediation analyses introduced an individual-difference mechanism underlying this intergenerational tension, implicating Succession attitudes in explaining this participant age effect.

Resource Scarcity and Intergenerational Interactions in the Workplace

Prior work (North & Fiske, 2013a) emphasizes how specific types of resource tensions can drive intergenerational resentment. The current work, centering on facilitating active Succession of enviable assets, limiting passive Consumption of shared assets, and avoidance of symbolic Identity activities, emphasizes that resource tensions can be exacerbated or minimized depending on perceived general availability of resources between generations. The findings mirror prior work showing that ageism arises under apparent intergenerational inequity (Garstka, Hummert, & Branscombe, 2005), albeit here from a prescriptive, work-specific standpoint. Moreover, the fact that resource abundance attenuates this prescriptive bias toward older adults (in addition to a lack of significant main effects for prescription violations versus adherences) suggests that older target prescriptions derive from default beliefs about resource scarcity between generations.

The current research also suggests that perceptions of intergenerational scarcity can manifest at multiple levels: specifically, via macro-level generational competition narratives as well as micro-level specific resource dynamics between older and younger workers. Consequently, getting generations to work together effectively may well require a multimodal approach. For example, policies might work to change broad, institutionalized beliefs about generational competition, while individual organizations work to devise creative ways of accommodating different-aged workers under seemingly scarce circumstances (e.g., offering flexible and part-time opportunities for mature workers; North & Hershfield, 2014). Future research can aid the goal by focusing on factors underlying intergenerational tensions, which threaten to inhibit ever-necessary collaboration, networking, and mentoring across generations.

Succession Attitudes and Intergenerational Treatment of Older Workers

Prior work has identified age as a strong predictor of prescriptive attitudes toward older generations, such that younger people harbor the strongest such beliefs. However, the current findings identify an important mechanism that might explain this relationship within a work context: Succession-focused resource attitudes. This makes sense; in analyses of intergenerational tensions in the modern workplace, Succession attitudes are arguably the most salient, as they represent expectations for the older generation to actively make way for younger generations and cede enviable employment or influence, by retiring or stepping down (North & Fiske, 2013a,b). Nevertheless, the current findings are the first to demonstrate the possibility of these attitudes translating into discriminatory workplace practices—that is, impacting the training opportunities of older workers.

The identification of a potential mechanism underlying intergenerational resentments also presents a hopeful message for future intervention work. Although changing one's chronological age (or correlates thereof, such as generational outlook or industry experience) is impractical, interventions geared toward changing prescriptive age-based expectations offer greater feasibility. As one example, social policies can work toward changing the default mindsets that workers should retire by the age of 65, a practice that is already becoming obsolete, due to demographic realities (North & Fiske, 2013c). Whatever the eventual solution, with modern workplaces often comprising as many as four different generations, overcoming intergenerational tension is becoming a managerial imperative.

Social Policy Implications

A few other, specific social policy implications emerge from the current work.

Emphasizing generational competition is not constructive for accommodating the aging workforce. The increased frequency of older generations in the workplace necessitates more intergenerational collaboration and greater utilization of older workers. Nevertheless, the findings indicate that a major barrier to this aim is the perception that zero-sum competition exists between generations. Recent evidence actually goes against such "lump of labor" mentalities: From a macro-perspective, labor outcomes between young and old are actually *positively* correlated, and thus not directly oppositional (Pew Charitable Trust, 2012). That is, when older workers prosper, so do younger ones. From the micro, workplace standpoint, too, worker outcomes tend to vary with the overall organizational performance; as older and younger workers tend to occupy different positions within companies, rises in wages for senior-level positions tend to predict commensurate rises for entry-level workers (Munnell & Wu, 2012). Thus, society should avoid institutionalized narratives of competition not only for purposes of being constructive, but also to be based on practical truths in accommodating multiple generations.

Policy initiatives should focus on connecting younger workers with older ones.   The first three studies of the current paper suggest that younger workers are not motivated to connect professionally with older ones who linger in ingroup spaces. At the same time, an increasingly intergenerational workforce necessitates a greater level of such interaction than ever before, and the organizational benefits of intergenerational interaction are becoming more clear (Ropes, 2013). Per the current work, a likely explanation for this barrier is the expectation among younger generations for older workers to step aside. Research-based policy initiatives should strive to unite generations, perhaps by emphasizing common goals of organizational productivity and fulfillment.

Recognize truths about age and organizational tenure.   Meanwhile, Study 2's results suggest that managers may be reluctant to invest in older workers' skill training investment, presumably due to beliefs that older workers will sooner leave the company via retirement. Although it is true that older workers are closer to this stage, recent research indicates that younger workers may not be a better investment, because older workers are generally more loyal to their current company (Pitt-Catsouphes et al., 2007) and statistically likely to stay with their employer for a longer period of time (U.S. Bureau of Labor Statistics, 2014). Nevertheless, the current findings suggest that people's default beliefs are that training resources are best invested in younger workers, and future work should focus on how to change such attitudes so that they are more strongly rooted in truths. For instance, rather than chronological age per se, individual-difference variables such as work centrality and age identity are likely the more predictive of how long older workers will remain (Macdonald & Levy, 2016).

Harnessing intergenerational productivity is a global issue.   Finally, although the immediate context of the current research is the United States, we note that workforce aging affects industrialized societies around the world. The current findings thus present considerations for countries worldwide that are grappling with how to utilize newly multigenerational workforces; these include India (Srinivasan, 2012), China (Dubberke, 2014), and much of Europe (Fraone, Hartmann, & McNally, 2008). Cultural factors inevitably will play a part in the development of particular solutions, but the dynamics and hurdles of networking and training between generations are clearly relevant worldwide.

Limitations

Both Study 1a–c's limited participant age range and Study 2's disproportionately scarce context might temper the strength of resulting conclusions. Future work aiming to disentangle the effects of scarcity versus abundance among different generations should rectify each of these limitations (e.g., for the latter, by providing ample resources to distribute among differentially-aged employees). Moreover, all four studies used online surveys designed to foster simulated interaction in a workplace context; future work might utilize a more interactive context to gauge the strength of current effects.

Another potential limitation was the current studies' reliance on male targets. As indicated, this was by design, as males represent the default member of the older adult category (North & Fiske, 2012). Nevertheless, future work is needed to explore whether subtle exclusion might target older female workers to an even greater extent. From a theoretical standpoint, it remains largely unknown whether older women face more extreme "gendered ageism" treatment than men (Duncan & Loretto, 2004; Levy & Macdonald, 2016). Understanding this issue is increasingly important from a workforce aging perspective as well, because dramatic increases in female, over-55 labor force participation from 1975 to 2010 have been a significant driver (Copeland, 2014).

Finally, the current research's reliance on work-related contexts might limit somewhat the scope of the findings. Although the SCI perspective would predict that resource scarcity should exacerbate intergenerational prescriptive age biases in general, future work is needed to know that this applies beyond work spheres per se.

Conclusion

This article identified two key factors fostering exclusion of older workers by younger generations: (1) intergenerational resource scarcity (both broad and context-specific) and (2) prescriptive beliefs about the older generation's resource use. Each significantly factored into younger people's receptiveness to intergenerational networking and investment in older worker skills training. Analyses on the training investment implicated turn-based Succession expectations to be an important mediator underlying intergenerational tensions, introducing avenues for future intervention work. More broadly, the findings hold practical relevance for developing a productive, ever-intergenerational workforce.

Appendix: Scarcity (News Article) Manipulation

Scarce Version (graphic)

Abundant Version (graphic)

WASHINGTON, DC (AP)—The proportion of people aged 65 and up is steadily increasing in the United States, the U.S. Census Bureau said Wednesday.

There are now 40.3 million people 65 and older in the United States, the bureau reported.

The figure accounts for 13% of the population and is larger than in any other decennial census, up from 31.2 million in 1990 and 35 million in 2000.

By 2030, the same age group is predicted to form a full 25% of the population. Projections also predict 88.5 million older Americans by 2050.

Though some experts are optimistic/pessimistic that a graying society will work smoothly, far more believe that there won't/will be enough resources to accommodate all generations.

"Unfortunately/fortunately, younger people **should suffer the most/shouldn't suffer much** from these demographic trends," said Dr. Kenneth Fields, a research professor at Georgetown University's Center for Population and Health. **"With more assets going to older Americans, there simply won't be as much to go around." / "Even with more assets going to older Americans, there should be plenty to go around."**

References

Abrams, D., Swift, H. J., & Drury, L. (2016). Old and unemployable? How age-based stereotypes affect willingness to hire job candidates. *Journal of Social Issues, 72*(1), 105–121.

Bendick, M., Jackson, C. W., & Romer, J. H. (1997). Employment discrimination against older workers. *Journal of Aging and Social Policy, 8*(4), 25–46. doi: 10.1300/J031v08n04_03.

Centre for European Economic Research (ZEW) (2013). Mixed-age teams are the best solution for firms to keep older employees working longer. *ZEWNews,* 3.

Copeland, C. (2014). Labor-force participation rates of the population ages 55 and older, 2013. *EBRI Notes, 35*(4). From http://www.ebri.org/pdf/notespdf/ebri_notes_04_apr-14_lbrpart.pdf. Accessed at December 31, 2015.

Dries, N., Pepermans, R., & De Kerpel, E. (2008). Exploring four generations' beliefs about career: Is "satisfied" the new "successful"?. *Journal of Managerial Psychology, 23*(8), 907–928. doi: 10.1108/02683940810904394.

Dubberke, S. (2014). Exploring China's multigenerational workforce. Worldwide ERC: The Association for Workforce Mobility. From http://www.worldwideerc.org/Resources /MOBILITYarticles/Pages/0714Dubberke.aspx. Accessed at December 31, 2015.

Duncan, C., & Loretto, W. (2004). Never the right age? Gender and age-based discrimination in employment. *Gender, Work and Organization, 11,* 95–115. doi: 10.1111/j.1468-0432.2004.00222.x.

Fiske, S. T., & Stevens, L. E. (1993). What's so special about sex? Gender stereotyping and discrimination. In S. Oskamp & M. Costanzo (Eds.), *Gender issues in contemporary society: Applied social psychology annual* (pp. 173–196). Newbury Park, CA: Sage.

Fraone, J., Hartmann, D., & McNally, K. (2008). *The multi-generational workforce: Management implications and strategies for collaboration.* Boston College Center for Work & Family. From https://www.bc.edu/content/dam/files/centers/cwf/research/publications/pdf/MultiGen_EBS. pdf. Accessed at December 31, 2015.

Garstka, T. A., Hummert, M. L., & Branscombe, N. R. (2005). Perceiving age discrimination in response to intergenerational inequity. *Journal of Social Issues, 61*(2), 321–342. doi: 10.1111/j.1540-4560.2005.00408.x. Accessed at December 31, 2015.

Grossmann, I., Na, J., Varnum, M. E. W., Park, D. C., Kitayama, S., & Nisbett, R. E. (2010). Reasoning about social conflicts improves into old age. *Proceedings of the National Academy of Sciences, 107*(16), 7246–7250. doi: 10.1073/pnas.1001715107.

Hagestad, G. O., & Uhlenberg, P. (2005). The social separation of old and young: A root of ageism. *Journal of Social Issues, 61*(2), 343–360. doi: 10.1111/j.1540-4560.2005.00409.x.

Helson, R., Kwan, V. S., John, O. P., & Jones, C. (2002). The growing evidence for personality change in adulthood: Findings from research with personality inventories. *Journal of Research in Personality, 36*(4), 287–306. doi: 10.1016/S0092-6566(02)00010-7.

Joshi, A., Dencker, J. C., & Franz, G. (2011). Generations in organizations. *Research in Organizational Behavior, 31,* 177–205. doi: 10.1016/j.riob.2011.10.002.

Kaufman, W. (2011). A successful job search: It's all about networking. *NPR.* From http://www.npr.org/2011/02/08/133474431/a-successful-job-search-its-all-about-networking. Accessed at December 31, 2015.

Kite, M. E., Stockdale, G. D., Whitley, B. E., Jr., & Johnson, B. T. (2005). Attitudes toward younger and older adults: An updated meta-analytic review. *Journal of Social Issues, 61,* 241–266. doi: 10.1111/j.1540-4560.2005.00404.x.

Kooji, D. T., & Zacher, H. (2016). Why and when do learning goal orientation and attitude decrease with age? The role of perceived remaining time and work centrality. *Journal of Social Issues, 72*(1), 146–168.

Kreamer, A. (2012). Looking for a job when you're no longer young. *Harvard Business Review.* From http://hbr.org. Accessed at December 31, 2015.

Lee, C. C., Czaja, S. J., & Sharit, J. (2008). Training older workers for technology-based employment. *Educational Gerontology, 35*(1), 15–31. doi: 10.1080/03601270802300091.

Levy, S. R., & Macdonald, J. L. (2016). Progress on understanding ageism. *Journal of Social Issues, 72*(1), 5–25.

Lieber, L. D. (2010). How HR can assist in managing the four generations in today's workplace. *Employment Relations Today, 36*(4), 85–91. doi: 10.1002/ert.20278.

Macdonald, J. L., & Levy, S. R. (2016). Ageism in the workplace: The role of psychosocial factors in predicting job satisfaction, commitment, and engagement. *Journal of Social Issues, 72*(1), 169–190.

MacKinnon, D. P., Lockwood, C. M., & Williams, J. (2004). Confidence limits for the indirect effect: Distribution of the product and resampling methods. *Multivariate Behavioral Research, 39*(1), 99–128. doi: 10.1207/s15327906mbr3901_4.

Maurer, T. J., & Rafuse, N. E. (2001). Learning, not litigating: Managing employee development and avoiding claims of age discrimination. *Academy of Management Executive, 15*(4), 110–121. doi: 10.5465/AME.2001.5898395.

Minkler, M. (2006). Generational equity and the new victim blaming. In H.R. Moody (Ed.), *Aging: Concepts and Controversies* (pp. 181–190). Newbury Park, CA: Pine Forge Press. (*Re-printed from Critical Perspectives on Aging*, pp. 67–79, by M. Minkler and C. Estes, Eds., 1991, Amityville, NY: Baywood.) doi: 10.2190/A9K3-M3UY-UR7M-TDP4.

Munnell, A. H., & Wu, A. Y. (2012). Are aging baby boomers squeezing young workers out of jobs? *Center for retirement research at Boston College.* Working paper, pp. 12–18.

Murphy, S. A. (2007). Leading a multigenerational workforce. *AARP.* From http://assets.aarp.org/www.aarp.org_/cs/misc/leading_a_multigenerational_workforce.pdf. Accessed at December 31, 2015.

Nelson, T. D. (Ed.). (2002). *Ageism: Stereotyping and prejudice against older adults.* Cambridge, MA: MIT Press.

Norton, M. I., & Sommers, S. R. (2011). Whites see racism as a zero-sum game that they are now losing. *Perspectives on Psychological Science, 6*(3), 215–218. doi: 10.1177/1745691611406922.

North, M. S., & Fiske, S. T. (2012). An inconvenienced youth? Ageism and its potential intergenerational roots. *Psychological Bulletin, 138*(5), 982–997. doi: 10.1037/a0027843.

North, M. S., & Fiske, S. T. (2013a). Act your (old) age: Prescriptive, ageist biases over succession, consumption, and identity. *Personality and Social Psychology Bulletin, 39*(6), 720–734. doi: 10.1177/0146167213480043.

North, M. S., & Fiske, S. T. (2013b). A prescriptive, intergenerational-tension ageism scale: Succession, identity, and consumption (SIC). *Psychological Assessment, 25*(3), 706–713. doi: 10.1037/a0032367.

North, M. S., & Fiske, S. T. (2013c). Subtyping ageism: Policy issues in succession and consumption. *Social Issues and Policy Review, 7*(1), 36–57. doi: 10.1111/j.1751-2409.2012.01042.x. Accessed at December 31, 2015.

North, M. S., & Hershfield, H. E. (2014). Four ways to adapt to an aging workforce. *Harvard Business Review.* From https://hbr.org/2014/04/four-ways-to-adapt-to-an-aging-workforce/. Accessed at December 31, 2015.

Olshansky, S. J., Biggs, S., Achenbaum, W. A., Davison, G. C., Fried, L., Gutman, G., Kalache, A., Khaw, K-. T., Fernandez, A., Rattan, S. I. S., Guimarães, R. M., Milner, C., & Butler, R. N. (2011). The Global Agenda Council on the Ageing Society: Policy principles. *Global Policy, 2*, 97–105. doi: 10.1111/j.1758-5899.2010.00053.x

Paluck, E. L., & Green, D. P. (2009). Prejudice reduction: What works? A review and assessment of research and practice. *Annual Review of Psychology, 60*, 339–367. doi: 10.1146/annurev.psych.60.110707.163607.

Pew Charitable Trust (2012. When baby boomers delay retirement, do younger workers suffer? *Economic Mobility Project*, Issue Brief. From http://www.pewstates.org/uploadedFiles/PCS_Assets/2012/EMP_retirement_delay.pdf. Accessed at December 31, 2015.

Pitt-Catsouphes, M., Smyer, M. A., Matz-Costa, C., & Kane, K. (2007). The National Study Report: Phase 2 of the national study of business strategy and workforce development. From http://www.bc.edu/content/dam/files/research_sites/agingandwork/pdf/publications/RH04_NationalStudy.pdf. Accessed at December 31, 2015.

Preacher, K. J., & Hayes, A. F. (2004). SPSS and SAS procedures for estimating indirect effects in simple mediation models. *Behavior Research Methods, Instruments, & Computers, 36*(4), 717–731. doi: 10.3758/BF03206553.

Preacher, K. J., & Hayes, A. F. (2008). Asymptotic and resampling strategies for assessing and comparing indirect effects in multiple mediator models. *Behavior Research Methods*, *40*(3), 879–891. doi: 10.3758/BRM.40.3.879.

Prentice, D. A., & Carranza, E. (2002). What women and men should be, shouldn't be, are allowed to be, and don't have to be: The contents of prescriptive gender stereotypes. *Psychology of Women Quarterly*, *26*(4), 269–281. doi: 10.1111/1471-6402.t01-1-00066.

Ropes, D. (2013). Intergenerational learning in organizations. *European Journal of Training and Development*, *37*(8), 713–727. doi: 10.1108/EJTD-11-2012-0081.

Rudman, L. A., & Glick, P. (2001). Prescriptive gender stereotypes and backlash toward agentic women. *Journal of Social Issues*, *57*(4), 743–762. doi: 10.1111/0022-4537.00239.

Scheiber, N. (2014). The brutal ageism of tech: Years of experience, plenty of talent, completely obsolete. *The New Republic*. From http://www.newrepublic.com/article/117088/silicons-valleys-brutal-ageism. Accessed at December 31, 2015.

Sedensky, M. (2014). Are older workers taking jobs from young? *USA Today*. From http://www.usatoday.com/story/money/business/2014/01/04/will-surge-of-older-workers-take-jobs-from-young/4305187/. Accessed at December 31, 2015.

Sherif, M., Harvey, O. J., White, B. J., Hood, W. R., & Sherif, C. W. (1961). *The Robbers Cave experiment: Intergroup conflict and cooperation*. Middletown, CT: Wesleyan University Press.

Srinivasan, V. (2012). Multi generations in the workforce: Building collaboration. *IIMB Management Review*, *24*(1), 48–66. doi: 10.1016/j.iimb.2012.01.004.

Tugend, A. (2013). Unemployed and older, and facing a jobless future. *New York Times*. From http://www.nytimes.com/2013/07/27/your-money/unemployed-and-older-and-facing-a-job less-future.html. Accessed at December 31, 2015.

Twenge, J. M. (2010). A review of the empirical evidence on generational differences in work attitudes. *Journal of Business and Psychology*, *25*(2), 201–210. doi: 10.1007/s10869-010-9165-6.

U.S. Bureau of Labor Statistics (2013). Labor force statistics from the current population survey. From http://www.bls.gov/web/empsit/cpseea10.htm. Accessed at December 31, 2015.

U.S. Bureau of Labor Statistics (2014). Employee tenure in 2014. From http://www.bls.gov/news.release/tenure.nr0.htm. Accessed at December 31, 2015.

Wilson, J. A., & Elman, N. S. (1990). Organizational benefits of mentoring. *The Executive*, *4*(4), 88–94.

Winerip, M. (2012). Boomers vs. Millennials: Who's really getting robbed? New York Times. From http://www.nytimes.com/2012/09/13/booming/13winerip.html. Accessed at December 31, 2015.

MICHAEL S. NORTH is an Assistant Professor of Management and Organizations at New York University Stern School of Business. He received his BA in Psychology from the University of Michigan, Ann Arbor, and his PhD in Psychology and Social Policy from Princeton University. He recently completed a 2-year postdoctoral position at Columbia University. His research focuses primarily on age, ageism, intergenerational tension, and related management and policy applications.

SUSAN T. FISKE is Eugene Higgins Professor, Psychology and Public Affairs, Princeton University. She investigates cognitive stereotypes and emotional prejudices, culturally, interpersonally, and neuroscientifically, with policy implications. Her books include *The HUMAN Brand: How We Relate to People, Products, and Companies* (with Chris Malone, 2013); *Envy Up, Scorn Down: How Status Divides Us* (2011); *Social Cognition* (with Shelley Taylor, 2013, 4/e). She edits

Annual Review of Psychology, PNAS, and *Policy Insights from Behavioral and Brain Sciences*, is President of the Federation of Associations in Behavioral and Brain Sciences, was elected to the National Academy of Sciences, the American Philosophical Society, and the American Academy of Arts and Sciences. Research requires a village, and her graduate students conspired for her winning Princeton University's Graduate Mentoring Award.

Journal of Social Issues, Vol. 72, No. 1, 2016, pp. 146–168
doi: *10.1111/josi.12160*

Why and When Do Learning Goal Orientation and Attitude Decrease with Aging? The Role of Perceived Remaining Time and Work Centrality

Dorien T.A.M. Kooij[*]
Tilburg University

Hannes Zacher
Queensland University of Technology

We conducted two studies to improve our understanding of why and when older workers are focused on learning. Based on socioemotional selectivity theory, which proposes that goal focus changes with age and the perception of time, we hypothesized and found that older workers perceive their remaining time at work as more limited than younger workers which, in turn, is associated with lower learning goal orientation and a less positive attitude toward learning and development. Furthermore, we hypothesized and found that high work centrality buffers the negative association between age and perceived remaining time, and thus the indirect negative effects of age on learning goal orientation and attitude toward learning and development (through perceived remaining time). These findings suggest that scholars and practitioners should take workers'. perceived remaining time and work centrality into account when examining or stimulating learning activities among aging workers.

Since the populations and workforces in many developed countries are aging, organizations must recognize that a majority of their talent and unique organizational knowledge resides within the group of older workers (Hedge & Borman, 2012). At the same time, today's fast changing work environment and constant evolution of technology requires older workers to participate in learning and development activities, particularly since older workers with obsolete skills will leave

───────────

[*]Correspondence concerning this article should be addressed to Dorien T.A.M. Kooij, Department of Human Resource Studies, Tilburg University, Warandelaan 2, 5037 AB, Tilburg, the Netherlands. Tel: +31 13 466 2827 [email: t.a.m.kooij@uvt.nl].

We thank Lylette van der Linden for her help with collecting the data.

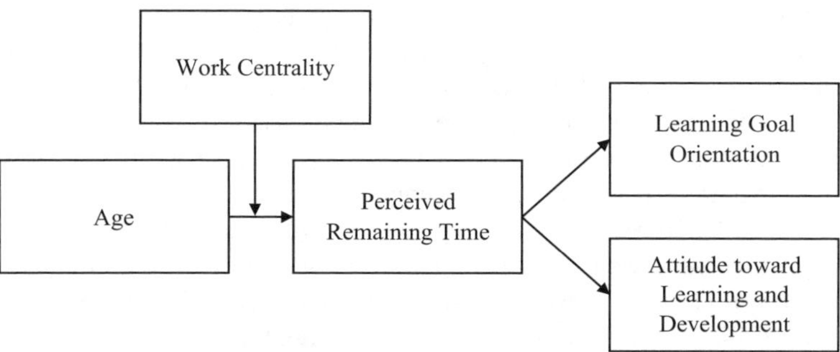

Fig. 1. Conceptual model and hypotheses.

the labor market (Maurer, 2001; Maurer, Weiss, & Barbeite, 2003). Unfortunately, age discrimination with regard to training and development, which is based on age stereotypes of older workers as incompetent and unwilling to learn, causes low organizational investments in older workers' human capital (Cuddy, Norton, & Fiske, 2005; Kite, Stockdale, & Whitley, 2005; Maurer, Wrenn, & Weiss, 2003; North & Fiske, 2016).

Besides these situational antecedents, older workers' lower participation in learning and development could also be explained by individual factors, such as decreased self-efficacy, lower career motivation, decreased learning orientation, stereotype threat, decreased work centrality, and limited future time perspective (Armstrong-Stassen & Schlosser, 2008; Kooij, Bal, & Kanfer, 2014; Maurer, Weiss et al., 2003; Van der Heijden, 2006; von Hippel, Kalokerinos, & Henry, 2013). In order to improve our understanding of why and when older workers are focused on learning, in this article, we examine associations between age, perceived remaining time at work, work centrality, and learning goal orientation and attitude toward learning and development. The studies we build on were mostly conducted in developed countries, and hence we conducted our research in a similar context (e.g., the Netherlands and United States). Despite some differences in pension systems, the Dutch and U.S. cultures are relatively similar and we expect similar results in our two samples. Our conceptual model is shown in Figure 1.

As outlined in this model and drawing on socioemotional selectivity theory (SST; Carstensen, Isaacowitz, & Charles, 1999), we argue that older workers perceive their remaining time at work as more limited than younger workers which, in turn, is associated with lower learning goal orientation (i.e., the tendency toward seeking to develop competence by acquiring new skills and mastering new situations; Dweck, 1986) and a more negative attitude toward learning and development (i.e., feeling favorably toward and having high interest in learning and development; Maurer et al., 2003). Furthermore, we argue that high work centrality, defined as "individual beliefs regarding the degree of importance that work plays in their lives" (Walsh & Gordon, 2008, p. 46), buffers the negative association between age and perceived remaining time, and thus the negative indirect effects of age on learning goal orientation and attitude toward learning and development (through perceived remaining time).

With this study we aim to contribute to the literature in a number of ways. First, we aim to extend research on age and engagement in learning and development at work (e.g., Maurer et al., 2003) by taking a lifespan perspective and hence applying a lifespan theory to explain age differences in learning orientation and attitude toward learning at work. By doing so, we shed light on the issue raised by Maurer (2002) of how to address and understand age differences in learning and development behavior, and answer Ng and Feldman's (2012) call to pay more attention to the fundamental reasons why age is related to motivation to keep learning.

Second, we aim to contribute to the literature on SST by examining how work centrality moderates the relationship between age and perceived remaining time. Specifically, we aim to provide more insight on how to mitigate the negative association between age and perceived remaining time found in previous research (Kooij et al., 2014; Zacher & Frese, 2009). Finally, we answer multiple calls (e.g., Kanfer & Ackerman, 2004; Raemdonck, Beausaert, Fröhlich, Kochoian, & Meurant, 2015) for more research on age-related constructs (i.e., perceived remaining time), aiming to explain additional variance in workers' learning goal orientation and attitude toward learning and development.

Age, Learning Goal Orientation, and Attitude toward Learning and
Development: The Mediating Role of Perceived Remaining Time at Work

Earlier research suggested that older workers are less oriented toward learning and development (Maurer, 2001). Ebner, Freund, and Baltes (2006), for example, found that with age, goal focus shifts from a focus on growth and performance optimization toward a focus on maintenance and counteracting performance losses. Similarly, Kanfer and Ackerman (2000) found that desire to learn was significantly lower among older adults compared to younger adults, and De Lange, Taris, Jansen, Kompier, Houtman, and Bongers (2010) showed that older workers were less motivated to learn. Finally, Kooij, De Lange, Jansen, Kanfer, and Dikkers (2011) conducted a meta-analysis and found that work-related growth motives, such as learning something new, decreased with age.

In this article, we use age as a continuous variable and hence we use younger and older workers simply as descriptive labels. There are three reasons for this. First, lifespan theories (as compared to life stage theories), such as SST, use age as a continuous variable. Second, cut-off ages distinguishing younger, middle-aged, and older workers used in previous studies are arbitrary and there are no universal cut-off points to distinguish younger, middle-aged, and older workers

(Shultz & Adams, 2007). However, in exploratory analyses, we additionally examine potential curvilinear relationships between age and perceived remaining time and learning outcomes (Cate & John, 2007). Third, distinguishing older workers and thus dichotomizing variables has negative consequences, such as loss of information on individual differences and associated reduction of statistical power (MacCallum, Zhang, Preacher, & Rucker, 2002).

Furthermore, we specifically focus on learning goal orientation and attitude toward learning and development. Dweck (1986) distinguished a learning orientation from a performance orientation. Individuals with a performance goal orientation seek to demonstrate and validate the adequacy of their competence by seeking favorable judgments and avoiding negative judgments about their competence, whereas individuals with a learning goal orientation seek to develop competence by acquiring new skills and mastering new situations. In a similar line of reasoning, Arygyris (1976) distinguished single-loop (i.e., focused on controlling tasks and on protecting the self) and double-loop learning (i.e., focused on valid information and internal commitment). Although both performance and learning goal orientation are likely to change with age (e.g., Kanfer & Ackerman, 2004), learning goal orientation or double-loop learning have more favorable outcomes in terms of affect and behavior (Arygyrs, 1976; Dweck, 1986) and thus we focus on learning goal orientation. Vandewalle (1997) applied this concept to the work domain and defined learning goal orientation as the general "desire to develop the self by acquiring new skills, mastering new situations and improving one's competence" (p. 1000). Although a learning goal orientation is often regarded as a relatively stable personality characteristic, to a certain extent it is also susceptible to manipulation and change (Maurer et al., 2003).

In addition to this rather stable construct, we also included the relatively more changeable construct of attitude toward learning and development. Maurer, Weiss et al. (2003) introduced this concept and defined it as feeling favorably toward and having high interest in learning and development. Attitude toward learning and development is very important, because attitudes toward a certain behavior influence intentions to perform that behavior (Ajzen, 1991). Building on the theory of planned behavior (Ajzen, 1991), Maurer, Weiss et al. (2003) indeed found that a higher attitude toward learning and development leads to greater intentions to engage in and actual engagement in learning and development activities.

To explain how and why learning orientation and attitude change with age, we build on SST (Carstensen et al., 1999). According to this theory, there are two main types of social goals in life: instrumental, future-oriented goals aimed at gaining resources, such as acquiring knowledge; and emotionally meaningful goals aimed at obtaining short-term, affective rewards, such as finding meaning in life and establishing feelings of social embeddedness (Carstensen et al., 1999). SST argues that FTP, defined as individuals' perceptions of remaining time in life, plays a fundamental role in the selection and pursuit of these goals (Lang &

Carstensen, 2002). Based on Carstensen and colleagues' work, Zacher and Frese (2009) distinguished between two dimensions of occupational future time perspective (FTP); perceived remaining opportunities at work and perceived remaining time at work. Consistent with SST theory and our focus on the work setting, we use perceived remaining time at work in this study. According to Zacher and Frese (2009), FTP is an age-related, flexible construct that is capable of modification and changes over time. These researchers hypothesized and found that perceived remaining time at work is negatively related to age.

According to SST, goals change with the perception of time as either limited or open-ended (Carstensen et al., 1999). More specifically, when time is perceived as open-ended, instrumental, preparatory goals related to the acquisition of knowledge, such as gathering information and experiencing novelty, are pursued, and when time is perceived as limited, emotionally meaningful goals, such as goals related to feeling states and experiencing emotional satisfaction, are prioritized (Carstensen et al., 1999). In line with this reasoning, Lang and Carstensen (2002) hypothesized and found that individuals who perceived their future time as being limited, prioritized emotionally meaningful goals, such as emotion regulation, whereas individuals who perceived their futures as open-ended, prioritized instrumental or knowledge-related goals. In a similar line of reasoning, Hershfield et al. (2011) found that priming future self-orientation enhances savings behavior. Adapting this to the work context, as retirement approaches and perceived remaining time at work decreases, workers will focus less on instrumental, future-oriented goals aimed at knowledge acquisition. Therefore, we hypothesize:

Hypothesis 1: Perceived remaining time is positively associated with (a) learning goal orientation and (b) attitude toward learning and development.

In sum, we expect that age is negatively related to perceived remaining time at work which, in turn, is positively associated with learning goal orientation and attitude toward learning and development. This line of reasoning is supported by SST (Carstensen et al., 1999), which proposes that age differences in goal focus can be explained by FTP. Similarly, Maurer, Weiss et al. (2003) noted that age-related factors, such as the number of years expected to be working until retirement from full-time work, could account for most of the relationships between age and individual and situational antecedents of attitude toward learning and development. Similarly, De Lange et al. (2010) suggested that older workers (who see retirement approaching quicker than middle-aged workers) may have a reduced FTP, resulting in motivational consequences like a lower motivation to learn (see also Zacher, Degner, Seevaldt, Frese, & Lüdde, 2009). Based on SST and these previous studies, we hypothesize:

Hypothesis 2: The negative associations between (a) age and learning goal orientation and between (b) age and attitude toward learning and development are mediated by perceived remaining time at work.

The Moderating Role of Work Centrality

Paullay, Alliger and Stone-Romero (1994) define work centrality as the general importance that work plays in an individual's life (see also Macdonald & Levy, 2016). Work centrality thus describes an individual's general commitment to work, the extent to which people perceive work as a main component of their life, and the degree of identification with the work role (Hirschfeld & Feild, 2000; Walsh & Gordon, 2008). Although work centrality has been found to influence the importance employees attach to training and development goals and intention to learn directly (Meurant, Raemdonck, Frenay, & Zacher, 2013), here we focus on the moderating role of work centrality in the negative association between age and perceived remaining time and in the negative indirect effects of age on learning orientation and attitude through perceived remaining time.

As individuals age, they face increasing loss of resources (Ebner et al., 2006), making the resources and energy they have more valuable (Bal & Kooij, 2011). Therefore, older workers will think carefully about which goals they allocate their resources to, and they will assign their resources to what they find important, dependent on what goals have priority in their lives (Kanfer & Ackerman, 2004). High work centrality means that one identifies with one's work role and sees work as an important aspect of life (Diefendorff, Brown, Kamin, & Lord, 2002). Hence, individuals who score high on work centrality devote more time and energy to their work role, rather than other life roles, such as family (Carlson & Kacmar, 2000). As a result, they invest in a long-term mutual relationship with their organization (Bal & Kooij, 2011). In line with this reasoning, positive associations have been found between work centrality and older workers' intention to remain in the company (e.g., Armstrong-Stassen & Schlosser, 2008). Since older employees with high work centrality maintain high levels of perceived remaining time at work, we hypothesize:

Hypothesis 3: Work centrality moderates the negative relationship between age and perceived remaining time, such that the relationship is stronger for low work centrality and weaker for high work centrality.

Moreover, building on our hypotheses that the associations between age and learning goal orientation and between age and attitude toward learning and development are mediated by perceived remaining time and that work centrality moderates the relationship between age and perceived remaining time, we propose a moderated mediation effect model (Figure 1). We argue that younger workers perceive a longer future ahead of them and are thus focused on learning, regardless of their level of work centrality. Older workers, on the other hand, have to deal with resource losses and will thus think more careful about where to allocate their time and energy. Therefore, work centrality will be crucial for how they perceive their remaining time at work and subsequently their focus on and attitude toward learning. In line with this reasoning, Armstrong-Stassen and Schlosser (2008) found that older workers with high work centrality have a higher development orientation. Therefore, we hypothesize:

Hypothesis 4: Work centrality moderates the indirect effects of age on (a) learning goal orientation and (b) attitude toward learning and development (through perceived remaining time), such that the indirect effects are stronger for low work centrality and weaker for high work centrality.

Method

Sample and Procedure

We used two samples to test our hypotheses. The first data set (i.e., Study 1) consisted of 175 employees in the Netherlands. The sample was a convenience sample acquired by a Master's student in Human Resource Studies. The initial sample consisted of 224 participants of which 49 questionnaires could not be used due to missing data. Attitudes toward learning and development were not gathered in this study. Of the participants, 45% were male and 55% were female. Mean age was 38.5 years ($SD = 13.5$) and ranged from 19 to 69 years. With respect to educational level, 32% had a higher vocational education, 46% a university education, and 22% had other education. The average hours worked per week was 32.6 hours ($SD = 11.6$), and the average years spent working for the current employer was 8.3 years ($SD = 9.4$). Participants were from a broad range of industries, including manufacturing, financial services, and healthcare.

The second data set (i.e., Study 2) consisted of 503 employees from the United States, including 214 (42.5%) men and 289 (57.5%) women. The age distribution ranged from 18 to 67 years, and the average age was 33 years ($SD = 10.6$). In terms of highest level of education, six (1.2%) employees indicated some high school, 64 (12.7%) had completed high school, 185 (36.8%) indicated some college, 182 (36.2%) had completed an undergraduate degree, and 66 (13.1%) completed a postgraduate university degree. The average number of hours worked per week was 36.6 hours ($SD = 11.2$), and the average years spent working for the current employer was 4.7 years ($SD = 5.4$). Employees worked in a broad range of jobs, including administrative assistant, customer service, engineer, graphic designer, manager, retail clerk, and teacher.

Participants were recruited using the crowdsourcing website Amazon's Mechanical Turk (MTurk; http://www.mturk.com). The use of MTurk to collect high-quality survey data in a fast and inexpensive way has been recommended by researchers (Buhrmester, Kwang, & Gosling, 2011; Mason & Suri, 2011). For example, Buhrmester et al. (2011) showed that data obtained using MTurk are at least as reliable as data obtained using traditional methods and that MTurk workers are generally more diverse than student samples (see also Landers & Behrend, 2015). In November 2012 (Time 1), participants received a link to the first online survey, and 503 provided usable data. Three months later, in February 2013, all of the T1 participants were contacted over MTurk and asked to complete a second online survey. Of the original respondents, 149 completed the second survey (response rate of 30%). Drop out analyses revealed that participants who participated at T2 were significantly older ($M = 35.4$ vs. 31.9 years, $t = 3.40$, $p = .001$), better educated ($M = 3.6$ vs. 3.4 years, $t = 2.05$, $p = .041$), and had lower work centrality ($M = 2.8$ vs. 3.0 years, $t = -2.09$, $p = .037$) than participants who did not participate at T2. Moreover, there was a greater proportion of women among those participants who also completed the T2 survey compared to those who dropped out.

Measures

Perceived remaining time at work.   Perceived remaining time was measured with the scale from Zacher and Frese (2009; based on Lang & Carstensen, 2002): "Most of my occupational life lies ahead of me," "My occupational future seems infinite to me," and "As I get older, I begin to experience time in my occupational future as limited" (reverse coded). These items were assessed on a 5-point scale ranging from 1 (*strongly disagree)* to 5 (*strongly agree)*. In Study 1, we deleted the third, reverse coded item, because the inclusion of this item resulted in unacceptable low internal consistency. The Spearman-Brown coefficient, which is the most appropriate reliability coefficient for two-item measures (Eisinga, te Grotenhuis, & Pelzer, 2013), was .70. Cronbach's alpha in Study 2 was .89.

Work centrality.   Work centrality was measured with 12 items based on the widely used scale of Paullay et al. (1994). Items included are "In my view, an individual's personal life goals should be work oriented" and "I would probably keep working even if I didn't need the money." These items were measured on a 6-point scale ranging from 1 (*strongly disagree*) to 6 (*strongly agree*). Cronbach's alphas were .80 in Study 1 and .87 in Study 2.

Learning goal orientation.   To measure learning goal orientation, the 5-item scale of Vandewalle (1997) was used. Example items are "I often look for opportunities to develop new skills and knowledge" and "I enjoy challenging and difficult tasks at work where I will learn new skills." These items were assessed on a 5-point scale ranging from 1 (*strongly disagree)* to 5 (*strongly agree)*. Cronbach's alpha was .84 in Study 1 and .89 (T1) and .92 (T2) in Study 2.

Attitude toward learning and development.   We measured attitude toward learning and development with the 8-item scale developed by Maurer, Weiss et al.

(2003). Example items are "I feel favorably toward the idea of improving my career skills" and "I am not very motivated in job or career-related learning and development activities (reverse coded)." These items were assessed on a 7-point scale ranging from 1 (*strongly disagree*) to 7 (*strongly agree*). Cronbach's alphas in Study 2 were .93 (T1) and .94 (T2).

Control and demographic variables.   Age was measured by asking individuals to fill in their age in years. Since Cate and John (2007) suggested that middle-aged people may still perceive high levels of remaining time in their lives (similar to young adults) and thus the relationship between age and perceived remaining time (as well as the indirect effects of age on learning outcomes through remaining time) may be curvilinear, we included age^2 as well as the interaction between age^2 and work centrality as control variables in both studies. Furthermore, we included gender (0 = *female*, 1 = *male*) as a control variable in Study 1 and gender and educational level (1 = *some high school,* 2 = *high school degree,* 3 = *some college,* 4 = *undergraduate degree,* 5 = *postgraduate university degree*) as control variables in Study 2.

Statistical Analyses.   We examined our hypotheses using regression and bootstrap analyses implemented in the PROCESS macro (Hayes, 2013). The macro tests direct, indirect, and conditional indirect (i.e., moderated mediation) effects. The significance of the indirect effects is tested using bias-corrected and bootstrapped 95% confidence intervals (CI). An indirect effect is considered significant when a CI does not include zero.

Results

The descriptive statistics and correlations of the Study 1 variables are shown in Table 1. Age correlated negatively with learning goal orientation ($r = $ -.16, $p = $ .039) and perceived remaining time ($r = $ -.64, $p < $ .001). Learning goal orientation correlated positively with perceived remaining time ($r = $ .27, $p < $ .001) and work centrality ($r = $ .17, $p = $ .026). Table 2 shows the results of regression and indirect effect analyses with the Study 1 data. In support of Hypothesis 1a, perceived remaining time positively predicted learning goal orientation above and beyond gender and age ($B = $ .23, $p < $ .001). The indirect effect of age on learning goal orientation through perceived remaining time was significant (-.15, 95% CI $= $ -.25, -.06). These findings provide support for Hypothesis 2a. Table 2 further shows that work centrality did neither moderate the relationship between age and perceived remaining time nor the indirect effect of age on learning goal orientation through perceived remaining time (i.e., the 95% CI included zero). Thus, Hypotheses 3 and 4a were not supported with the Study 1 data. Age^2 had a significant effect on perceived remaining time ($B = $ -.27, $p < $ .001), but not on learning goal

Table 1. Descriptive Statistics and Correlations of Study 1 Variables

Variable (endpoints of scale)	M	SD	1	2	3	4	5
1. Age	38.54	13.47	–				
2. Gender	0.45	0.50	–.01	–			
3. Perceived remaining time (1 – 5)	3.21	1.19	–.64**	.00	(.68)		
4. Work centrality (1 – 6)	3.27	0.60	.11	.12	.07	(.80)	
5. Learning goal orientation (1 – 5)	4.25	0.62	–.16*	.15*	.27**	.17*	(.84)

Notes. N = 175.
For gender, 0 = female, 1 = male.
Reliability estimates (α), where available, are shown in parentheses along the diagonal.
*p < .05; **p < .01.

Table 2. Results of Regression and Indirect Effect Analyses (Study 1)

Predictor variable	B	SE	t	p	R^2
Effects on perceived remaining time					
Gender	–.02	.06	0.30	.765	
Age	–.67	.06	–11.48	<.001	
Age^2	–.27	.06	–4.25	<.001	
Work centrality	.17	.06	2.78	.006	
Age × work centrality	.02	.06	0.40	.690	
Age^2 × work centrality	.05	.05	0.92	.361	
					.47**
Effects on learning goal orientation					
Gender	.08	.04	1.77	.079	
Age	.05	.06	0.83	.408	
Age^2	.07	.05	1.44	.152	
Perceived remaining time	.23	.06	3.79	<.001	
					.12**
Indirect effect of age on learning goal orientation (through perceived remaining time)	–.15	.05	95% CI = –.25, –.06		
Index of moderated mediation (for age)	.01	.01	95% CI = –.02, .03		
Indirect effect of age^2 on learning goal orientation (through perceived remaining time)	–.06	.03	95% CI = –.13, –.02		
Index of moderated mediation (for age^2)	.01	.01	95% CI = –.01, .05		

Notes. N = 175.
For gender, 0 = female, 1 = male.
CI = confidence interval.
All variables were z-standardized. Number of bootstrap samples for bias-corrected bootstrap CI: 5,000.
**p < .01.

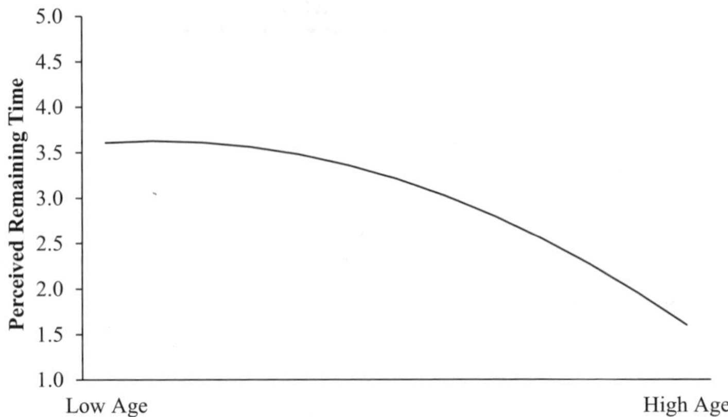

Fig. 2. Relationship between age and perceived remaining time (Study 1).
Note. "High age" and "low age" refer to age ±1 *SD*, respectively.

orientation. As shown in Figure 2, the negative relationship between age and perceived remaining time had a slight inverted U-shape, suggesting that young and middle-aged employees perceived more remaining time at work than older employees. Finally, age^2 also had a significant indirect effect on learning goal orientation (through perceived remaining time; -.06, 95% CI = -.13, -.02).

Table 3 shows the descriptive statistics and correlations of the Study 2 variables. Age correlated negatively with perceived remaining time ($r = -.51, p <$ .001) but not with work centrality, learning goal orientation at T1 and T2, and attitude toward learning and development at T1 and T2. Perceived remaining time correlated positively with work centrality ($r = .13, p < .001$), learning goal orientation at T1 and T2 ($rs = .28$ and .34, respectively, $ps < .001$), and attitude toward learning and development at T1 and T2 ($rs = .34$ and .45, respectively, $ps < .001$). Work centrality correlated positively with learning goal orientation at T1 ($r = .21$, $p < .001$) but not at T2, and with attitude toward learning and development at T1 and T2 ($r = .21, p < .001$, and $r = .17, p = .035$).

Tables 4 and 5 show the results of regression and moderated mediation analyses with the Study 2 data. In the first step, we regressed perceived remaining time on the control variables (gender and education), age, work centrality, and the interaction between age and work centrality (Table 4). Age had a negative effect on perceived remaining time ($B = -.52, p < .001$). Moreover, age^2 had a weak but significant effect on perceived remaining time ($B = -.09, p = .026$), and the negative relationship between age and perceived remaining time had a slight inverted U-shape (Figure 3). In the next steps, we regressed the control variables, age, and perceived remaining time on learning goal orientation at T1 and T2 and attitude toward learning and development at T1 and T2 (Tables 4 and 5). When

Table 3. Descriptive Statistics and Correlations of Variables (Study 2)

Variable (endpoints of scale)	M	SD	1	2	3	4	5	6	7	8	9
1. Age	32.96	10.61	–								
2. Gender	0.42	0.49	$-.10^*$	–							
3. Education	3.47	0.92	$.11^*$	.04	–						
4. Perceived remaining time $(1-5)$	3.99	0.91	$-.51^{**}$	$-.03$	$-.04$	(.89)					
5. Work centrality $(1-6)$	2.92	0.79	$-.05$	$.13^{**}$	$.09^*$	$.13^{**}$	(.37)				
6. Learning goal orientation T1 $(1-5)$	4.00	0.66	$-.03$	$-.06$	.09	$.28^{**}$	$.21^{**}$	(.89)			
7. Attitude toward learning and development T1 $(1-7)$	5.52	0.93	$-.07$	$-.09$	$.09^*$	$.34^{**}$	$.21^{**}$	$.74^{**}$	(.93)		
8. Learning goal orientation T2 $(1-5)$	3.95	0.70	$-.02$	$-.11$	.11	$.34^{**}$	.08	$.83^{**}$	$.69^{**}$	(.92)	
9. Attitude toward learning and development T2 $(1-7)$	5.54	1.03	$-.11$	$-.09$	.05	$.45^{**}$	$.17^*$	$.69^{**}$	$.73^{**}$	$.79^{**}$	(.94)

Notes. $N_{Time1} = 503$; $N_{Time2} = 149$; T1 = Time 1; T2 = Time 2 (3 months later).
Reliability estimates (α), where available, are shown in parentheses along the diagonal.
$^*p < .05$. $^{**}p < .01$.

Table 4. Results of Regression and Moderated Mediation Analyses Predicting T1 Outcomes (Study 2)

Predictor variable	B	SE	t	p	R^2
Effects on perceived remaining time					
Gender	.10	.04	2.64	.009	
Education	.01	.04	0.17	.867	
Age	−.52	.04	−13.57	<.001	
Age^2	−.09	.04	−2.24	.026	
Work centrality	.12	.04	3.03	.003	
Age × work centrality	.10	.04	2.55	.011	
Age^2 × work centrality	−.01	.03	−0.22	.822	
					.30**
Effects on learning goal orientation T1					
Gender	.03	.03	0.94	.349	
Education	.06	.03	1.95	.052	
Age	.09	.03	2.55	.011	
Age^2	−.01	.03	−0.42	.677	
Perceived remaining time	.23	.03	6.83	<.001	
					.10**
Indirect effect of age on learning goal orientation at T1 (through remaining time)	−.12	.02	95% CI = −.16, −.08		
Index of moderated mediation (for age)	.02	.01	95% CI = .01, .04		
Indirect effect of age^2 on learning goal orientation at T1 (through remaining time)	−.02	.01	95% CI = −.04, −.004		
Index of moderated mediation (for age^2)	−.002	.01	95% CI = −.02, .01		
Effects on attitude toward learning and development T1					
Gender	.06	.04	1.54	.125	
Education	.08	.04	2.13	.033	
Age	.11	.05	2.36	.019	
Age^2	−.06	.04	−1.61	.108	
Perceived remaining time	.37	.05	8.16	<.001	
					.15**
Indirect effect of age on attitude toward learning at T1 (through remaining time)	−.19	.03	95% CI = −.25, −.14		
Index of moderated mediation (for age)	.04	.01	95% CI = .01, .06		
Indirect effect of age^2 on attitude toward learning at T1 (through remaining time)	−.03	.01	95% CI = −.06, −.005		
Index of moderated mediation (for age^2)	−.003	.01	95% CI = −.03, .02		

Notes. N_{Time1} = 503; T1 = Time 1.
CI = confidence interval.
For gender, 0 = *female*, 1 = *male*.
All variables were z-standardized. Number of bootstrap samples for bias-corrected bootstrap CI: 5,000.
**p < .01.

Table 5. Results of Regression and Moderated Mediation Analyses Predicting T2 Outcomes (Study 2)

Predictor variable	B	SE	t	p	R^2
Effects on learning goal orientation T2					
Gender	.02	.03	0.65	.519	
Education	.04	.03	1.03	.304	
Age	.03	.04	0.79	.433	
Age^2	.02	.03	0.60	.548	
Learning goal orientation T1	.53	.04	15.14	<.001	
Perceived remaining time	.03	.04	0.77	.441	
					.69**
Indirect effect of age on learning goal orientation at T2 (through remaining time)	−.02	.03	95% CI = −.08, .04		
Index of moderated mediation (for age)	.005	.01	95% CI = −.007, .03		
Indirect effect of age^2 on learning goal orientation at T2 (through remaining time)	.0001	.005	95% CI = −.01, .01		
Index of moderated mediation (for age^2)	.003	.01	95% CI = −.003, .02		
Effects on attitude toward learning and development T2					
Gender	.03	.06	0.55	.580	
Education	−.002	.06	−0.04	.971	
Age	.04	.07	0.60	.548	
Age^2	.03	.06	0.54	.592	
Attitude toward learning and development T1	.66	.07	10.13	<.001	
Perceived remaining time	.20	.08	2.63	.010	
					.56**
Indirect effect of age on attitude toward learning at T2 (through remaining time)	−.13	.06	95% CI = −.26, −.02		
Index of moderated mediation (for age)	.02	.02	95% CI = .001, .07		
Indirect effect of age^2 on attitude toward learning at T2 (through remaining time)	.005	.02	95% CI = −.03, .05		
Index of moderated mediation (for age^2)	.01	.02	95% CI = −.01, .06		

Notes. N_{Time2} = 149. T1 = Time 1; T2 = Time 2.
CI = confidence interval. For gender, 0 = *female*, 1 = *male*.
All variables were z-standardized. Number of bootstrap samples for bias-corrected bootstrap CI: 5,000.
**p < .01.

predicting T2 outcomes, we additionally controlled for the outcome variables assessed at T1. Results showed that perceived remaining time positively predicted learning goal orientation at T1 (B = .23, p < .001) but not at T2, as well as attitude toward learning and development at T1 (B = .37, p < .001) and T2 (B = .20, p = .010). These findings provide partial support for Hypothesis 1a and full support for Hypothesis 1b. Tables 4 and 5 further show that age had significant indirect

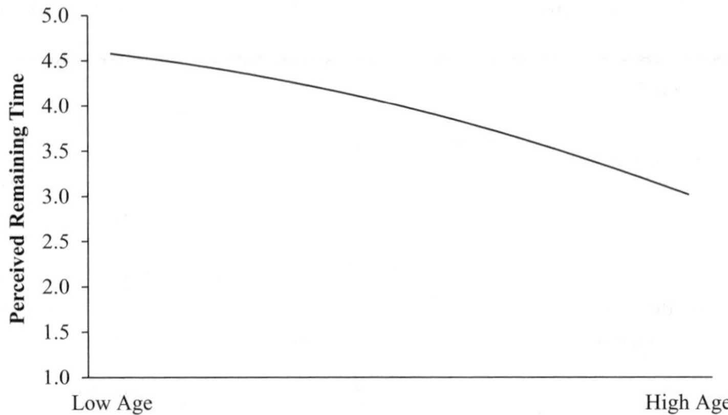

Fig. 3. Relationship between age and perceived remaining time (Study 2).
Note. "High age" and "low age" refer to age ±1 *SD*, respectively.

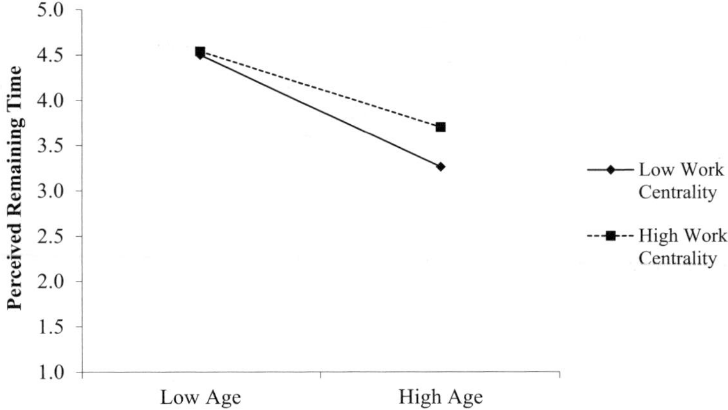

Fig. 4. Relationship between age and perceived remaining time moderated by work centrality (Study 2).
Note. "High age" and "low age" refer to age ±1 *SD*, respectively.

effects through perceived remaining time on learning goal orientation at T1 (-.12, 95% CI = -.16, -.08) but not at T2, as well as on attitude toward learning and development at T1 (-.19, 95% CI = -.25, -.14) and at T2 (-.13, 95% CI = -.26, -.02). Thus, Hypothesis 2a was partially and Hypothesis 2b was fully supported. Age^2 did neither predict learning goal orientation nor attitude toward learning and development at T1 and T2; however, age^2 had significant indirect effects on T1 learning goal orientation (-.02, 95% CI = -.04, -.004) and T1 attitude toward learning and development (-.03, 95% CI = -.06, -.005). Age^2 did not have indirect effects on change in learning goal orientation and attitude toward learning and development (at T2).

Table 4 further shows that work centrality had a positive effect on perceived remaining time ($B = .12$, $p = .003$), and the interaction effect of age and work centrality on perceived remaining time was also significant ($B = .10$, $p = .011$). Figure 2 shows the interaction effect. We further probed the interaction effect by regressing perceived remaining time on age at low (i.e., -1 SD) and high (i.e., + 1 SD) values of work centrality. The results of this simple slopes analysis showed that the relationship between age and perceived remaining time was stronger negative for low work centrality ($B = -.56$, $p < .001$) than for high work centrality ($B = -.39$, $p < .001$). Together, these results provide support for Hypothesis 3. Age^2 did not interact with work centrality in predicting perceived remaining time (Table 4).

Finally, we examined whether perceived remaining time also mediated the interaction effect of age and work centrality on outcomes (i.e., moderated mediation). Tables 4 and 5 show that moderated mediation was present (i.e., the 95% CI did not include zero) for learning goal orientation at T1 but not at T2, as well as for attitude toward learning and development at T1 and T2. For learning goal orientation at T1, the indirect effect of age (through perceived remaining time) was stronger negative at low work centrality (-.14, 95% CI $= -.19$, -.10) compared to high work centrality (-.10, 95% CI $= -.14$, -.06). For attitude toward learning and development at T1, the indirect effect of age (through perceived remaining time) was also stronger negative at low work centrality (-.23, 95% CI $= -.30$, -.17) compared to high work centrality (-.16, 95% CI $= -.22$, -.11). Finally, for attitude toward learning and development at T2, the indirect effect of age (through perceived remaining time) was stronger negative at low work centrality (-.14, 95% CI $= -.30$, -.02) compared to high work centrality (-.10, 95% CI $= -.23$, -.02). Overall, these findings provide partial support for Hypothesis 4a and full support for Hypothesis 4b. Work centrality did not moderate any of the indirect effects of age^2 on learning outcomes (Tables 4 and 5).

Discussion

The goal of this study was to test a moderated mediation model of age, perceived remaining time, work centrality, and learning orientation and attitude (Figure 1). Results based on cross-sectional employee data from two different countries showed that age was negatively related to perceived remaining time at work which, in turn, was positively associated with learning goal orientation (Study 1 and 2) and attitude toward learning and development (Study 2). In addition, we found that the negative relationship between age and perceived remaining time at work had a slight inverted U-shape, such that remaining time, and thus learning goal orientation and attitude toward learning and development, was relatively high for both young and middle-aged workers, and lower among older workers. Thus, consistent with SST (Carstensen et al., 1999), perceived remaining time appears to be an age-related individual difference characteristic that links age with employees' focus on workplace learning. Moreover, perceived remaining time mediated the effects of age (but not age^2) on change in attitude toward learning and development across 3 months, but not the effects of age on change in learning goal orientation (Study 2). A potential reason for these diverging findings may be that learning goal orientation is a more stable characteristic than attitude toward learning and development (Ajzen, 1991; Maurer, Weiss et al., 2003).

Results of Study 2 (but not Study 1) further showed that work centrality moderated the negative relationship between age and perceived remaining time, as well as the indirect effects of age on learning goal orientation (at Time 1) and attitude toward learning and development (at both Time 1 and Time 2). Specifically, the negative effects were weaker among employees with high compared to low work centrality, suggesting that the importance of work in older employees' lives is an important factor with regard to their focus on workplace learning. We did not find the moderating role of work centrality in the Dutch sample, which might be due to the fixed retirement age system of the Netherlands causing age and perceived remaining time at work to be more highly related and more difficult to influence compared to the United States.

Limitations and Future Research

This study has a number of limitations that should be addressed in future research. First, cross-sectional designs do not allow conclusions about causality and age-related changes over time (i.e., aging). Moreover, the time lag of 3 months used in Study 2 may have been too short to capture a meaningful effect of perceived remaining time on learning goal orientation. Future research should, therefore, assess employees' learning orientation and attitude over longer time periods and across critical transition phases (e.g., transition from early to mid-career, or from mid- to late-career). Second, several other factors aside from perceived remaining time may mediate the complex relationships between age and learning orientation and attitude. For instance, the FTP construct includes several additional dimensions such as foci on opportunities and limitations in the remaining time at work (Zacher, 2013) and also relates to subjective age, which is an important age-related variable in the workplace (Staudinger, 2015). Moreover, future research should examine whether perceived remaining time can explain variance in learning outcomes above and beyond established predictors such as self-efficacy (Maurer et al., 2003) and discriminative decisions by managers (Maurer & Barbeite, 2001). Third, as also mentioned by Maurer et al. (2003), our sample might be biased, because it excludes workers who have left the workforce voluntarily or involuntarily (e.g., because of health problems, "healthy worker effect"). Since older workers participate less in training and development, they are more likely to have left the labor market because of obsolete skills (Maurer et al., 2003). Future studies should include working as well as nonworking individuals to test whether the learning orientation and attitude toward learning and development of these groups differ. Furthermore, like most other studies on aging at work, we did not examine the intersection of multiple group identities (Marcus & Fritzsche, 2015). Employees are not only young or old; they are also male or female, White or non-White, and have low or high socioeconomic status. Multiple-group membership influences individual employees' perceptions, attitudes, emotions, and behaviors (e.g., perceptions of an older White male might differ considerably from an older non-White female; Marcus & Fritzsche, 2015). For example, older women might be more disadvantaged compared to older men with respect to learning opportunities at work, because stereotypes on incompetency and inability to learn are more prevalent among older women (Hummert, 1990). Future research should therefore examine the role of age intersectionality in associations between age, perceived remaining time, and learning goal orientation and attitudes toward learning and development. In addition, we conducted our research in Western contexts. Although we deliberately focused on developed countries, because research on associations between age and learning orientation and attitudes is mostly conducted in developed countries, future research should replicate our findings in other contexts (e.g., Asian or Eastern European countries). Since previous studies support basic tenets of SST in other contexts as well (e.g., Fung, Lai, & Ng, 2001), we expect to find similar results. Finally, work centrality may only be one of several factors that may moderate associations between age and FTP dimensions. For instance, Zacher and Frese (2009) found that job complexity moderated the negative relationship between age and focus on opportunities, but not perceived remaining time. Thus, future research on work-related boundary conditions of the age–FTP association is needed.

Theoretical and Practical Implications

With this study, we contributed to the literature in a number of ways. First, we contributed to the literature on age and engagement in learning and development at work. We demonstrated that older workers perceive their time at work as more limited, which in turn leads to a lower learning orientation and attitude toward learning and development (also over time). With this we provide additional insight in the underlying process explaining age differences in motivation to keep learning (Ng & Feldman, 2012) and learning and development behavior (Maurer, 2002). Since older workers perceive that their time at work is running out, they are less likely to invest resources in future-oriented goals, such as knowledge acquisition. Moreover, by applying SST, and thus taking a lifespan perspective to explain these differences, we revealed that lifespan theories are suitable to understand learning attitudes and behavior at work (see also Raemdonck et al., 2015).

Second, we contributed to the literature on SST by demonstrating that work centrality moderates the relationship between age and perceived remaining time at work. Age and perceived remaining time both in general and at work are strongly negatively related (Kooij et al., 2014; Zacher & Frese, 2009). Because of the profound influence of perceived remaining time on important outcomes, such as life satisfaction, physical exercise, and learning orientation and attitude, it is important to know how to mitigate this strong negative association. Our study results show that older workers, who see work as an important aspect of their lives, are able to maintain relatively high levels of perceived remaining time at work, and thus high levels of learning goal orientation and attitude toward learning and development. Finally, we contribute to the literature on aging by answering multiple calls (e.g., Kanfer & Ackerman, 2004) for more research on conceptualizations related to age, and found that age has a negative influence on learning orientation and attitude toward learning and development via perceived remaining time.

This study also has some practical implications. First of all, we found that it is perceived remaining time and not age that determines lower learning orientation and attitude toward learning and development (age even had a positive influence on learning orientation and attitude at Time 1 in the U.S. sample when controlling for perceived remaining time). Organizations should thus be careful with stereotypical views that older workers have no desire to learn anymore and are less motivated to work than younger workers. In addition, organizations can stimulate learning and development by offering Human Resource Management practices that lengthen perceived remaining time, such as career counseling to discuss future career opportunities and favorable employment and working conditions. Governments can stimulate and help organizations by providing resources, such as subsidies and best practice reports. Moreover, governments can lengthen perceived remaining time at work and thus stimulate learning and development of older workers by increasing retirement ages. Currently, many European countries have an official retirement age of about 65 years (OECD, 2014). Actual or effective retirement ages are mostly even below 65 (Phillips & Siu, 2012). Governments of several European countries, such as the Netherlands and Germany, are now in the process of increasing their official retirement ages. In the United States, no mandatory retirement age exists and the self-reported actual retirement age has increased to about 62 years (Riffkin, 2014). However, attitudes and norms with respect to retirement age need to change as well. Lifelong learning and continuing working rather than depreciation of older workers and early retirement should be the norm. Since U.S. and European citizens are starting to recognize, although reluctantly, the need to increase retirement age (Vaupel & Loichinger, 2006), the time seems right for more severe policy measures, such as the abolishment of fixed retirement ages.

Second, we found that work centrality mitigates the strong negative association between age and perceived remaining time. Although work centrality is a rather stable construct, it can be developed through individual experiences of employees (Paullay et al., 1994). Since Sharabi and Harpaz (2010) found that experiencing more autonomy, responsibility, and interesting and varied work leads to higher work centrality, organizations should ensure that older workers' jobs increasingly consist of these elements or stimulate job crafting so that older workers can change their task boundaries themselves Kooij, Tims, & Kanfer, 2015. In addition, governments should urge older workers to take their responsibility to participate in the workforce. Instead of preparing for an early retirement, older workers should continue to contribute value to and actively engage in the workforce (potentially part-time). Therefore, government campaigns emphasizing the tremendous value of older workers and the opportunities for older workers to enjoy and fully use their remaining time at work would be helpful. These types of social policies might increase older worker work centrality, and thus their learning orientation and attitudes, stimulating learning activities among older workers.

References

Ajzen, I. (1991). The theory of planned behavior. *Organizational Behavior and Human Decision Processes, 50*, 179–211. doi: 1016/0749-5978(91)90020-T.

Armstrong-Stassen, M., & Schlosser, F. (2008). Benefits of a supportive development climate for older workers. *Journal of Managerial Psychology, 23*, 419–437. doi: 10.1108/02683940810869033.

Arygyris, C. (1976). Single-loop and double-loop models in research on decision making. *Administrative Science Quarterly, 21*, 363–375.

Bal, P. M., & Kooij, D. (2011). The relations between work centrality, psychological contracts, and job attitudes: The influence of age. *European Journal of Work and Organizational Psychology, 20*, 497–523. doi: 10.1080/13594321003669079.

Buhrmester, M., Kwang, T., & Gosling, S. D. (2011). Amazon's Mechanical Turk: A new source of inexpensive, yet high-quality, data? *Perspectives on Psychological Science, 6*(1), 3–5. doi: 10.1177/1745691610393980.

Carlson, D. S., & Kacmar, K. M. (2000). Work-family conflict in the organization: Do life role values make a difference? *Journal of Management, 26*(5), 1031–1054. doi: 10.1177/0149206300026000502.

Carstensen, L. L., Isaacowitz, D. M., & Charles, S. T. (1999). Taking time seriously: A theory of socioemotional selectivity. *American Psychologist, 54*, 165–181. doi: 10.1037/0003-066X.54.3.165.

Cate, R. A., & John, O. P. (2007). Testing models of the structure and development of future time perspective: Maintaining a focus on opportunities in middle age. *Psychology and Aging, 22*, 186–201. doi: 10.1037/0882-7974.22.1.186.

Cuddy, A. J. C., Norton, M. I., & Fiske, S. T. (2005). This old stereotype: The pervasiveness and persistence of the elderly stereotype. *Journal of Social Issues, 61*, 267–285. doi: 10.1111/j.1540-4560.2005.00405.x.

De Lange, A. H., Taris, T. W., Jansen, P. G. W., Kompier, M. A. J., Houtman, I. L. D., & Bongers, P. M. (2010). On the relationships among work characteristics and learning-related behavior: Does age matter? *Journal of Organizational Behavior, 31*, 925–950. doi: 10.1002/job.649.

Diefendorff, J. M., Brown, D. J., Kamin, A. M., & Lord, R. G. (2002). Examining the roles of job involvement and work centrality in predicting organizational citizenship behaviors and job performance. *Journal of Organizational Behavior*, *23*, 93–108. doi: 10.1002/job.123.

Dweck, C. S. (1986). Motivational processes affecting learning. *American Psychologist*, *41*, 1040–1048. doi: 10.1037/0003-066X.41.10.

Ebner, N. C., Freund, A. M., & Baltes, P. B. (2006). Developmental changes in personal goal orientation form young to late adulthood: From striving for gains to maintenance and prevention of losses. *Psychology and Aging*, *21*, 664–678. doi: 10.1037/0882-7974.21.4.664.

Eisinga, R., te Grotenhuis, M., & Pelzer, B. (2013). The reliability of a two-item scale: Pearson, Cronbach, or Spearman-Brown? *International Journal of Public Health*, *58*, 637–642. doi: 10.1007/s00038-012-0416-3.

Fung, H. H., Lai, P., & Ng, R. (2001). Age differences in social preferences among Taiwanese and Mainland Chinese: The role of perceived time. *Psychology and Aging*, *16*, 351–356. doi: 10.1037/0882-7974.16.2.351.

Hayes, A. F. (2013). *Introduction to mediation, moderation, and conditional process analysis: A regression-based approach*. New York: Guilford Press.

Hedge, J. W., & Borman, W. C. (2012). *The Oxford handbook of work and aging*. New York: Oxford University Press.

Hershfield, H. E., Goldstein, D. G., Sharpe, W. F., Fox, J., Yeykelis, L., Carstensen, L. L., & Bailenson, J. N. (2011). Increasing saving behavior through age-progressed renderings of the future self. *Journal of Marketing Research*, *48*, S23–S37. doi: 10.1509/jmkr.48.SPL.S23.

Hirschfeld, R. R., & Feild, H. S. (2000). Work centrality and work alienation: Distinct aspects of a general commitment to work. *Journal of Organizational Behavior*, *21*, 789–800. doi: 10.1002/1099-1379.

Hummert, M. L. (1990). Multiple stereotypes of elderly and young adults: A comparison of structure and evaluations. *Psychology and Aging*, *5*, 182–193. doi: 10.1037/0882-7974.5.2.182.

Kanfer, R., & Ackerman, P. L. (2000). Individual differences in work motivation: Further explorations of a trait framework. *Applied Psychology: An International Review*, *49*, 470–482. doi: 10.1111/1464-0597.00026.

Kanfer, R., & Ackerman, P. L. (2004). Aging, adult development and work motivation. *Academy of Management Review*, *29*, 440–458. doi: 10.5465/AMR.2004.13670969.

Kite, M. E., Stockdale, G. D., & Whitley, B. E. (2005). Attitudes toward younger and older adults: An updated meta-analytic review. *Journal of Social Issues*, *61*, 241–266. doi: 10.1111/j.1540-4560.2005.00404.x.

Kooij, D. T. A. M., De Lange, A. H., Jansen, P. G. W., Kanfer, R., & Dikkers, J. S. E. (2011). Age and work-related motives: Results of a meta-analysis. *Journal of Organizational Behavior*, *32*, 197–225. doi: 10.1002/job.665.

Kooij, D. T. A. M., Bal, P. M., & Kanfer, R. (2014). Future time perspective and promotion focus as determinants of intraindividual change in work motivation. *Psychology and Aging*, *29*, 319–328. doi: 10.1037/a0036768.

Kooij, D. T. A. M., Tims, M., & Kanfer, R. (2015). Successful aging at work: The role of job crafting. In P. M. Bal, D. T. A. M. Kooij, & D. M. Rousseau (Eds.), *Aging workers and the employee–employer relationship* (pp. 145–161). New York: Springer.

Landers, R. N., & Behrend, T. S. (2015). An inconvenient truth: Arbitrary distinctions between organizational, Mechanical Turk, and other convenience samples. *Industrial and Organizational Psychology: Perspectives on Science and Practice*, *8*(2), 142–164. doi: 10.1017/iop.2015.13.

Lang, F. R., & Carstensen, L. L. (2002). Time counts: Future time perspective, goals, and social relationships. *Psychology and Aging*, *17*, 125–139. doi: 10.1037/0882-7974.17.1.125.

MacCallum, R. C., Zhang, S., Preacher, K. J., & Rucker, D. D. (2002). On the practice of dichotomization of quantitative variables. *Psychological Methods*, *7*, 19–40. doi: 10.1037/1082-989X.7.1.19.

Macdonald, J. L., & Levy, S. R. (2016). Ageism in the workplace: The role of psychosocial factors in predicting job satisfaction, commitment, and engagement. *Journal of Social Issues*, *72*(1), 169–190.

Marcus, J., & Fritzsche, B. A. (2015). One size doesn't fit all: Toward a theory on the intersectional salience of ageism at work. *Organizational Psychology Review, 5,* 168–188. doi: 10.1177/2041386614556015.

Maurer, T. J. (2001). Career-relevant learning and development, worker age, and beliefs about self-efficacy for development. *Journal of Management, 27,* 123–140. doi: 10.1177/014920630102700201.

Maurer, T. J. (2002). Employee learning and development orientation: Toward an integrative model of involvement in continuous learning. *Human Resource Development Review, 1,* 9–44. doi: 10.1177/1534484302011002.

Maurer, T. J., Weiss, E. M., & Barbeite, F. G. (2003). A model of involvement in work-related learning and development activity: The effects of individual, situational, motivational and age variables. *Journal of Applied Psychology, 88,* 707–724. doi: 10.1037/0021-9010.88.4.707.

Maurer, T. J., Wrenn, K. A., & Weiss, E. M. (2003). Toward understanding and managing stereotypical beliefs about older workers' ability and desire for learning and development. *Research in Personnel and Human Resources Management, 22,* 253–285. doi: 10.1016/S0742-7301(03)22006-5.

Meurant, C., Raemdonck, I., Frenay, M., & Zacher, H. (2013). The relative importance of work-related learning goals across the career: Does age really matter? *Paper presented at the Conference of the European Association of Work and Organizational Psychology,* Münster, May 22-25.

Ng, T. W. H., & Feldman, D. C. (2012). Aging and participation in career development activities. In J. W. Hedge & W. C. Borman (Eds.), *The Oxford handbook of work and aging* (pp. 137–150). New York: Oxford University Press.

North, M. S., & Fiske, S. T. (2016). Resource scarcity and prescriptive attitudes generate subtle, intergenerational older-worker exclusion. *Journal of Social Issues, 72*(1), 122–145.

OECD (2014). Statistics on average effective age of retirement. Retrieved from oecd.org. Accessed November 20, 2014.

Paullay, I. M., Alliger, G. M., & Stone-Romero, E. F. (1994). Construct validation of two instruments designed to measure job involvement and work centrality. *Journal of Applied Psychology, 79,* 224–228. doi: 10.1037/0021-9010.79.2.224.

Phillips, D. R., & Siu, O. (2012). Global aging and aging workers. In J. W. Hedge & W. C. Borman (Eds.), *The Oxford handbook of work and aging* (pp. 11–32). New York: Oxford University Press.

Raemdonck, I., Beausaert, S., Fröhlich, D., Kochoian, N., & Meurant, C. (2015). Aging workers' learning and employability. In P. M. Bal, D. T. A. M. Kooij, & D. M. Rousseau (Eds.), *Aging workers and the employment relationship* (pp. 163–184). Dordrecht: Springer.

Riffkin, R. (2014). Average U.S. retirement age rises to 62. US: Gallup. Retrieved from http://www.gallup.com/poll/168707/average-retirement-age-rises.aspx. Accessed at November 20, 2014.

Sharabi, M., & Harpaz, I. (2010). Improving employees' work centrality improves organizational performance: Work events and work centrality relationships. *Human Resource Development International, 13,* 379–392. doi: 10.1080/13678868.2010.501960.

Shultz, K. S., & Adams, G. A. (2007). In search of a unifying paradigm for understanding aging and work in the 21st century. In K. S. Shultz & G. A. Adams (Eds.), *Aging and work in the 21st century* (pp. 303–319). Mahwah, NJ: Lawrence Erlbaum.

Staudinger, U. M. (2015). Images of aging: Outside and inside perspectives. *Annual Review of Gerontology and Geriatrics, 35,* 187–209. doi: 10.1891/0198-8794.35.187.

Van der Heijden, B. I. J. M. (2006). Age differences in career activities among higher-level employees in the Netherlands. A comparison between profit sector an non-profit sector staff. *International Journal of Training and Development, 10,* 98–120. doi: 10.1111/j.1468-2419.2006.00247.x.

Vandewalle, D. (1997). Development and validation of a work domain goal orientation instrument. *Educational and Psychological Measurement, 57,* 995–1015. doi: 10.1177/0013164497057006009.

Vaupel, J. W., & Loichinger, E. (2006). Redistributing work in aging Europe. *Science, 312*(5782), 1911–1913. doi: 10.1126/science.1127487.

Von Hippel, C., Kalokerinos, E. K., & Henry, J. D. (2013). Stereotype threat among older employees: Relationship with job attitudes and turnover intentions. *Psychology and Aging, 28*, 17–27. doi: 10.1037/a0029825.

Walsh, K., & Gordon, J. R. (2008). Creating an individual work identity. *Human Resource Management Review, 18*, 46–61. doi: 10.1016/j.hrmr.2007.09.001.

Zacher, H. (2013). Older job seekers' job search intensity: The interplay of proactive personality, age, and occupational future time perspective. *Ageing & Society, 33*, 1139–1166. doi: 10.1017/S0144686×12000451.

Zacher, H., & Frese, H. (2009). Remaining time and opportunities at work: Relationships between age, work characteristics, and occupational future time perspective. *Psychology and Aging, 24*, 540–55. doi: 10.1037/a0015425.

Zacher, H., Degner, M., Seevaldt, R., Frese, M., & Lüdde, J. (2009). Was wollen jüngere und ältere Erwerbstätige erreichen? Altersbezogene Unterschiede in den Inhalten und Merkmalen beruflicher Ziele [What do younger and older workers want to accomplish? Age-related differences in content and characteristics of occupational goals]. *Zeitschrift für Personalpsychologie, 8*, 191–200. doi: 10.1026/1617-6391.8.4.191.

DORIEN T.A.M. KOOIJ is Assistant Professor at the Department of Human Resource Studies of Tilburg University, the Netherlands. Her research focuses on aging at work, and in particular on HR practices for older workers, on how work motivation changes with aging, and on job crafting. She has published in international peer-reviewed journals such as *Journal of Organizational Behavior, Work & Stress*, and *Psychology and Aging*.

HANNES ZACHER is Professor of Innovation and Human Resource Management in the School of Management at Queensland University of Technology. His research program investigates sustainability in and of organizations, with foci on career adaptability, occupational well-being, and successful aging at work; leadership, innovation, and entrepreneurship; and proenvironmental employee behavior. He is a research fellow at the Sloan Center on Aging & Work at Boston College and member of the founding editorial board of *Work, Aging and Retirement*.

Journal of Social Issues, Vol. 72, No. 1, 2016, pp. 169–190
doi: 10.1111/josi.12161

Ageism in the Workplace: The Role of Psychosocial Factors in Predicting Job Satisfaction, Commitment, and Engagement

Jamie L. Macdonald* and **Sheri R. Levy**
Stony Brook University

With a worldwide aging population and increasingly youth-centered societies around the world, there are mounting concerns about how perceptions of age and aging may influence the workplace. Using an age diverse national sample of workers (n = 800) from a wide range of occupations and socioeconomic backgrounds in the United States, this study investigated understudied psychosocial factors (age identity, aging anxiety, perceived age discrimination, perceived social support at work, and work centrality) that may buffer or hinder job satisfaction, commitment, and engagement. Identity variables, both age identity and work centrality, as well as perceived social support at work, were found to be positively associated with job satisfaction, commitment, and engagement, while both perceived age discrimination and anxiety about aging were negatively associated with these three job longevity variables. The results suggest that psychosocial factors such as age identity, work centrality, and perceived social support could be targeted to improve job satisfaction, commitment, and engagement, while it would be beneficial for organizational policies to continue to focus on reducing age discrimination as well as reducing anxiety about aging in the workplace.

Internationally, many adults spend a substantial amount of their time working. In the United States, for example, adults (ages 15 and over) spend on average 8.12 hours working per weekday (Bureau of Labor Statistics, 2014). Thus, the workplace and its effect on individuals is an important area of study. With a worldwide aging population and increasingly youth-centered societies around the world (e.g., Nelson, 2002, 2009; WHO, 2012), there are mounting concerns about how perceptions of age and aging may influence the work environment

*Correspondence concerning this article should be addressed to Jamie L. Macdonald, Department of Psychology, Stony Brook University, Stony Brook, NY 11794–2500. Tel: +631-632-4355 [e-mail: jamie.macdonald@stonybrook.edu].

including job satisfaction, commitment, and engagement (e.g., Bal & Kooji, 2011). Researchers are increasingly considering the role that psychosocial factors play on job longevity.

One psychosocial factor is perceived age discrimination in the workplace including discriminatory practices based on age, such as firing and lack of hiring, as well as perceived lack of support of supervisors of employees of a certain age (e.g., North & Fiske, 2012; Roscigno, 2010). There is evidence that perceived age discrimination influences workers in many age groups with a negative impact on job satisfaction, commitment, and engagement (e.g., Hassell & Perrewè, 1993; Snape & Redman, 2003), whereas perceived social support may help to alleviate these negative effects (e.g., Redman & Snape, 2006; Schaufeli, Taris, & van Rhenen, 2008). Another related factor that influences workers is how anxiety about aging may undermine job satisfaction and commitment (e.g., Gendron, 2014). Both perceived age discrimination in the workplace and concerns about aging can undermine people's identification with work. There is a smaller but growing body of research examining the role of identification with work and one's age group, showing that social identification influences work engagement and outcomes (e.g., Bal & Kooji, 2011; Bayl-Smith & Griffin, 2014; Desmette & Gaillard, 2008). For example, greater work centrality, or how central one sees work, is related to more positive attitudes towards one's occupation, increased job satisfaction, work engagement, commitment to one's organization, and reduced turnover intentions (e.g., Bal & Kooji, 2011; Hirschfeld & Field, 2000). Taken together, these findings point to the importance of studying psychosocial factors affecting job satisfaction, commitment, and engagement among workers along the age continuum.

Building and expanding on past research, the present investigation focuses on whether these psychosocial factors (age identity, aging anxiety, perceived age discrimination, perceived social support at work, and work centrality) bolster or hinder job satisfaction, commitment, and engagement. Moreover, this study includes an age diverse community sample of workers from a wide range of occupations and socioeconomic backgrounds from across the United States. In the next sections, we provide a brief review of past research and theorizing on these psychosocial factors in turn and how this study aims to fill gaps in the literature toward a better understanding of how perceptions of age and aging influence individuals in the workplace.

Social Identity

Long-standing research on social identity theory (e.g., Hogg & Abrams, 1988; Tajfel & Turner, 1979) has shown that people develop affiliations or identities with relevant groups (e.g., with their age group; with an occupation or as a worker) and that different social contexts (e.g., the workplace) can elicit thoughts, goals, and behaviors consistent with these identities. Likewise, having a strong and positive identity (e.g., as a worker) can set in motion a positive set of thoughts (e.g., increased satisfaction and engagement at work) and behaviors (e.g., remaining in the job for long periods of time) that maintain that identity. Past research, for example, has shown that having a positive ethnic identity can act as a protective factor against perceived discrimination (e.g., Romero, Edwards, Fryberg, & Orduna, 2014). Although there is substantial research demonstrating the pivotal role of social identity (e.g., gender, race) within environments such as academic ones (e.g., London, Rosenthal, Levy, & Lobel, 2011), there is relatively little research on social identity in the workplace, with some research on work centrality (Bal & Kooji, 2011; Hirschfeld & Field, 2000; Witt, Patti, & Farmer, 2002) and minimal research on age identity in the workplace (Bayl-Smith & Griffin, 2014; Desmette & Gaillard, 2008; Gaillard & Desmette, 2008). Below, we focus on the study of two types of identity—age and work—that may offer insights into understanding job longevity variables in an age diverse workforce.

The little research on age identity has been limited in scope, examining older workers with a focus on how greater age identity could be a barrier to job satisfaction, commitment, and engagement. The age group of older adults, which in the workplace can be conceived to be 55 years or older depending on the study and occupation (e.g., Duncan & Loretto, 2004), is generally thought to be a lower status group, who face mistreatment and stereotyping in this particular domain (e.g., Roscigno, 2010; Lamont, Swift, & Abrams, 2015). There are a few studies that show that identification as an older or late career worker has negative consequences for job engagement and retirement intentions. For example, two studies in Belgium of workers nearing retirement, ages 45–59 (Gaillard & Desmette, 2008) and ages 50–59 (Desmette & Gaillard, 2008), found that participants who identified as an "older worker" were more likely to report intentions to retire early, which in these studies was viewed as the negative consequence of withdrawing from the workforce. Other research findings also suggest that identification as a late career worker may have a negative effect on job engagement (Bayl-Smith & Griffin, 2014). Taken together, this past research has highlighted that identification with a stigmatized identity ("late career worker") in the workplace can be detrimental to job outcomes.

Expanding this line of research and drawing on social identity theory (Hogg & Abrams, 1988; Tajfel & Turner, 1979), this study examines age identity in a more general way, which is not explicitly linked to a specific stigmatized identity such as a late career worker. That is, this study focuses on assessing people's level of identification with an age group and how important or central that identity is to their self-concept (e.g., Garstka, Schmitt, Branscombe, & Hummert, 2004). Age identity in particular is unique, compared to other identities like gender and race/ethnicity, in that individuals move through age groups that vary by high or low status as they age. Although no studies have yet assessed age identity in this general sense in the workplace, past research has assessed age identity without focusing on a specific context showing that increased identification with one's age group for younger adults is related to increased self-esteem and for older adults is related to both increased self-esteem and life satisfaction in a U.S.-based sample (Garstka et al., 2004). Given this and past research from social identity theory, we expect increased age identity to positively influence job satisfaction, commitment, and engagement in the workplace. For example, having a strong and positive identity with one's age group could create positive buffers that are realized in the workplace such as facilitating engagement, commitment and satisfaction at work.

Although there is little research on age identification among workers, and no specific research on age identity as a distinct construct in the workplace in age diverse samples, there is research on identification with one's occupation, or work centrality (e.g., Bal & Kooji, 2011). Consistent with the way identity is conceptualized within social identity theory, we use Paullay, Alliger, and Stone-Romero's (1994) definition which conceptualizes work centrality as "beliefs that individuals have regarding the degree of importance that work plays in their lives" and that "individuals may come to believe, through their own experiences, that work to them is a central component of their lives." (p. 225). Research has suggested that work centrality is related to more positive attitudes towards one's occupation, increased job satisfaction, job engagement, job commitment, and reduced turnover intentions. For example, in samples from the United States, higher work centrality was found to be related to increased job commitment (Hirschfeld & Field, 2000; Witt et al., 2002). A study in the Netherlands, which is also a youth-centered culture similar to the United States and other Western countries (see Kooij & Zacher, 2016), found that work centrality was positively related to both job satisfaction and job engagement and negatively associated with turnover intentions (Bal & Kooji, 2011). Building on this research, the present investigation for the first time to our knowledge examines work centrality along with age identity as well as other psychosocial factors, as discussed next, in the context of workplace issues.

Aging Beliefs and Treatment in the Workplace

Beliefs about aging and treatment in the workplace are relatively well-documented as powerful factors affecting job satisfaction, commitment, and engagement, and understanding these factors is increasingly important as the workforce continues to become more age diverse. Ageism in the workplace in particular continues to be a worldwide problem (e.g., McCann & Giles, 2002). In the United States, for example, according to the U.S. Equal Employment Opportunity Commission (2013), age discrimination claims are on the rise increasing from 15,785 in 1997 to 21,396 in 2013. Rising reports of age discrimination may be due in part to the growing older population (WHO, 2012) or age discrimination laws shifting to include claims from younger age groups (ages 45 and up) in the United States (EEOC, n.d.), or including age discrimination claims from working individuals of any age in the United Kingdom (Duncan & Loretto, 2004) and Australia (Encel, 2001) for example. At the same time, recent shifts in the economy and workforce in many countries have led to dramatic increases in job turnover and sometimes even forced early retirement, which have negatively affected and potentially increased discrimination toward workers across age groups (e.g., Rampell, 2010; Roscigino, 2010). There is some evidence that young workers have been hit the hardest during the poor economy with great difficulty securing jobs (e.g., Greenhouse, 2009). Workers over 55 years of age who have lost a job on the other hand, if rehired, tend often to experience a downgrade when taking a new position such as, part-time work, lower salaries, and less benefits (e.g., Roscigno, 2010). Older workers on the job market may also face discrimination in hiring based on stereotypes associated with specific skill sets generally associated with older workers (see Abrams, Swift, & Drury, 2016).

Also as a result of the poor worldwide economy, workers may be more motivated to continue to work and delay retirement. Workers may also wish to work longer than the traditional retirement age of 65 in the United States for other reasons such as good health (e.g., WHO, 2012). Thus, despite facing expectations from employers and even younger workers to retire, older workers may decide to continue to work (North & Fiske, 2013). This may increase tension between younger and older age groups, particularly since younger age groups may see older age groups as infringing upon resources such as job opportunities (e.g., North & Fiske, 2012, 2013, 2016; Scrutton, 1999). This confluence of factors suggests it is vital to make progress in understanding perceived age discrimination affecting a wide range of age groups in today's workplace environment.

Perceived age discrimination in the workplace has been shown to negatively affect job satisfaction, commitment, and engagement (e.g., Bayl-Smith & Griffin, 2014; Hassell & Perrewè, 1993; Kunze, Boehm, & Bruch, 2011; Orpen, 1995; Redman & Snape, 2006; Snape & Redman, 2003). Past research has more often focused on particular age groups, such as older adults, since studies suggest that ageism and discrimination against this group is the most pernicious (e.g., Nelson, 2005). However, a select few studies assessing age discrimination in the workplace in age diverse samples have found that internationally other age groups, for example, young adults and middle-age adults, also report experiencing age discrimination (Duncan & Loretto, 2004; Gee, Pavalko, & Long, 2007; Hassell & Perrewé, 1993). Young adults report being treated as too young and inexperienced as a reason for negative treatment in the workplace, while older adults more often cite negative stereotypes of incompetence; however, both young adults and older adults report less opportunity for promotions in the workplace based on their age (Duncan & Loretto, 2004). For example, in a study of workers 45 years and older in Australia, perceived age discrimination in the workplace was related to reduced work engagement (Bayl-Smith & Griffin, 2014). In a sample of police officers, ages 19–57 in England, perceived age discrimination was associated with reduced job satisfaction and commitment (Redman & Snape, 2006). In a study assessing a representative age-diverse sample of workers in the United Kingdom, perceived age discrimination in the workplace was shown again to reduce commitment (Snape & Redman, 2003). These findings highlight the importance of assessing how factors such as age discrimination affect job satisfaction, commitment, and engagement across age groups. Furthermore, past studies have tended to only focus on certain occupations or organizations such as police officers (e.g., Redman & Snape, 2006), employees at large companies, or at government agencies and assess unrepresentative samples, such as white-collar workers (e.g., Bayl-Smith & Griffin, 2014; Post, Schneer, Reitman, & Ogilvie, 2013).

A related factor in the workplace is perceived social support from both coworkers and supervisors, which can potentially buffer the negative effects of age discrimination and foster positive relations among workers of different age groups. Past work has found that social support in the workplace is negatively related to age discrimination (Chou & Choi, 2011). Social support in the workplace has also been shown to have positive effects on job satisfaction and job commitment (Redman & Snape, 2006; Schaufeli et al., 2008). Increased perceived supervisor support, for example, has also been shown to be related to increased job engagement (James, McKechnie, & Swanberg, 2011). Lack of social support should be expected to have the opposite effect and potentially could make workers more vulnerable to negative influences on job longevity variables at work, particularly for both older and younger age groups who report the most age discrimination (Gee et al., 2007).

Although both age discrimination and social support are somewhat well-studied, another related factor, aging anxiety, has rarely been investigated in this context. Aging anxiety can include anxiety about aging in general, reduced mental and physical capabilities, and effects on physical appearance (Lasher & Faulkender, 1993). Aging anxiety is found not just among middle age and older adults, but young adults as well (Bousfield & Hutchison, 2010) likely due to youth-oriented cultures of Westernized countries (Nelson, 2009). Aging anxiety is rarely studied, particularly in the workplace, but it has been shown to be negatively related to job longevity variables. One study of workers in gerontological fields, ages 20–83, in the United States found that aging anxiety was negatively related to both job satisfaction and commitment (Gendron, 2014).

The Current Study

To obtain a more complete understanding of the psychosocial factors influencing job satisfaction, commitment, and engagement, this study utilizes an age diverse national community sample of 800 workers from a range of occupations, organizations, and socioeconomic backgrounds in the United States. This study is consistent with calls for a "lifespan" approach to studying ageism across the life course (Giles & Reid, 2005; Levy & Macdonald, 2016) and calls for the use of social psychological theories to better understand psychosocial factors in the workplace (Abben, Brown, Graupmann, Mockler, & Fernandes, 2013).

Based on past research, we hypothesize that identity—age identity and work centrality—will be positively related to job longevity variables examined in terms of job satisfaction, commitment and engagement. We expect both perceived age discrimination at work and aging anxiety to be negatively related and likewise for perceived social support at work to be positively related to job longevity variables. Furthermore, we expect identity factors to predict job satisfaction, commitment and engagement over and above aging beliefs and treatment in the workplace factors. In testing our hypotheses, we also assessed other variables that are related to ageism including gender, race/ethnicity, and socioeconomic status (e.g., see Chrisler, Barney, & Palatino, 2016).

Method

Participants

Participants ($N = 1,246$) were internet users recruited through craigslist ($n = 780$) or Amazon's Mechanical Turk (Mturk; $n = 466$) living in the United States. Some participants began the study and only answered a few questions; thus, data from those participants were not included in the analyses ($n = 184$ from craigslist and $n = 54$ from Mturk). Data were not included from participants who reported being younger than 18 years of age ($n = 5$), who did not include usable demographic information ($n = 96$), and who reported that their health was "poor" ($n = 29$) in response to the question "In general, would you say your health is" on a scale of 1 (*poor*) to 5 (*excellent*) (see Ware & Sherbourne, 1992) because poor health may require an individual to take more time off of work and thus affect job longevity variables. Data were not included for participants who indicated that they were not currently working at the time of the study ($n = 78$). The final sample included 800 participants ($n = 451$ from craigslist; $n = 349$ from Mturk). The sample was diverse in terms of age ($M = 38.94$, $SD = 14.21$, range 18–75). Participants were also diverse in terms of occupation (e.g., accounting associates, bankers, computer programmers, construction workers, engineers, nurses, real estate agents, sales representatives, teachers, and writers). The samples came from across the United States with craigslist participants living in 33 states and Mturk participants living in 45 states. See Table 1 for demographic information of the sample.

Table 1. Descriptive Statistics of Sample (Craigslist $n = 451$, Mturk $n = 349$, Total $n = 800$)

	Craigslist n (%)	Mturk n (%)	Total n (%)
Age			
18–24	107 (23.7)	29 (8.3)	136 (17.0)
25–34	133 (29.5)	112 (32.1)	245 (30.6)
35–44	60 (13.3)	72 (20.6)	132 (16.5)
45–54	65 (14.4)	61 (17.5)	126 (15.8)
55+	86 (19.1)	75 (21.5)	161 (20.1)
Gender			
Male	125 (27.7)	125 (35.8)	250 (31.3)
Female	326 (72.3)	224 (64.2)	550 (68.7)
Race/ethnicity			
White/European American	310 (68.7)	275 (78.8)	585 (73.1)
Black/African American	43 (9.5)	36 (10.3)	79 (9.9)
Latino/Hispanic	47 (10.4)	14 (4.0)	61 (7.6)
Asian	19 (4.2)	14 (4.0)	33 (4.1)
East Indian	16 (3.5)	2 (0.6)	18 (2.3)
Native American	9 (2.0)	6 (1.7)	15 (1.9)
Caribbean	5 (1.1)	2 (0.6)	7 (0.9)
Middle Eastern	2 (0.4)	0 (0.0)	2 (0.3)
SES			
Lower class	39 (8.6)	42 (12.0)	81 (10.1)
Lower middle class	93 (20.6)	97 (27.8)	190 (23.8)
Middle class	225 (49.9)	178 (51.0)	403 (50.4)
Upper middle class	89 (19.7)	30 (8.6)	119 (14.9)
Wealthy	5 (1.1)	2 (0.6)	7 (0.9)
Education			
Some middle/high school	6 (1.3)	8 (2.3)	14 (1.7)
High school degree	30 (6.7)	34 (9.7)	64 (8.0)
Some college	119 (26.4)	96 (27.5)	215 (26.9)
2-Year college degree	36 (8.0)	34 (9.7)	70 (8.8)
4-Year college degree	160 (35.5)	120 (34.4)	280 (35.0)
Master's degree	76 (16.9)	47 (13.5)	123 (15.4)
Doctorate or professional degree	17 (3.8)	9 (2.6)	26 (3.3)
No answer	7 (1.6)	1 (0.3)	8 (1.0)
Working status			
Part-time	155 (34.4)	111 (31.8)	266 (33.3)
Full-time	296 (65.6)	238 (68.2)	534 (66.7)

Procedure

For participants recruited through craigslist, an advertisement named "Volunteer for online research survey on Age Issues" was placed in the volunteer section of www. craigslist.com in states across the United States including California, Colorado, Florida, Hawaii, Illinois, Massachusetts, Minnesota, Missouri, North Carolina, Nevada, New York, Oklahoma, and Texas. After potential participants clicked the link to the study, they were brought to www.qualtrics.com, a secure online data collection site, and were instructed to read through the consent form, which described the study and offered a chance to win an Amazon gift card for completion of the survey, which was typical for completing surveys of this length on craigslist. The procedure was the same for Mturk participants, but given that they were recruited through a volunteer website, the advertisement read "Research: reflecting on age issues." Participants were paid for successful completion of the survey, which was typical for completing surveys of this length on Mturk. After participants consented to participate, they completed the identity measures (age identity and work centrality), the aging beliefs and treatment in the workplace measures (anxiety about aging, age discrimination, social support in the workplace), the job longevity measures (job satisfaction, work commitment, work engagement), and demographic measures. Measures were shortened for use in this brief internet study. The last page of the survey for all participants was a debriefing page, which described the goals of the study and contact information of the investigators.

Measures

Identity Measures

Age group identity. Participants completed a 5-item shortened version of the established 13-item measure of age group identity (Garstka, Branscombe, & Hummert, 1997). On a scale of 1 (*strongly disagree*) to 7 (*strongly agree*), participants rated "I value being a member of my age group," "My age group membership is important to me," "My age group is central to who I am as a person," "I have a strong sense of belonging to my own age group," and "I identify with being a member of my age group."

Work centrality. Participants completed a 5-item (2 reversed scored items) shortened version (Bal & Kooji, 2011) of the established 13-item measure of work centrality (Paullay et al., 1994). On a scale of 1 (*strongly disagree*) to 5 (*strongly agree*) participants rated "The major satisfaction in my life comes from my job," "The most important things that happen to me involve my work," "I have other activities more important than my work," "I consider work to be central to my life," and "To me, my work is only a small part of who I am."

Aging Beliefs and Treatment in the Workplace Measures

Aging anxiety. Participants completed a 4-item (1 reverse score item) established measure of aging anxiety (Bousfield & Hutchison, 2010). On a scale of 1 (*strongly disagree*) to 7 (*strongly agree*) participants rated "I am relaxed about getting old," "I am worried that I will lose my independence when I am old," "I am concerned that my mental abilities will suffer when I am old," and "I do not want to get old because it means that I am closer to dying."

Perceived age discrimination at work.   To assess perceived age discrimination, participants answered the following question: "How often have you been treated poorly or been negatively discriminated at work because of your age?" on a scale of 1 (*never*) to 7 (*daily*).

Social support at work.   Participants completed a 4-item shortened version of an established 6-item measure of perceived social support in the workplace (Bosma et al., 1997). On a scale of 1 (*never*) to 5 (*all the time*) participants answered "How often are your co-workers willing to listen to your work-related problems?," "How often do you get the information you need from your supervisor or superiors?," "How often do you get help support from your immediate supervisor?," and "How often is your immediate supervisor willing to listen to your work-related problems?"

Job Longevity Measures

Job satisfaction.   To assess job satisfaction, participants completed a 4-item shortened version of an established 6-item measure of job satisfaction (Bal & Kooji, 2011). On a scale of 1 (*strongly disagree*) to 5 (*strongly agree*) participants rated "I am satisfied with my current job," "I am satisfied with my work environment," "I am satisfied with my career so far," and "I am satisfied with my learning opportunities."

Job commitment.   Participants completed a 4-item shortened version of an established 8-item measure of affective organizational commitment (Allen & Meyer, 1990). On a scale of 1 (*strongly disagree*) to 7 (*strongly agree*) participants rated "I enjoy discussing my organization with people outside it," "This organization has a great deal of personal meaning for me," "I feel emotionally attached to this organization," and "I would be very happy to spend the rest of my career with this organization."

Job engagement.   Participants completed a 6-item shortened version of the established UWES 9-item measure of work engagement (Schaufeli, Bakker, & Salanova, 2006), which included 3 items from the absorption subscale and 3 items from the dedication subscale. On a scale of 1 (*never*) to 7 (*always*) participants rated "I am enthusiastic about my job," "My job inspires me," "I feel happy when

I am working intensely," "I am proud of the work I do," "I am immersed in my work," and "I get carried away when I am working."

Results

Table 2 displays means, standard deviations, Cronbach's α, and bivariate correlations for all study measures for all study participants. The means of all items in each measure were summed and averaged to create a composite score for that measure.

The pattern of correlations mostly fit with our hypotheses and is consistent with prior relevant research. As expected, greater age identification overall was positively correlated with job longevity variables— job satisfaction, commitment, and engagement. As expected and replicating past research (Bal & Kooji, 2011; Hirschfeld & Field, 2000), greater work centrality overall was strongly positively correlated with the job longevity variables. Aging anxiety, as expected and consistent with past work (Gendron, 2014), was negatively related to job longevity variables. In line with past research (Hassell & Perrewè, 1993; Redman & Snape, 2006; Snape & Redman, 2003) age discrimination at work was negatively related to job satisfaction and job commitment; however, it was not significantly related to job engagement. Social support as expected was positively related to job longevity variables, which is consistent with past work (Redman & Snape, 2006).

Sequential Regression Analyses

Next, we turned to the key analyses of how psychosocial factors (age identity, aging anxiety, perceived age discrimination, perceived social support at work, and work centrality) bolster or hinder job satisfaction, commitment, and engagement. We conducted three sequential regression analyses regressing all predictors separately on each of our dependent variables (job satisfaction, job commitment, and job engagement). For each set of analyses, control variables, age, gender (coded $0 = male$, $1 = female$), race/ethnicity (coded $0 = numeric\ minority$, $1 = numeric\ majority$) and socioeconomic status (see Ramírez & Palacios-Espinosa, 2016), were entered in the first step. Aging beliefs and treatment in the workplace variables, age discrimination at work, aging anxiety, and social support at work were entered in the second step, and identity variables, age identity and work centrality, were entered in the third step. Results from the sequential regression analysis predicting job satisfaction are shown in Table 3. The first model which included demographic control variables, explained 3% of the variance in job satisfaction ($F(4, 795) = 5.37, p < .001$), with socioeconomic status as a significant predictor. With the addition of aging beliefs and treatment in the workplace variables in the second step, variance in job satisfaction significantly increased to 15% ($F(3, 792) = 37.28, p < .001$). As expected, age discrimination at work, aging anxiety, and

Table 2. Bivariate Correlations among Variables, Descriptive Statistics, and Internal Reliability

Variable	1	2	3	4	5	6	7	8	9	10	11	12
1. Age identity	–											
2. Work centrality	.08[*]	–										
3. Age discrimination at work	−.01	.07	–									
4. Aging anxiety	−.13[**]	.01	.10[**]	–								
5. Social support at work	.23[**]	.11[**]	−.23[**]	−.14[**]	–							
6. Job satisfaction	.20[**]	.28[**]	−.18[**]	−.13[**]	.34[**]	–						
7. Job commitment	.27[**]	.32[**]	−.10[**]	−.07[*]	.39[**]	.54[**]	–					
8. Job engagement	.24[**]	.40[**]	−.05	−.14[**]	.41[**]	.54[**]	.71[**]	–				
9. Age	.04	−.09[*]	.05	.05	−.05	.002	.06	.03	–			
10. Gender	.001	−.002	.10[**]	.11[**]	.03	.02	.03	.02	−.06	–		
11. Race/ethnicity	−.13[**]	−.04	−.02	.16[**]	.02	.06	.03	−.01	.23[**]	.01	–	
12. SES	.09[**]	.05	−.04	−.03	.11[**]	.15[**]	.18[**]	.18[**]	.06	−.02	.05	–
Mean	4.69	2.50	1.87	4.30	3.49	3.34	4.26	4.73	38.94	0.69	0.73	2.72
SD	1.36	0.82	1.45	1.32	0.88	0.98	1.53	1.25	14.21	0.46	0.44	0.87
Cronbach's α	.91	.81	–	.69	.86	.86	.87	.92	–	–	–	–

[*]$p < .05$, [**]$p < .01$.

Table 3. Sequential Regression Analysis for Job Satisfaction

Predictors	Model 1 β	Model 2 β	Model 3 β
Age	−.02	.01	.02
Gender	.02	.03	.04
Race/ethnicity	.06	.06	.08[*]
SES	.15[***]	.11[***]	.09[**]
Age discrimination at work		−.10[**]	−.13[***]
Aging anxiety		−.09[**]	−.09[**]
Social support at work		.29[***]	.23[***]
Age identity			.11[***]
Work centrality			.25[***]
R^2	.03	.15	.22
Adjusted R^2	.02	.14	.21
$\triangle R^2$	.03[***]	.12[***]	.08[***]

[*]$p < .05$, [**]$p \leq .01$, [***]$p \leq .001$.

Table 4. Sequential Regression Analysis for Job Commitment

Predictors	Model 1 β	Model 2 β	Model 3 β
Age	.05	.07[*]	.08[**]
Gender	.04	.03	.04
Race/ethnicity	.01	.003	.04
SES	.17[***]	.13[***]	.11[***]
Age discrimination at work		−.01	−.05
Aging anxiety		−.02	−.02
Social support at work		.37[***]	.30[***]
Age identity			.17[***]
Work centrality			.28[***]
R^2	.04	.18	.28
Adjusted R^2	.03	.17	.27
$\triangle R^2$	.04[***]	.14[***]	.11[***]

[*]$p < .05$, [**]$p \leq .01$, [***]$p \leq .001$.

social support at work significantly predicted job satisfaction. With the addition of identity variables, variance significantly increased to 22% ($F(2, 790) = 38.84$, $p < .001$). Both identity variables significantly predicted job satisfaction.

For job commitment (see Table 4), the first model, including demographic control variables, explained 4% of the variance ($F(4, 795) = 7.17$, $p < .001$)

Table 5. Sequential Regression Analysis for Job Engagement

Predictors	Model 1 β	Model 2 β	Model 3 β
Age	.03	.05	.07[*]
Gender	.03	.02	.03
Race/ethnicity	−.03	−.03	.001
SES	.18[***]	.14[***]	.11[***]
Age discrimination at work		.05	.01
Aging anxiety		−.09[**]	−.09[**]
Social support at work		.40[***]	.32[**]
Age identity			.11[***]
Work centrality			.36[***]
R^2	.03	.20	.34
Adjusted R^2	.03	.19	.33
$\triangle R^2$	.03[***]	.16[***]	.14[***]

[*]$p < .05$, [**]$p \leq .01$, [***]$p \leq .001$.

with only socioeconomic status as a significant predictor. With the addition of aging beliefs and treatment in the workplace variables to the model, variance explained significantly increased to 18% ($F(3, 792) = 44.71$, $p < .001$); yet, age discrimination at work and aging anxiety were not significant while social support at work was a significant predictor of job commitment. With the addition of identity factors explained variance significantly increased to 28% ($F(2, 790) = 57.68$, $p < .001$), and both age identity and work centrality were significant predictors of job commitment.

For job engagement (see Table 5), the first model, including demographic control variables, explained only 3% of the variance ($F(4, 795) = 7.09, p < .001$). With the addition of aging beliefs and treatment in the workplace variables to the model, variance explained increased to 20% ($F(3, 792) = 53.91, p < .001$). Age discrimination at work was not a significant predictor, but aging anxiety, and social support at work were significant predictors of job engagement. With the addition of identity factors variance increased to 34% ($F(2, 790) = 83.71, p < .001$), and both age identity and work centrality significantly predicted job engagement.

Discussion

Given that the workplace is where people spend a great deal of time and earn their livelihood, it is important to understand factors that influence job longevity among an age diverse workforce across occupations and socioeco-nomic backgrounds. Building on past research, this study focused on the relatively understudied role of psychosocial factors including identity factors as well as beliefs and treatment about aging in the workplace. Above and beyond the contribution of demographic variables and aging beliefs and treatment in the workplace (age discrimination, aging anxiety, and social support), age identity and work centrality significantly predicted job longevity variables. Increased identification with one's age group and with one's occupation significantly predicted increased job satisfaction, job commitment, and job engagement.

Age identity was most strongly related to job commitment which may be because having a positive social identity can lead to behaviors that maintain that identity, such as increased commitment to one's occupation, and workers of all ages might be motivated to prove that they are valuable workers to others and their organization, at any age. Work centrality was a strong predictor of job longevity variables in this study, which is consistent with past research (Bal & Kooji, 2011; Hirschfeld & Field, 2000). Workers who see their occupation as an important aspect of their self-concept and a central component in their lives seem likely to show increased job commitment, and job engagement to maintain that identity and as a result would report more job satisfaction as well.

Findings from this study also showed the contributing roles of aging beliefs and treatment in the workplace on job longevity variables. Increased aging anxiety predicted decreased job satisfaction and job engagement, although it did not significantly predict job commitment. Generally, aging anxiety was weakly related to the job longevity variables, which may suggest that aging anxiety may not affect these directly, but through another variable. For example, stereotypic beliefs about aging and older adults have been shown to be related to increased aging anxiety (Bousfield & Hutchison, 2010) and this may moderate the relationship between aging anxiety and job longevity variables, particularly if one has negative perceptions of aging. Aging anxiety, while weakly related to job longevity variables, should continue to be investigated, especially with regard to other variables such as individual differences, particularly since findings from this study and past research has suggested that females and racial/ethnic minorities tend to report more aging anxiety (Bergman, Bodner, & Cohen-Fridel, 2013; Lynch, 2000).

Findings with regard to perceived age discrimination were mixed. Consistent with past research it negatively, although weakly, predicted decreased job satisfaction (Hassell & Perrewè, 1993; however, it was not significantly related to job commitment or engagement. These inconsistencies in findings may be due to the small number of participants (30%) who reported ever experiencing age discrimination, which may also reflect the underreporting of age discrimination in the workplace (Nicholson, 2003). There may be an underreporting issue in that people are hesitant to report on the survey or to themselves that they have been discriminated against. It may also be that people placed a high threshold on what discrimination means in the workplace such as a blatant firing because of one's age or explicit ageist feedback on work performance. More subtle forms of age discrimination, like ageist remarks from a coworker, may not be recognized as age discrimination despite the potential negative effects on individuals, due to the institutionalization of ageism in the United States (Nelson, 2002, 2009).

In contrast, perceived social support at work was a strong significant predictor of job satisfaction, job commitment and job engagement, which is consistent with past research (Redman & Snape, 2006; Schaufeli et al., 2008). Workers who perceive that they can turn to either their supervisor or other co-workers when work-related problems arise, would likely be better able handle such situations and stay more committed, engaged, and satisfied.

Limitations and Future Directions

There are several limitations of this study. First due to the design of the study, it is not possible to determine causality. Although our sample was diverse in some ways (e.g., age, socioeconomic status, workers from diverse fields), the sample was not diverse in terms gender or race/ethnicity, limiting the analyses and investigation of the potentially important role of these individual differences (see Chrisler et al., 2016). Although this study included established measures from the literature, the measures were shortened to allow for a brief internet-based survey. Furthermore, a one item measure was used to assess age discrimination at work, which is sometimes used in past work (Gee et al., 2007), although this potentially limits our understanding of this social problem. Future studies should assess age discrimination with longer more detailed measures including qualitative measures that can capture nuances of this social issue. Finally, the sample consisted of individuals living in the United States, and may not generalize to other countries and cultures. Results from the current study did replicate some findings from past research which was largely from international samples in Westernized countries. It is likely that results would be similar in other Westernized countries; however, studying these constructs in nonindividualistic cultures could yield different results. Perceptions and the importance of age identity and work centrality may vary based on culture, and studies have suggested that there are differences about beliefs of aging in the workplace and stereotypes of workers as they age based on culture (Chiu, Chan, Snape, & Redman, 2001).

Another fruitful future direction is to expand the exploration of identity issues. In this study, identity explained unique variance over and above demographic controls and aging beliefs and treatment in the workplace variables. As age identification continues to be investigated, future studies may consider defining what is meant by an "age group" for participants (see Levy & Macdonald, 2016). In the current study participants were not prompted with any indication of what an "age group" meant, although they did fill out a free response follow up question asking what age group they were thinking of while rating items. Assessment of the free responses indicated that perceptions of what an "age group" meant varied among participants. For example, some participants viewed this to mean just their own chronological age, while others viewed it as meaning individuals within a ten year span of their chronological age. Future research should also assess variations by age identity with regard to culture among age diverse samples. There has also been some research to suggest that age identification among young adults varies by culture and gender (McCann, Kellerman, Giles, Gallois, & Viladot, 2004). Researchers have continued to call for more research on intersectionality, or individuals who are identified with multiple stigmatized groups based on gender or race/ethnicity, and have noted that studies assessing ageism in relation to sexism or racism are rare (see Chrisler et al., 2016). Thus, assessing social identity relating to one's gender and race ethnicity in the workplace is important to future studies.

Work centrality played a significant role in predicting job longevity variables. Work centrality has been found to be a buffer of negative effects of aging on work outcomes (see Kooij & Zacher, 2016), which opens up avenues for policy implications as discussed next.

Implications for Workplace Policies

There are a number of policy implications that grow out of the present investigation. As just noted, the findings on work centrality, along with a solid base of past research (e.g., Kooij & Zacher, 2016), increasingly suggest that employers and organizations who focus on creating positive, inclusive work environments, where employees feel their work is valued, regardless of individual differences, can increase the importance that one's occupation plays in an individual's self-concept and thereby increase work outcomes.

Similarly, the findings on social identity also suggest that increasingly social identification with one's age group could be a worthwhile avenue for organizations seeking to improve worker's satisfaction, commitment and engagement. For example, policies explicitly stating that workers of all ages are valued and respected members of a workplace organization or zero tolerance policies for ageist remarks and age-based discrimination would help to facilitate and reinforce a strong positive identification with one's age group and working at the organization.

Governments internationally have acknowledged age discrimination in the workplace as a pressing social issue with policies aimed at protecting individuals in this context, although it seems that these policies need to be updated to help alleviate the problem, particularly in the United States (e.g., Rothenberg & Gardner, 2011), which only protects workers over the age of 40 (EEOC, n.d.). In the United Kingdom (Duncan & Loretto, 2004) and Australia (Encel, 2001) workers of all ages are protected from age discrimination at work.

However, more subtle forms of ageism in the workplace, such as ageist remarks toward an employee, not connected to concrete aspects of one's job like retirement decisions are often difficult to prove in age discrimination suits (e.g., North & Fiske, 2012, 2013). Furthermore, although it is important to protect older workers, it is also important to acknowledge that younger individuals can experience age discrimination as well. Age itself can be a tricky categorization, since it can be argued that one's age is apparent externally, however an individual can sometimes look younger or older than their chronological age. It is possible that an individual younger than the age of 40, who may appear significantly older than their chronological age for instance, is potentially at risk for age discrimination, however in the United States they would not be protected based on their chronological age. Another aspect that is problematic with regard to age discrimination laws, as researchers have noted, is the tendency to not attend to individual differences of older workers and instead treat this group as homogeneous and without attention to its intersection with other forms of discrimination by gender or race (Spencer, 2013).

Since perceived social support at work, which includes support from both supervisors and coworkers in the current study, appears to be a key component in increasing job longevity variables (Redman & Snape, 2006; Schaufeli et al., 2008), policies aimed to increase support in this context should be a focus of organizations. Increasing contact, particularly in the form of diversity training (age, gender, race/ethnicity) among workers and creating mixed groups for training may foster support and respect from workers (e.g., Brooke & Taylor, 2005).

Conclusion

With a national community sample which was diverse in terms of age, occupation, and socioeconomic status, findings from the present investigation advance our understanding of the role of psychosocial factors in the workplace. Work centrality, age identity, and perceived social support at work were found to be buffers of satisfaction, commitment, and engagement at work, whereas perceived age discrimination and anxiety about aging were barriers to these key job longevity variables. Accordingly, these findings have implications for social policies and programs in the workplace, and these findings are especially relevant in today's workplace which may include non-trivial levels of age discrimination and lack of social support for workers across an increasingly age diverse workforce. Given these findings, and that psychosocial factors as a whole are understudied, we hope that future studies continue to investigate these factors in the workplace setting in the United States as well as other countries.

References

Abben, D. R., Brown, S. G., Graupmann, V., Mockler, S. A., & Fernandes, G. F. (2013). Drawing on social psychology literature to understand and reduce workplace discrimination. *Industrial and Organizational Psychology*, 6(4), 476–479. doi: 10.1111/iops.12088.

Abrams, D., Swift, H. J., & Drury, L. (2016). Old and unemployable? How age-based stereotypes affect willingness to hire job candidates. *Journal of Social Issues, 72*(1), 105–121.

Allen, N. J., & Meyer, J. P. (1990). The measurement and antecedents of affective, continuance and normative commitment to the organization. *Journal of Occupational Psychology, 63*(1), 1–18. doi: 10.1111/j.2044-8325.1990.tb00506.x.

Bal, P. M., & Kooji, D. (2011). The relations between work centrality, psychological job contracts, and job attitudes: The influence of age. *European Journal of Work and Organizational Psychology, 20*(4), 497–523. doi: 10.1080/13594321003669079.

Bayl-Smith, P. H., & Griffin, B. (2014). Age discrimination in the workplace: Identifying as a late career worker and its relationship with engagement and intended retirement age. *Journal of Applied Social Psychology, 44*(9), 588–599. doi: 10.1111/jasp.12251.

Bergman, Y. S., Bodner, E., & Cohen-Fridel, S. (2013). Cross-cultural ageism: Ageism and attitudes towards aging among Jews and Arabs in Israel. *International Psychogeriatrics, 25*(1), 6–15. doi: 10.1017/S1041610212001548.

Bosma, H., Marmot, M. G., Hemingway, H., Nicholson, A. C., Brunner, E., & Stansfeld, S. A. (1997). Low job control and risk of coronary heart disease in Whitehall ii (prospective cohort) study. *British Medical Journal, 314*(7080), 558–565. doi: 10.1136/bmj.314.7080.558.

Bousfield, C., & Hutchison, P. (2010). Contact, anxiety, ad young people's attitudes and behavioral intentions towards the elderly. *Educational Gerontology, 36*(6), 451–466. doi: 10.1080/03601270903324362.

Brooke, L., & Taylor, P. (2005). Older workers and employment: Managing age relations. *Ageing and Society, 25*(3), 415–429. doi: 10.1017/S0144686×05003466.

Bureau of Labor Statistics (2014). American time use survey summary. *Economic News Release.* Retrieved from: http://www.bls.gov/news.release/atus.nr0.htm. Accessed at October 16, 2014.

Chiu, W. C. K., Chan, A. W., Snape, E., & Redman, T. (2001). Age stereotypes and discriminatory attitudes towards older workers: An east-west comparison. *Human Relations, 54*(5), 629–661. doi: 10.1177/0018726701545004.

Chou, R. J., & Choi, N. G. (2011). Prevalence and correlates of perceived workplace discrimination among older workers in the United States of America. *Ageing and Society, 31*, 1051–1070. doi: 10.1017/S0144686×10001297.

Chrisler, J. C., Barney, A., & Palatino, B. (2016). Ageism can be hazardous to women's health: Ageism, sexism, and stereotypes of older women in the health care system. *Journal of Social Issues, 72*(1), 86–104.

Desmette, D., & Gaillard, M. (2008). When a "worker" becomes an "older worker": The effects of age-related social identity on attitudes towards retirement and work. *Career Development International, 13*(2), 168–185. doi: 10.1108/13620430810860567.

Duncan, C., & Loretto, W. (2004). Never the right age? Gender and age-based discrimination in employment. *Gender, Work, and Organization, 11*(1), 95–115. doi: 10.1111/j.1468-0432.2004.00222.x.

Equal Employment Opportunity Commission (n.d.). The Age Discrimination in Employment Act of 1967. Retrieved from: http://www.eeoc.gov/laws/statutes/adea.cfm. Accessed at October 16, 2014.

Equal Employment Opportunity Commission (2013). Age Discrimination in Employment Act. Retrieved from: http://www.eeoc.gov/eeoc/statistics/enforcement/adea.cfm Accessed at October 16, 2014.

Encel, S. (2001). Age discrimination in Australia: Law and practice. In Z. Hornstein (Ed.), *Outlawing age discrimination: Foreign lessons, U.K. choices* (pp. 12–29). Bristol: Policy Press.

Gaillard, M., & Desmette, D. (2008). Intergroup predictors of older workers' attitudes towards work and early exit. *European Journal of Work and Organizational Psychology, 17*(4), 450–481. doi: 10.1080/13594320801908564.

Garstka, T. A., Branscombe, N. R., & Hummert, M. L. (1997). *Age group identification across the lifespan.* Paper presented at the annual meeting of the American Psychological Society, Washington, D.C.

Garstka, T. A., Schmitt, M. T., Branscombe, N. R., & Hummert, M. L. (2004). How young and older adults differ in their responses to perceived age discrimination. *Psychology and Aging, 19*(2), 326–335. doi: 10.1037/0882-7974.19.2.326.

Gee, G. C., Pavalko, E. K., & Long, J. S. (2007). Age, cohort, and perceived age discrimination: Using the life course to assess self-reported age discrimination. *Social Forces, 86*(1), 265–290. doi: 10.1353/sof.2007.0098.

Gendron, T. (2014). *The development of a discipline: Examination of the profession of gerontology and gerontological professionals.* Doctoral Dissertation. Retrieved from ProQuest Dissertations and Theses. (Accession Order No. 3610741)

Giles, H., & Reid, S. A. (2005). Ageism across the lifespan: Towards a self-categorization model of ageing. *Journal of Social Issues, 61*(2), 389–404. doi: 10.1111/j.15404560.2005.00412.x.

Greenhouse, S. (2009). Young and Old Are Facing Off for Jobs. *New York Times,* Retrieved from: http://www.nytimes.com/2009/03/21/business/21age.html/pagewanted = all&module = Search&mabReward = relbias%3Aw. Accessed at August 12, 2014.

Hassell, B. L., & Perrewè, P. L. (1993). An examination of the relationship between older workers' perceptions of age discrimination and employee psychological states. *Journal of Managerial Issues, 5*(1), 109–120.

Hirschfeld, R. R., & Field, H. S. (2000). Work centrality and work alienation: Distinct aspects of a general commitment to work. *Journal of Organizational Behavior, 21*(7), 789–800. doi:10.1002/1099-1379(200011)21:7<789::AID-JOB59>3.0.CO;2-W

Hogg, M. A., & Abrams, D. (1988). *Social identifications: A social psychology of intergroup relations and group processes.* Florence, KY: Taylor & Frances/Routeledge.

James, J. B., McKechnie, S., & Swanberg, J. (2011). Predicting employee engagement in an age-diverse retail workforce. *Journal of Organizational Behavior, 32,* 173–196. doi: 10.1002/job.681.

Kooij, D. T. A. M., & Zacher, H. (2016). Why and when do learning goal orientation and attitude decrease with age? The role of perceived remaining time and work centrality. *Journal of Social Issues, 72*(1), 146–168.

Kunze, F., Boehm, S. A., & Bruch, H. (2011). Age diversity, age discrimination climate and performance consequences—A cross organizational study. *Journal of Organizational Behavior, 32*(2), 264–290. doi: 10.1002/job.698.

Lamont, R. A., Swift, H. J., & Abrams, D. (2015). A review and meta-analysis of age-based stereotype threat: Negative stereotypes, not facts, do the damage. *Psychology and Aging, 30,* 180–193. doi: 10.1037/a0038586.

Lasher, K. P., & Faulkender, P. J. (1993). Measurement of aging anxiety: Development of the anxiety about aging scale. *The International Journal of Aging and Human Development, 37*(4), 247–259.

Levy, S. R., & Macdonald, J. L. (2016). Progress on understanding ageism. *Journal of Social Issues, 72*(1), 5–25.

London, B., Rosenthal, L., Levy, S. R., & Lobel, M. (2011). The influences of perceived identity compatibility and social support on women in non-traditional fields during the college transition. *Basic and Applied Social Psychology, 33,* 304–321. doi: 10.1080/01973533.2011.614166.

Lynch, S. M. (2000). Measurement and prediction of aging anxiety. *Research on Aging, 22*(5), 533–558. doi: 10.1177/0164027500225004.

McCann, R. M., & Giles, H. (2002). Ageism in the workplace: A communication perspective. In T. D. Nelson (Ed.), *Ageism: Stereotyping and prejudice against older persons* (pp. 163–199). Cambridge, MA, US: The MIT Press.

McCann, R. M., Kellermann, K., Gile, H., Gallois, C., & Viladot, M. A. (2004). Cultural and gender influences on age identification. *Communication Studies, 55*(1), 88–105. doi: 10.1080/10510970409388607.

Nicholson, T. (2003). Boomers Discover Age Bias: Age Complaints Surge as Midlife Workers Find the Going Harder, AARP Bulletin. Retrieved from: http://www.globalaging.org/elderrights/us/boomersbias.htm. Accessed October 16, 2014.

Nelson, T. D. (2002). *Ageism: Stereotyping and prejudice against older persons.* Cambridge, MA, US: The MIT Press.

Nelson, T. D. (2005). Ageism: Prejudice against our feared future self. *Journal of Social Issues*, *61*(2), 207–221. doi: 10.1111/j.1540-4560.2005.00402.x.

Nelson, T. D. (2009). Ageism. In T. D. Nelson (Ed.), *Handbook of prejudice, stereotyping, and discrimination* (pp. 431–440). New York, NY, US: Psychology Press.

North, M. S., & Fiske, S. T. (2012). An inconvenienced youth? Ageism and its potential intergenerational roots. *Psychological Bulletin*, *138*(5), 982–997. doi: 10.1037/a0027843.

North, M. S., & Fiske, S. T. (2013). Subtyping ageism: Policy issues in succession and consumption. *Social Issues and Policy Review*, *7*(1), 36–57. doi: 10.1111/j.1751-2409.2012.01042.x.

North, M. S., & Fiske, S. T. (2016). Resource scarcity and prescriptive attitudes generate subtle, intergenerational older-worker exclusion. *Journal of Social Issues*, *72*(1), 122–145.

Orpen, C. (1995). The effects of perceived age discrimination on employee job satisfaction, organizational commitment, and job involvement. *Psychology: A Journal of Human Behavior*, *32*(3-4), 55–56.

Paullay, I. M., Alliger, G. M., & Stone-Romero, E. F. (1994). Construct validation of two instruments designed to measure job involvement and work centrality. *Journal of Applied Psychology*, *79*(2), 224–228. doi: 10.1037/0021-9010.79.2.224.

Post, C., Schneer, J. A., Reitman, F., & Ogilvie, D. (2013). Pathways to retirement: A career stage analysis of retirement age expectations. *Human Relations*, *66*(1), 87–112. doi: 10.1177/0018726712465657.

Ramírez, L. F., & Palacios-Espinosa, X. (2016). Stereotypes about old age, social support, aging anxiety, and evaluations of one's health. *Journal of Social Issues*, *72*(1), 47–68.

Rampell, C. (2010). In Job Market Shift, Some Workers Are Left Behind. *New York Times*, Retrieved from: http://www.nytimes.com/2010/05/13/business/economy/13obsolete.html? pagewanted = all&_r = 0. Accessed August 12, 2014.

Redman, T., & Snape, E. (2006). The consequences of perceived age discrimination amongst older police officers: Is social support a buffer? *British Journal of Management*, *17*(2), 167–175. doi: 10.1111/j.1467-8551.2006.00492.x.

Romero, A. J., Edwards, L. M., Fryberg, S. A., & Orduna, M. (2014). Resilience to discrimination stress across ethnic identity stages of development. *Journal of Applied Social Psychology*, *44*(1), 1–11. doi: 10.1111/jasp.12192.

Roscigino, V. J. (2010). Ageism in the American workplace. *Contexts*, *9*(1), 16–21. doi: 10.1525/ctx.2010.9.1.16.

Rothenberg, J. Z., & Gardner, D. S. (2011). Protecting older workers: The failure of the Age Discrimination in Employment Act of 1967. *Journal of Sociology and Social Welfare*, *38*(1), 9–30.

Schaufeli, W. B., Bakker, A. B., & Salanova, M. (2006). The measurement of work engagement with a short questionnaire: A cross-national study. *Educational and Psychological Measurement*, *66*(4), 701–716. doi: 10.1177/0013164405282471.

Schaufeli, W. B., Taris, T. W., & van Rhenen, W. (2008). Workaholism, burnout, and work engagement: Three of a kind or three different kinds of well-being? *Applied Psychology: An International Review*, *57*(2), 173–203. doi: 10.1111/j.1464-0597.2007.00285.x.

Scrutton, S. (1999). *Counseling older people* (2nd ed.). London: Gower Publishing.

Snape, E., & Redman, T. (2003). Too old or too young? The impact of perceived age discrimination. *Human Resource Management Journal*, *13*(1), 78–89. doi: 10.1111/j.1748-8583.2003.tb00085.x.

Spencer, C. (2013). Legal and legislative issues in protecting older adults in the workplace: An international perspective. In P. Brownell & J. J. Kelly (Eds.), *Ageism and mistreatment of older workers: Current reality, future solutions* (pp. 145–164). Dordrecht: Springer.

Tajfel, H., & Turner, J. C. (1979). An integrative theory of intergroup conflict. In W. G. Austin & S. Worchel (Eds.), *The social psychology of intergroup relations* (pp. 33–47). Monterey, CA: Brooks/Cole.

Ware, J. E., & Sherbourne, C. D. (1992). The MOS 36-item short-form health survey (SF-36): I. Conceptual framework and item selection. *Medical Care*, *30*(6), 473–483.

World Health Organization. (2012). 10 facts on ageing and the life course. Retrieved from: http://www.who.int/features/factfiles/ageing/en/ and http://www.who.int/features/factfiles/ageing/ageing_facts/en/. Accessed November 3, 2014.

Witt, L. A., Patti, A. L., & Farmer, W. L. (2002). Organizational politics and work identity as predictors of organizational commitment. *Journal of Applied Social Psychology, 32*(3), 486–499. doi: 10.1111/j.1559-1816.2002.tb00226.x.

JAMIE L. MACDONALD is a Graduate Student in the Department of Psychology at Stony Brook University, USA. She studies prejudice, stereotyping, discrimination, and intergroup relations. Her research focuses on ageism, and how it affects individuals in different contexts throughout the life course.

SHERI R. LEVY is an Associate Professor in the Department of Psychology at Stony Brook University, USA. She studies factors that cause and maintain prejudice, stigmatization, and negative intergroup relations and that can be harnessed to reduce bias, marginalization, and discrimination. Her research focuses on bias based on age, ethnicity, gender, nationality, race, sexual orientation, social class, and weight. Building on her research on ageism, she founded an organization called the *Wise Owls* to bring cheer and support to our older adult community (www.thewiseowls.org; thewiseowls.org@gmail.com). Levy was Editor of *Journal of Social Issues* from 2010–2013.

Journal of Social Issues, Vol. 72, No. 1, 2016, pp. 191–198
doi: 10.1111/josi.12162

The Age of Ageism

Todd D. Nelson[*]

California State University

*This article discusses how research on ageism has gained more attention, espe-
cially as the baby boomers have started retiring, shepherding in an era that some
call "the graying of America." As the population of the country aged 65 and over
is projected to double by 2030, it is especially important to study and help reduce
age prejudice, so that the lives of older people can be improved. The papers presented in this issue represent some of the best empirical and theoretical work on
the influence of ageism on the workplace environment and on healthcare for the
older adult. These papers are summarized, and their recommendations for change
in policy, law, and education are further highlighted.*

Since the term "ageism"[1] was coined by Butler in 1969, research on prejudice
against older persons has proceeded at a comparatively glacial pace compared to
the attention given to the other two ways we automatically categorize people: by
race and gender (Nelson, 2015). While there are likely many explanations for this,
the simplest reason, it seems to me, is that ageism is much more institutionalized
than the other two types of prejudice, and as such, people don't even notice that it
is a prejudice or a form of discrimination when it occurs. Thus, ageism has flown
under the radar among the public, and even among most prejudice researchers.

Why is ageism condoned and even promoted in American culture? One reason
is that we don't see ageism as an "-ism" in the same way we see racism, sexism,
and other types of prejudice. We joke about older people having "senior moments"
(memory problems), and we joke about being "over the hill" (our best years are
behind us). One marketing research firm predicted that in 2015, Americans will

---

[*]Correspondence concerning this article should be addressed to Todd D. Nelson, Department
of Psychology, California State University – Stanislaus Turlock, CA 95382. Tel: 209-667-3442;
[e-mail: tnelson@csustan.edu].

[1]Ageism is defined as prejudice against someone based on their age. So it can refer to any
age group. While there is a literature on prejudice against young people (called "juvenile ageism";
Westman, 1991), the bulk of the research on ageism refers to prejudice against older persons, and that
is the focus of this article, and this special issue.

spend 114 billion dollars on products dedicated to hiding the physical signs of aging on our face and bodies (Crary, 2011). Our birthday cards convey the same underlying message: I'm sorry to hear you are another year older. Consider the following hypothetical, to illustrate the institutionalization of ageism: a commercial comes on television designed to promote a cream that can hide the fact that you are an African American. Similarly, you go to the greeting card section of your drug store and find a whole section of cards promoting the message: sorry to hear you are a woman. Of course, those scenarios are outrageous, but these are the messages that are conveyed in multiple ways everyday (as I mentioned above) for older persons. Older people are told they are not valued, they are leeching off of society, they are useless, and that they should just die already.

On a positive note, the picture is improving with regard to our understanding of ageism. Since Butler's 1969 paper, a small but rapidly growing group of other researchers have drawn attention to ageism (e.g., Nelson, 2002; North & Fiske, 2013; Palmore, 1999). This increased attention is likely also due to the fact that a huge segment of the U.S. population (approximately 77 million people born between 1946 and 1964 called the "baby boomers") has recently started retiring. This is bringing unprecedented challenges to our economy, our healthcare system, and to policy makers and legislators. The massive influx of older people will change the demographics of the United States to such an extent that some refer to it as the "greying of America (Williams, 2014)." A recent U.S. Bureau of the Census report (May, 2014) indicates that by 2050, the number of people over age 65 will double what it was in 2012.

As the population demographics shift, it is increasingly urgent that researchers understand the origin and maintenance of ageism, and especially ways to reduce or eliminate it. While it is beyond the scope of this special issue to address all the ways in which ageism influences the quality of life of older adults (e.g., legal, economic, political, mental and physical health, & education), the papers presented here highlight the most recent and outstanding empirical efforts to understand how ageism influences the health and employment of older adults.

How Ageism Interferes with Healthy Aging

A long-standing belief about Asian cultures is that they traditionally revere and greatly respect elderly persons (Levy & Langer, 1994). However, research indicates that young people in Eastern cultures have a more mixed, and even negative view of older adults (Ng, 2002; Williams et al., 1997). Indeed, Williams and colleagues 1997 found that Koreans reported the strongest need to be polite and deferential toward older adults, followed by those in Japan, and then citizens of the Philippines. Chinese persons reported the weakest obligation to show the elderly such respect. Indeed, one recent study (Luo, Zhou, Jin, Newman, & Liang,

2013) found that Chinese college students held even more negative views toward older adults than their American counterparts.

Set against this backdrop, it is important to ask how these changing views of older Chinese influence the way those older adults think about themselves? To address this question, Bai, Lai, and Guo (2016) surveyed 954 Chinese adults older than 60. Bai et al. found that older adults were more likely to internalize the increasingly negative views (e.g., seeing older people as a burden to families and society) of older people in China. This, in turn, was a strong predictor of depression and other mental health issues in the older person. Interestingly, to the extent that the older person has available family support and better self-family relationships, the older adult was much less susceptible to depression and the negative effects of stress.

Bai et al. suggest that, in order for older Chinese adults to avoid these negative self-views and negative outcomes, changes need to occur in the way older people are viewed by society in general. For example, older people should be counseled against buying into negative stereotypes about aging, and instead they should focus on volunteering, and other empowering activities that promote increased self-esteem and feelings of self-worth. The community should be educated to promote positive views of aging and to dispel myths about aging. Programs that promote intergenerational contact would help younger people develop more positive views of aging. Finally, family support and positive family relations should be encouraged, as that has been shown to be a strong buffer against negative self-views and negative mental and physical health outcomes in older adults.

It is interesting to note that while research attention on ageism is still (relative to research on racism and sexism) lacking, there have been no shortage of studies in recent years looking at the incidence and prevalence of ageism in countries outside the United States. For example, researchers have examined ageism in Turkey (Polat, Karadag, Ulger, & Demir, 2014), Israel (Bergman, Bodner, & Cohen-Fridel, 2013), Poland (Wilinska & Cedersund, 2010), Australia (Petersen & Warburton, 2012), and Qatar (Musaiger, D'Souza, & Al-Roomi, 2013). To address the dearth of research on ageism in Columbia, Ramírez and Palacios-Espinosa (2016) surveyed 215 men and women ages 44 to 89 in Bogota, Columbia about their stereotypes of older adults, the amount of perceived social support currently and also when they are older. Participants were also asked about their current and expected mental and physical health (when they are older). Ramírez and Palacios-Espinosa found that negative stereotypes about older adults were associated with greater concern about aging. As one might expect, participants who said they had higher expectations of good mental and physical health tended to be less concerned about aging. Similarly, those who were concerned about not having social support when they were older were much more anxious about getting older. The researchers suggest that these data provide support for the notion that it is important to provide solid care for people up to the end of their life, and that people need to be made aware that such care is both reliable and attainable. This is important in that it provides a much-needed sense of security and control in the aging adult, and that can do much for staving off feelings of loneliness, helplessness, depression, and anxiety about one's physical and mental health.

Some believe that our attitudes toward aging when we are young adults often predict what kind of older person we will be. So, for example, if one dislikes older people he/she would likely grow to be a crotchety, disagreeable older person. A fascinating study by Ng, Monin, Allore, and Levy (2016) examines the degree to which attitudes about retirement are predictive of later mental and physical well-being. Using a sample of 1,011 people over the age of 50, Ng and colleagues examined data obtained in 1975 from participants in the Ohio Longitudinal Study of Aging and Retirement (Atchley, 1999). Ng et al. then compared those answers to the information the respondents provided 23 years later. Ng and colleagues found that people who had positive stereotypes about their mental and physical health during retirement actually lived 2.5 and 4.5 years longer, respectively. Positive work attitudes were associated with lower mortality risk. Older people appeared to be psychologically unprepared for retirement, and they also tended to feel negatively about retirement. Like Ramírez and Palacios-Espinosa, Ng and colleagues call for social policies to promote retirement preparation, with a specific focus on psychological well-being. Society should be encouraged to promote the positive aspects of retirement. The goal is to facilitate the older adult internalizing those positive views of retirement, with a resulting positive expectation about their physical and mental well-being as they get older.

Unfortunately for women, there exists a double whammy, as it were, in terms of the prejudice they endure if they live to be older women. In addition to sexist stereotypes and prejudice, older women must also contend with ageism (Palmore, 1997). For example, a study of children's literature revealed that women, not men, tended to be presented in stereotypical terms, and when an older woman was depicted in a story, she was invariably without power, agency, and was diminished on a number of dimensions (Henneberg, 2010). This pattern of perception of women, and older women is even found among those whose job it is to help others. That is, some mental health therapists are reluctant to take on female clients due to negative stereotypes about women (e.g., their concerns are unimportant, overblown, or she is just "over emotional"), and these therapists are also much less likely to work with older women due to ageist views (e.g., older people are just lonely, and their concerns are not important; Nelson, 2015; Steuer, 1982).

In a review paper, Chrisler, Barney, and Palatino (2016) show how ageism and sexism can have significant effects on the physical and mental health of older women. While women make up a majority of older adults, they have less power and opportunities than their older male counterparts. Older actresses in Hollywood have very few (if any) roles offered to them, while older actors continue to work steadily well into their senior years. Women are told by society to hide signs of aging, while gray hair, and even some wrinkles are said to make a man look "distinguished." Chrisler and colleagues detail the many ways that some healthcare professionals show ageist and sexist stereotypes toward some patients, and how these attitudes can have real consequences on the mental and physical health of older women. More research is needed at the intersection of ageism and sexism. Chrisler and colleagues further suggest that mental and physical health professionals (and even older people themselves) need more education on the pernicious effects of these negative attitudes on the well-being of their female patients. Finally, the stereotypes that prevent some older women (compared to younger women) from participating in clinical trials need to be addressed, so that scientists can obtain the needed research data from older women, and these data can be used to enhance the quality of life for older women.

Ageism in the Workplace

In recent years, an interesting theory has been introduced that attempts to show when and why younger people feel prejudice against older persons. The Succession, Identity, and Consumption model by North and Fiske (2012, 2013) suggests that ageism arises in younger people because older people fail to pass down (or, in the workplace, retire, so that younger people can have the job) enviable resources (succession), they consume more than their fair share of limited resources in society (consumption), and they fail to act their age (identity). In a series of four experiments, North and Fiske (2016) wanted to find out how older workers were perceived by younger people when the older worker violated the prescriptive behavior of the SIC model. The researchers found that when younger people perceived that an older worker believed the older worker had violated the expected behaviors for older people, younger workers were more likely to avoid the older person. This effect was strongest when resources were portrayed as being especially scarce. North and Fiske say that these results also indicate that policies directed at changing prescriptive beliefs can have a meaningful, positive impact on the increasingly intergenerational workplace, such that ageist stereotypes can be reduced, and younger people can increasingly see the value and benefit of working with and learning from their older coworkers, and to be less inclined to see the workplace as an "us-versus-them" battlefield.

Another way that ageist stereotypes influence older workers is that they bias the employers' perception of the older worker as incompetent (decreasing physical and mental capabilities) and untrainable (can't "teach an old dog new tricks"). Such beliefs then tend to lead employers to be less inclined to invest in the continuing education or training of those persons, which then may hasten the likelihood that the older person would have to leave the workplace. In three studies, Abrams, Swift, and Drury (2016) asked people to imagine that they were an employer, and were tasked with deciding between two different, equally qualified (one young, one old) job applicants. The results revealed that participants preferred to hire a younger applicant, even when the job was cast as a "low-status position." The researchers also found that the only instance where participants would hire an older person is if the job was specifically subordinate to that of a young supervisor. One might imagine that an employer would want to hire a younger person over an older person because they would get more out of their investment of time and money training the younger person who would work many years longer than a soon-to-retire older person. However, Abrams et al. (2016) found that the job duration (short vs. long term) did not make a difference in hiring, and that participants preferred the younger applicant in both instances.

In two studies, Kooij and Zacher (2016) set out to understand how ageism influences the self-perception of the older workers, and how this affects their motivation and dedication to their position in the workplace. Kooij and Zacher found that, because older workers perceive their remaining time at work as more limited, they had lower goals or expectations for learning and developing new skills. Equally interesting is their finding that the older worker's work centrality (degree to which their work is important to them, and to which it forms their identity) can buffer the effects of negative stereotypes on their motivation and learning.

In a similar study, Macdonald and Levy (2016) found that work centrality, and perceived social support tend to enhance job longevity. On the other hand, perceived age discrimination and one's anxiety about aging tend to be associated with lower job longevity. The results of these two studies provide further support for the idea that education of workers (young and older) and the employers about dispelling ageist beliefs can have a tremendous influence on reducing the harmful effects of ageism on the experiences of the older worker, and can be a more cost-effective way to retain experienced workers.

Conclusion

As Levy and Macdonald (2016) write in their review of the ageism literature, much progress has been made in ageism research in the relatively short time it was first brought to mainstream attention with Butler's (1969) coining the term "ageism." The pace of research on ageism has increased to the degree that an observer might agree that research on ageism is coming out from under the radar, and into mainstream consciousness. As the 77 million baby boomers continue to retire every day, and the demographic complexion of the country changes accordingly, politicians, policy makers, legal experts, mental and health professionals, and other researchers are realizing with increasing urgency the importance of understanding the pernicious influence that age prejudice has on the life and well-being of older persons. The research and theory presented in this issue represents some of the finest work aimed at understanding and reducing ageism as it influences older people in two important areas: in their jobs and in their mental and physical health. As in most research endeavors, we have learned much, but there is much yet we do not know, and more research is needed. It is the hope of the editors that this issue helps ignite further theoretical and empirical work on ageism. In so doing, perhaps we can help shift the long-standing American fear of aging and (as a by-product of that fear,) stereotyping of older persons so that aging is regarded by young and old as a period of continued positive growth and vitality. The resulting influence on the lives of both young and old people can be life-changing.

References

Abrams, D., Swift, H. J., & Drury, L. (2016). Old and unemployable? How age-based stereotypes affect willingness to hire job candidates. *Journal of Social Issues*, *72*(1), 105–121.

Atchley, R. C. (1999). *Continuity and adaptation in aging: Creating positive experiences.* Baltimore, MD: Johns Hopkins University Press.

Bai, X., Lai, D. W. L., & Guo, A. (2016). Ageism and depression: Perceptions of older people as a burden in China. *Journal of Social Issues*, *72*(1), 26–46.

Bergman, Y. S., Bodner, E., & Cohen-Fridel, S. (2013). Cross-cultural ageism: Ageism and attitudes toward aging among Jews and Arabs in Israel. *International Psychogeriatrics*, *25*(1), 6–15. doi: 10.1017/S1041610212001548.

Butler, R. (1969). Age-ism: Another form of bigotry. *The Gerontologist*, *9*(4), 243–246. doi: 10.1093/geront/9.4_Part_1.243.

Chrisler, J. C., Barney, A., & Palatino, B. (2016). Ageism can be hazardous to women's health: Ageism, sexism, and stereotypes of older women in the health care system. *Journal of Social Issues*, *72*(1), 86–104.

Crary, D. (2011, August 22). Boomers will be spending billions to counter aging. *USA Today*. Retrieved from http://www.usatoday.com.

Henneberg, S. (2010). Moms do badly, but grandmas do worse: The nexus of sexism and ageism in children's classics. *Journal of Aging Studies*, *24* (2), 125–134. doi: 10.1016/j.jaging.2008.10.003.

Kooij, D. T. A. M., & Zacher, H. (2016). Why and when do learning goal orientation and attitude decrease with age? The role of perceived remaining time and work centrality. *Journal of Social Issues*, *72*(1), 146–168.

Levy, B., & Langer, E. (1994). Aging free from negative stereotypes: Successful memory in China and among the American deaf. *Journal of Personality and Social Psychology*, *66* (6), 989–997. doi: 10.1037/0022-3514.66.6.989.

Levy, S. R., & Macdonald, J. L. (2016). Progress on understanding ageism. *Journal of Social Issues*, *72*(1), 5–25.

Luo, B., Zhou, K., Jin, E., Newman, A., & Liang, J. (2013). Ageism among college students: A comparative study between U.S. and China. *Journal of Cross Cultural Gerontology*, *28*(1), 49–63. doi: 10.1007/s10823-013-9186-5.

Macdonald, J. L., & Levy, S. R. (2016). Ageism in the workplace: The role of psychosocial factors in predicting job satisfaction, commitment, and engagement. *Journal of Social Issues*, *72*(1), 169–190.

Musaiger, A. O., D'Souza, R., & Al-Roomi, K. (2013). Perception of aging and ageism among women in Qatar. *Journal of Women & Aging*, *25* (3), 273–280. doi: 10.1080/08952841.2013.791602.

Nelson, T. D. (Ed.) (2002). *Ageism: Stereotyping and prejudice against older persons.* Cambridge, MA: MIT Press.

Nelson, T. D. (Ed.) (2015). Ageism. *Handbook of prejudice, stereotyping, and discrimination* (2nd ed.). New York: Psychology Press.

Ng, S. H. (2002). Will families support their elders? Answers from across cultures. In T. D. Nelson (Ed.), *Ageism: Stereotyping and prejudice against older persons* (pp. 295–309). Cambridge, MA: MIT Press.

Ng, R., Monin, J. K., Allore, H. G., & Levy, B. R. (2016). Retirement as meaningful: Positive retirement stereotypes associated with longevity. *Journal of Social Issues, 72*(1), 69–85.

North, M. S., & Fiske, S. T. (2012). An inconvenienced youth? Ageism and its potential intergenerational roots. *Psychological Bulletin, 138*(5), 982–997. doi: 10.1037/a0027843.

North, M. S., & Fiske, S. T. (2013). Act your (old) age: Prescriptive, ageist biases over succession, consumption, and identity. *Personality and Social Psychology Bulletin, 39*(6), 720–734. doi: 10.1177/0146167213480043.

North, M. S., & Fiske, S. T. (2016). Resource scarcity and prescriptive attitudes generate subtle, intergenerational older-worker exclusion. *Journal of Social Issues, 72*(1), 122–145.

Palmore, E. (1997). Sexism and ageism. In J. M. Coyle, (Ed.), *Handbook of woman and aging* (pp. 3–13). Westport, CT: Greenwood Press.

Palmore, E. (1999). *Ageism: Positive and negative* (2nd ed.). New York: Springer.

Petersen, M., & Warburton, J. (2012). Residential complexes in Queensland, Australia: A space of segregation and ageism? *Ageing & Society, 32*(1), 60–84. doi: 10.1017/S0144686×10001534.

Polat, U., Karadag, A., Ulger, Z., & Demir, N. (2014). Nurses' and physicians' perceptions of older people and attitudes toward older people: Ageism in a hospital in Turkey. *Contemporary Nurse, 48*(1), 88–97. doi: 10.1080/10376178.2014.11081930.

Ramírez, L. F., & Palacios-Espinosa, X. (2016). Stereotypes about old age, social support, aging anxiety and evaluations of one's own health. *Journal of Social Issues, 72*(1), 47–68.

Steuer, J. L. (1982). Psychotherapy with older women: Ageism and sexism in traditional practice. *Psychotherapy: Theory, Research, and Practice, 19*(4), 429–436. doi: 10.1037/h0088455.

U.S. Bureau of the Census (May, 2014). *An aging nation: The older population in the United States.* Washington DC: U.S. Bureau of the Census.

Westman, J. C. (1991). Juvenile ageism: Unrecognized prejudice and discrimination against the young. *Child Psychiatry and Human Development, 21*(4), 237–256. doi: 10.1007/BF00705929.

Wilinska, M., & Cedersund, E. (2010). 'Classic ageism' or 'brutal economy'? Old age and older people in the Polish media. *Journal of Aging Studies, 24*(4), 335–343. doi: 10.1016/j.jaging.2010.07.003.

Williams, T. (2014). Graying of America is speeding, report says. New York Times, May 6. Retrieved from http://www.nytimes.com/2014/05/07/us/graying-of-america-is-speeding-report-says.html?_r=0.

Williams, A., Ota, H., Giles, H., Pierson, H., Gallois, C., Ng, S., Lim, T., Ryan, E. B., Somera, L., Maher, J., Cai, D., & Harwood, J. (1997). Young people's beliefs about intergenerational communication: An initial cross-cultural comparison. *Communication Research, 24*(4), 370–393. doi: 10.1177/009365097024004003.

TODD D. NELSON is a Professor of Psychology at California State University – Stanislaus. His research focuses on stereotypes and prejudice against older adults (ageism). He is a fellow of the society for experimental social psychology, and has published extensively on ageism.

Journal of Social Issues, Vol. 72, No. 1, 2016, pp. 199–222
doi: 10.1111/josi.12163

When Passionate Advocates Meet Research on Diversity, Does the Honest Broker Stand a Chance?

Alice H. Eagly[*]
Northwestern University

In an ideal world, social science research would provide a strong basis for advocacy and social policy. However, advocates sometimes misunderstand or even ignore scientific research in pursuit of their goals, especially when research pertains to controversial questions of social inequality. To illustrate the chasm that can develop between research findings and advocates' claims, this article addresses two areas: (a) the effects of the gender diversity of corporate boards of directors on firms' financial performance and (b) the effects of the gender and racial diversity of workgroups on group performance. Despite advocates' insistence that women on boards enhance corporate performance and that diversity of task groups enhances their performance, research findings are mixed, and repeated meta-analyses have yielded average correlational findings that are null or extremely small. Therefore, social scientists should (a) conduct research to identify the conditions under which the effects of diversity are positive or negative and (b) foster understanding of the social justice gains that can follow from diversity. Unfortunately, promulgation of false generalizations about empirical findings can impede progress in both of these directions. Rather than ignoring or furthering distortions of scientific knowledge to fit advocacy goals, scientists should serve as honest brokers who communicate consensus scientific findings to advocates and policy makers in an effort to encourage exploration of evidence-based policy options.

---

[*]Correspondence concerning this article should be addressed to Alice H. Eagly, Department of Psychology, Northwestern University, 2029 Sheridan Road, Evanston, IL 60208. Tel: +847-467-5026; [E-mail: eagly@northwestern.edu].

This manuscript is based in the Presidential Address that Alice H. Eagly delivered at the 2015 conference of the Society for the Psychological Study of Social Issues, "A Road Less Traveled: Forging Links between Psychological Science and Social Policy," Washington, DC.

The author thanks John Antonakis, Linda Carli, Lindsay Chase-Lansdale, Susan T. Fiske, Leire Gartzia, Jack Glaser, Madeline Heilman, David Matsa, David Miller, Douglas Medin, Corinne Post, Sabine Sczesny, Gabriel Twose, and Hans van Dijk for the comments on a draft of this article.

199

Fostering social policy based on science is a central goal of many social scientists. Commitment to joining sound social science to responsible policy is the fundamental undertaking of the Society for the Psychological Study of Social Issues, in alliance with public interest missions of organizations such as the American Psychological Association and the Association for Psychological Science. Despite the increasing effort that psychologists and many other social scientists are devoting to social policy, relations of science to policy are often troubled. On politically charged issues, science and policy are not linked by a smooth highway but by a more treacherous route where issue advocates hold sway.

Advocates are often ideologically polarized players who eagerly invoke social scientific data that support their objectives but whose use of science can be selective and thus unrepresentative of the available scientific knowledge. Researchers, in turn, may fail to communicate effectively to advocates and policy makers, at least in part because research can yield findings that are more complex and less affirming of advocates' goals than what they desire and expect. Under such circumstances, is it possible for social scientists to serve as honest brokers who communicate research findings to invite creative thinking about evidence-based policy? Is it more common that researchers are shunted to the sidelines, with their findings exploited and often inaccurately portrayed by ideologically polarized advocates?

I approach these matters by analyzing two research questions relating to the social disadvantage of some social groups. The first question pertains to the "woman on boards" issue that has yielded a large research literature on the gender integration of corporate boards of directors. The second question pertains to the workgroup diversity issue that has yielded a large research literature on the integration of groups by gender and race/ethnicity. In these two important research areas, there are surprising contradictions between what advocates claim and what research has demonstrated. Therefore, I argue that social scientists should more assertively communicate the scientific consensus about diversity's relations to corporate financial success and group productivity. Then researchers should proceed to address the conditions under which diversity produces its varied effects on outcomes that include gains for social justice as well as group and organizational performance.

Women on Corporate Boards

Advocacy to include more women on boards of directors is extensive in the United States and many other Western nations. This advocacy makes sense given the low representation of women as directors, currently 19% in the Fortune 500 (Catalyst, 2015) but only 9% if smaller firms are included (Adams & Kirchmaier, 2015). Although social justice arguments could be deployed to favor increasing women's share of board memberships, advocates have typically focused on the so-called "business case," by indicating that companies with more women on their boards perform better—that is, they have better financial outcomes (e.g., Ernst & Young, 2014). This attention to the economic value of diversity reflects the capitalist societal context in which shareholder value and profits are the measures of corporate success.

The business-case claim that adding women increases corporate success appears often in daily newspapers. In one example, Claire Cain Miller (2014) wrote in the New York Times, "Several studies have shown that diversity on boards improves decision making and profits." Also, Jena McGregor (2014) offered in the Washington Post, "Researchers have long found ties between having women on a company's board of directors and better financial performance." And Tiffany Hsu (2012) added in the Los Angeles Times, "Need a balance sheet boost? Try adding some women to the board of directors."

What is the source of these claims? The advocacy organization Catalyst (2004) produced a study showing that among Fortune 500 firms, those in the top quartile of female representation on their boards of directors performed better than those in the bottom quartile. The reported performance data consisted of the financial outcomes of returns on equity, sales, and invested capital. This initial report and its replications (Catalyst, 2007, 2011) claimed "a link" between women on boards and corporate performance. Also, the management consulting company McKinsey produced a related study of large European publicly traded corporations that demonstrated better financial outcomes for the 89 firms with the highest level of gender diversity in their top management (including on boards), compared with the average of European listed firms (Desvaux, Devillard-Hoellinger, & Baumgarten, 2007; see also Desvaux, Devillard, & Sancier-Sultan, 2010). Similar data came from the 2020 Women on Boards advocacy organization (Kurth, 2015) and the Credit Suisse financial services organization (Dawson, Kersley, & Satella, 2014). These reports were further disseminated in the business press (e.g., Taylor, 2012; Wittenberg-Cox, 2014) and by consulting firms (e.g., International Finance Corporation, 2014).

The reports from advocacy and consulting organizations offered comparisons of groups of firms that differed in the gender diversity of their corporate boards—for example, between the top and bottom quartiles in the Catalyst (2004) research. These studies would certainly not be publishable in academic journals because of the elementary form of their data presentations. Such group comparisons do not reveal the strength of the relation between the participation of women and financial success. The analyses lacked even correlations relating the percentages of women on corporate boards to corporate outcomes or simple scatter plots of these relationships. Such studies do not meet the standards of the relevant academic disciplines, which are economics and management. Does it matter that the studies are academically substandard? The answer to this question is an emphatic yes.

Statistically trained investigators, and perhaps even students who have had one or two statistics courses, would recommend at least the presentation of correlation coefficients and furthermore would raise questions about two matters: (a) possible reverse causation from financial success to the inclusion of women and (b) possible confounding of the percentage of women on boards with omitted variables that may influence corporate success. On the first point of reverse causation, which advocacy and consulting organizations have acknowledged (e.g., Catalyst, 2004; Desvaux et al., 2007), firms that are more profitable may have the resources to seek out and attract women with the requisite corporate executive experience. On the second point, omitted variables might include, for example, firm size, given that women directors are more common on the boards of larger firms (Adams, 2015; Hillman, Shropshire, & Cannella, 2007). Any positive correlation between board gender diversity and financial outcomes might not survive controls for firm size and many other variables potentially correlated with the percentage of women directors.

Social scientists routinely analyze such correlational data using statistical techniques designed to rule out such ambiguities, which economists refer to as *endogeneity* (Antonakis, Bendaham, Jacquart, & Lalive, 2014). For example, given data over time, researchers can exploit these repeated observations while controlling for the stable differences between firms (in so-called "firm fixed effects" analyses). In addition, to address omitted variables, they also may introduce *instrumental variables* that are correlated with the predictor of interest (gender diversity) and with the outcome variables (financial success) only through their relation with gender diversity. Using such methods, investigators can eliminate many confounds and thus discern causal relations with some certainty, whereas investigators have little basis for inferring causality from correlations or comparisons of firms grouped by their level of diversity.

An exemplary study that invoked statistically appropriate techniques examined 1,939 firms from the United States for the period 1996–2003 (Adams & Ferreira, 2009). The observed positive relation between the percentage of female directors and financial outcomes became negative when statistical controls for endogeneity were introduced—that is, greater gender diversity was associated with poorer firm outcomes. The findings also showed that women had better attendance at board meetings and were more likely to sit on monitoring committees; their presence was associated with more CEO resignations after poor company performance. The increased monitoring associated with the increase in the presence of women on boards appeared to have positive effects on firms with weak governance but negative effects otherwise. In the aggregated data, these negative effects outweighed the positive ones. Consistent with these findings, effects of gender diversity on financial outcomes can be causally related to the behavior of female versus male directors and their placement on board committees. Other causal possibilities include a negative effect of female directors on stock prices because of investor gender bias, especially by institutional investors, who are especially attentive to corporate governance (Dobbin & Jung, 2011).

Board gender diversity has become a hot topic among economists and management researchers, with many studies conducted in many nations. A meta-analysis integrated the results of 140 such studies (45 with U.S. data; Post & Byron, 2015). These published and unpublished studies were methodologically diverse, ranging from the Catalyst (2004) report with its simple group comparisons to studies using multiple regression techniques (e.g., Stanwick & Stanwick, 1998) as well as a few more sophisticated studies with controls for endogeneity (e.g., Adams & Ferreira, 2009). Examining only the zero-order correlations from these studies, which are vulnerable to endogeneity effects, the Post and Byron meta-analysis obtained a very small, but significant, positive relation of board gender diversity to firm financial performance ($r = .03$). This relation was slightly higher for accounting outcomes, such as profit and loss ($r = .05$) but smaller and nonsignificant for outcomes indicating market performance, such as stock price and returns to shareholders ($r = .01$). In addition, a smaller meta-analysis that included only 20 studies (4 with U.S. data) published in peer-reviewed academic journals found a near-zero, nonsignificant correlation ($r = .01$) between board gender diversity and financial outcomes (Pletzer, Nikolova, Kedzior, & Voelpel, 2015). Also, an extensive narrative review of the same research literature reached the conclusion that findings are mixed, with no clear trend toward positive or negative relations (Rhode & Packel, 2014).

Given that the findings of studies included in these two meta-analyses varied around these average results, an accurate description of this extensive empirical literature is that correlational findings relating percentages of women on corporate boards to firms' financial performance are mixed, and on the average lean very slightly in the positive direction but only for companies' accounting outcomes. The sign and magnitude of the correlations related to a few moderators: For example, in the Post and Byron (2015) meta-analysis, the null relation between female board representation and market performance became positive in countries with greater gender equality. Despite such moderation, these correlational findings do not reveal causation.

Establishing that the presence of women on corporate boards causes any of the positive or negative outcomes is far more challenging (see Adams, 2015). As in many other domains of nonexperimental research, relatively few researchers have addressed endogeneity in a manner that allows claims about causation (Antonakis, Bendahan, Jacquart, & Lalive, 2010). However, the "business case"—that is, the boldly causal claim that including women on corporate boards improves firms' financial outcomes, lives on in communications directed to the public and business community (e.g., Committee for Economic Development, 2015), most often supported by citations of the least informative studies, which are those containing only simple group comparisons (e.g., Catalyst, 2004; Desvaux et al., 2007).

Gender Diversity of Task Groups

Given the ambiguities and complexities of relations between corporate board gender diversity and company performance, social scientists might turn to simpler situations for examining the impact of diversity. Findings might be clearer if the diversity independent variables and the outcome dependent variables were closer in time and space, thereby presenting fewer possibilities for confounding variables and complicated mediation than with corporate performance. One such domain is the study of workgroups, where the question is whether demographically diverse groups perform better than groups composed on a homogeneous basis. In these correlational and experimental studies, diversity is typically proximate to the group outcomes because the workgroups themselves generate the products (e.g., solutions to problems) that are the basis of the outcome variables.

The view that diversity improves group performance appears often in news media. For example, Nicholas Kristoff (2013) wrote in the *New York Times*, "Scholarly research suggests that the best problem-solving doesn't come from a group of the best individual problem-solvers, but from a diverse team whose members complement each other. That's an argument for leadership that is varied in every way—in gender, race, economic background and ideology." And, in *Financial Times* ("Definition of diverse teams," n.d.), "Research shows that diversity [of all types] results in better performance on complex decisions and problems, just the type of challenges faced by global firms."

These opinions were fueled in part by Scott Page's claims, presented in his journal articles (e.g., Hong & Page, 2004; Page, 2007) and book, *The Difference: How the Power of Diversity Creates Better Groups, Firms, Schools, and Societies* (Page, 2008). These writings featured abstract, theory-driven arguments from mathematics, computer science, and economics supporting the idea that groups of diverse individuals are more effective in solving problems and predicting events than are homogeneous groups, even when those homogeneous groups are made up of the best individual problem solvers. Page's reasoning was based on the assumption that diversity of all types brings *cognitive heterogeneity*—differences between group members in their knowledge, perspectives, and heuristics, which yield more tools and resources for doing the work of the group. Critics quickly faulted the unidimensionality of Page's reasoning: While prioritizing groups' cognitive resources, he failed to consider that diversity's potential is often compromised by social processes that follow from in-group favoritism and status disparities within groups (Klein & Harrison, 2007).

In-group favoritism is critical because increasing diversity often means that female and minority individuals enter groups composed primarily of white men, as is the case for many decision-making boards and committees. Such newcomers are vulnerable to being categorized as members of an out-group. These intergroup phenomena reflect people's derivation of their identities and esteem from their group memberships (see review by Hogg, 2006). Because gender and racial group memberships serve as important bases of collective identity (Ashmore, Deaux, & McLaughlin-Volpe, 2004; Howard, 2000), in-group preferences are often organized around these identities. Therefore, women and minority individuals can be disadvantaged in groups composed mainly of the other gender or the majority race/ethnicity, and this disadvantage can hamper their contributions.

As social psychological research has demonstrated (see review by Bodenhausen, Kang, & Peery, 2012), out-group members generally receive less positive evaluations and inferior rewards and support, compared with objectively equivalent in-group members. These processes are typically compounded by status differences that are correlated with membership in gender and race/ethnicity groupings (van Dijk & van Engen, 2013). Although status differences that reflect genuine competence differences can serve a valuable coordination function, status differences that arise from demographic groupings often do not reflect competence differences among those who are members of decision-making bodies (Correll & Ridgeway, 2006). Nevertheless, women and minorities may be regarded with some skepticism and marginalized in discussions and negotiations (see Karpowitz & Mendelberg, 2014). Under these circumstances, these individuals may find it difficult to engage productively in the work of the group, and any potentially valuable cognitive heterogeneity that they bring to the group can dissipate.

Much earlier diversity research had given clear signs that all is not simple when it comes to effects on performance. For example, a classic study by Allmendinger and Hackman (1995) examined the inclusion of women in symphony orchestras in the second half of the 20th Century, fostered by the introduction of blind auditions conducted behind a screen that obscured musician gender (Goldin & Rouse, 2000). In this project, which encompassed 78 professional symphony orchestras in the United States and Europe, the outcome measures included players' reports about their orchestra's functioning, the quality of their relationships, and their own motivation and satisfaction. In cross-sectional comparisons of orchestras that differed in the extent of their inclusion of women, these outcome measures declined with the inclusion of more women. However, on some measures, this decline flattened and the trend even turned upward as the percentage of women approached 50%. Apparently, gender integration proved to be destabilizing, but some of these negative reactions moderated when women became at least a substantial minority of players.

Over the years, a very large research literature has accumulated relating workgroup diversity to group performance, published in academic journals mainly in industrial-organizational psychology and management. These investigators have distinguished two types of diversity: *job-related*, which pertains to differences in knowledge and expertise related to the problems that work groups are charged with solving, and *demographic*, which pertains to differences in attributes such as gender, race, and age (e.g., Mannix & Neale, 2005). Research has extensively examined both of these forms of diversity.

Several meta-analyses of the diversity-performance relation have been prominently published, with the latest and most inclusive produced by van Dijk, van Engen, and van Knippenberg (2012). Among this project's 146 studies, there were three types of settings: (a) laboratory experiments (b) field studies, and (c) studies conducted on teams composed of undergraduate or MBA students. These field and student studies generally provided correlational data relating amount of diversity to group performance. The finding that the classification of studies by these three types of settings did not moderate diversity-performance relations eases concerns about endogeneity, given the greater ability of the laboratory experiments to rule out alternative explanations based on uncontrolled variables.

The meta-analysis produced mainly very small average effect sizes: The key overall findings were that demographic diversity yielded a small negative relation to performance outcomes ($r = -.02$), which was present for both gender diversity ($r = -.01$) and racial/ethnic diversity ($r = -.05$); all of these relations were nonsignificant. In contrast, job-related diversity produced a significant, but small, positive relation ($r = .05$). These findings replicated four prior meta-analyses based on smaller samples of studies (Bell, Villado, Lukasik, Belau, & Briggs, 20100; Horwitz & Horwitz, 2007; Hülsheger, Anderson, & Salgado, 2009; Joshi & Roh, 2009). In addition, a meta-analysis of 68 studies produced a nonsignificant relation between gender diversity and team performance (r = -.01; Schneid, Isidor, Li, & Kabst, 2015). Moreover, these meta-analytic results were generally consistent with earlier narrative reviewers' cautions that demographic diversity had yielded mixed and inconclusive effects (Harrison & Klein, 2007; Mannix & Neale, 2005; Milliken & Martins, 1996; Williams & O'Reilly, 1998).

Novel results emerged when van Dijk van Engen, and van Knippenberg (2012) separated outcome variables according to (a) subjective ratings by team members and leaders, and (b) objective measures, such as financial outcomes or numbers of problems solved. Subjective measures produced more extreme data—that is, an accentuation of the positive effects for job-related diversity and of the negative effects for demographic diversity. To account for these more extreme findings, these authors argued that subjective ratings, especially when performed by raters external to the team, tended to be biased against demographic diversity and in favor of job-related diversity. Yet, even on the objective measures, demographic diversity related nonsignificantly and slightly negatively to performance for both gender ($r = -.02$) and racial/ethnic ($r = -.01$) diversity.

The van Dijk van Engen and van Knippenberg (2012) meta-analysis examined moderation by variables that might produce conditions that especially benefit from diversity. Task complexity is one such variable: with greater complexity, job-related diversity had more positive effects. Because job-related diversity generally involves choosing group members for their differing knowledge and expertise, these gains are consistent with Page's (2007) reasoning about cognitive hetero-geneity. However, comparable gains were absent for demographic diversity.

In summary, when aggregated across studies, an extensive research literature on group performance has shown no overall advantage for demographically di-verse groups, with a small tendency toward disadvantage, especially on subjective measures of performance. However, these meta-analytic averages encompassed heterogeneous outcomes, whereby some studies did produce positive effects of diversity. Yet, approximately as many studies yielded negative effects, producing average effects that were near zero. In this respect, these findings are similar to the correlations between the representation of women as corporate directors and financial outcomes.

Social Scientists' and Advocates' Responses to These Research Literatures

Given these findings on diversity in corporate boards and task groups more generally, what is the current state of discourse on diversity in these contexts? How do advocates, policy makers, and scientists cope with clear evidence that broad, simple claims about diversity's positive relations to corporate financial outcomes and group effectiveness are not supported by scientific research?

Understandably, the findings that have accumulated may be troubling, espe-cially for the researchers who have produced studies with negative outcomes and the meta-analysts who have failed to produce support for blanket claims about gains from diversity. Because many academic researchers in the social sciences are of a decidedly liberal bent (Duarte et al., 2015; Gross & Fosse, 2012), they presumably hope that their research will support progressive agendas to increase diversity and inclusion. From advocacy and policy perspectives, there is an obvious appeal in simple, straightforward claims that diversity in groups and organizations produces performance gains.

Given this appeal, simplistic renditions of scientific findings on diversity con-tinue to find favor among diversity's advocates and the legions of practitioners and consultants engaged in helping organizations meet their diversity goals. Presented as if they were evidence-based findings, broad claims about the advantages of diversity for group and organizational performance appear regularly in promo-tional materials of consultants and advocates (e.g., Kirby & Burns, 2012; Lee, n.d.). Also, their scientific allies may engage in selective citations of those studies or portions of studies that have shown the hoped-for performance gains, without hinting at the general pattern of findings across studies. However, the scientific consensus inherent in multiple meta-analyses and narrative reviews drawing con-sistent conclusions surely pressures scientists to be even-handed. Yet, scientists, like advocates, may fear that acknowledging the lack of support for broad claims about diversity's gains could undermine efforts to promote diversity.

At least some policy makers, whose knowledge of and access to the scientific literatures on diversity may be quite limited, appear to have accepted these broad claims as a basis for their policy recommendations. For example, in a document of the European Commission (2012, p. 5), "The proposed Directive [to include more women on corporate boards] will lead to breaking down the barriers that women face when aiming for board positions and to improved corporate governance, as well as enhanced company performance." In a U.K. government-sponsored report (Davies, 2011, p. 7), "There is a strong business case for balanced boards."

Despite the chorus of advocacy that has enjoyed at least some limited success in relation to policy, social scientists who are dedicated to fostering social policy based on sound social science should assiduously avoid misrepresenting research. While foreswearing misrepresentation and selective citations of studies with congenial results, social scientists who support inclusive agendas might pursue two responsible directions: (a) Carry out and identify research that discerns the conditions under which diversity does produce positive outcomes and communicate the resulting findings to advocates and policy makers, and (b) encourage broadening the focus of advocacy by arguing that gains of profit and productivity are not the only or most appropriate place to look for diversity's benefits.

Discovering Moderators of Diversity–Performance Relationships

Simplistic claims about diversity's benefits can discourage new research by suggesting that diversity has consistently positive effects on corporate performance and group effectiveness. Instead, awareness of the inconsistencies in the research literature is needed to foster the challenging and important task of uncovering the conditions under which demographic diversity has positive or negative effects. To illustrate this direction, I note three areas of investigation that offer promise for discovering moderators—specifically, research on (a) sex-related differences in styles of social interaction and leadership, (b) the duration of interaction, and (c) diversity mindsets and climate for inclusion.

Although demographic diversity may not have generally positive effects on group effectiveness, some aspects of diversity may have such effects under some conditions. In particular, research has considered whether the participation of women may be advantageous when groups' tasks are socially complex. Consistent with women's relatively relational self-construal (Cross & Madson, 1997; Gabriel & Gardner, 1999), they are more likely than men to emphasize collaborative teamwork and to have a participative and interpersonally concerned leadership style (see meta-analyses by Eagly, Johannescen-Schmit, & van Engen, 2003; Eagly & Johnson, 1990; van Engen & Willemsen, 2004). These relational tendencies of women may be advantageous for group performance if groups' tasks entail social complexity, for example, by requiring discussion and negotiation or coordination between functionally diverse or geographically dispersed units (Post, 2015). (In contrast, the task complexity variable assessed in the van Dijk van Engen & van Knippenberg (2012) meta-analysis pertained only to cognitive demands, or "mental labor," and did not moderate the effects of gender diversity on group performance.)

Although these ideas about female advantage with social complexity require more exploration, existing findings are promising. Specifically, under socially complex conditions, women experienced less disadvantage in emerging as group leaders (see meta-analysis by Eagly & Karau, 1991) and their leadership yielded improved communication and group cohesiveness (Post, 2015), likely precursors to performance gains. Also, in Wood's (1987) group performance meta-analysis, interaction in all-female groups, but not in all-male groups, facilitated performance on socially complex tasks (see also Wood, Polek, & Aiken, 1985). Finally, in a large sample of U.S. firms, greater female representation in their top management teams predicted better firm performance for those firms that focused on innovation, a context that may reward participative leadership and collaborative social interaction (Dezső & Ross, 2012; but see van Dijk van Engen & van Knippenberg, 2012, for absence of analogous moderation by innovative vs. in-role group tasks).

Another potential moderator of diversity's effects is the time spent in interaction. Diversity's gains for group and organizational performance may emerge gradually over time. Short-term measures can reflect the challenges that people often initially experience when they encounter coworkers who are not part of their cultural in-group. Such challenges have emerged in research on interracial interaction showing heightened stress and anxiety compared with same-race interaction, especially for whites (see meta-analysis by Toosi, Babbitt, Ambady, & Sommers, 2012; Trawalter, Richeson, & Shelton, 2009). Such reactions can produce process losses that lower group effectiveness.

With continued interaction, people from different demographic groups may discover bases of similarity that lessen negative effects and foster positive ones. As argued by MacInnis and Page-Gould (2015), the heightened anxiety and resulting process losses that often accompany integration can dissipate over time. Also, this reasoning about the passage of time is consistent with demonstrations that intergroup contact generally lessens intergroup prejudice (see meta-analysis by Pettigrew & Tropp, 2006). Relatedly, it is this attitudinal and social rationale for diversity that was influential in the Supreme Court's *Grutter v. Bollinger* 2003 decision that achieving student body diversity justifies preferential student admissions of minorities to colleges and universities (Levinson, 2011). The Court thus appeared to accept research evidence that diversity reduces prejudice, promotes intergroup understanding, and counters racial stereotyping (Gurin, Nagda, & Lopez, 2004). Although such reduction of prejudice may help the positive effects of diversity on group performance to emerge over time, unfortunately direct support is lacking because the great majority of studies of prejudice have either not assessed group performance outcomes or have assessed them on a short-term basis.

Even though diversity may often improve intergroup attitudes, organizational researchers have argued that favorable intergroup attitudes are not sufficient to unleash positive effects on group performance. In view of research on the effects of diversity-relevant beliefs and attitudes (van Knippenberg, van Ginkel, & Homan, 2013), valuing diversity is only a first step toward establishing conditions under which positive outcomes can manifest (Homan, van Knippenberg, van Kleef, & De Dreu, 2007). Specifically, positive effects of diversity appear to be dependent on group members developing a so-called *diversity mindset*, which encompasses knowledge about the ways in which diversity can have positive or negative effects on team processes and performances. Another concept that captures social relational contexts allowing diversity to become an asset is *climate for inclusion*, by which workgroups create norms that foster personal ties and the exchange of ideas across identity groups (Nishii, 2013). Without such conditions, majority group members often dominate discussions and fail to share their leadership and decision-making power. In such ways, majority group members can unwittingly weaken the potential contributions of diverse group members, who may in turn become discontent or discouraged and lessen their effort and cooperation. Accurate knowledge of such pitfalls, combined with an attitudinally positive, promotion-focused and inclusive outlook, can foster favorable outcomes to the extent that these conditions are shared among group members.

As these examples illustrate, some diversity researchers have moved beyond simple (and false) generalizations about consistently positive effects of diversity on group and organizational performance toward more nuanced hypotheses that reflect growing understanding of the processes by which diversity can have positive or negative effects (e.g., Galinsky et al., 2015). As such research cumulates, social scientists will be in a position to offer meaningful advice to advocates, trainers, and policy makers. However, as I detail in the next section, scientists who participate in discussions about the implications of diversity research findings should in addition promote understanding of the importance of outcomes beyond group and organizational performance.

Diversity's Gains for Social Justice

A fundamental rethinking of potential gains from diversity questions the typical emphasis on competitive advantage, corporate profits, or group effectiveness. Given near-exclusive emphasis on these tangible utilitarian ends, the absence of consistently positive effects of this type would undermine the very basis of efforts to increase diversity.

Issues of inclusion were traditionally framed in terms of fairness and social justice (van Dijk, van Engen, & Paauwe, 2012). The rationale for affirmative action and antidiscrimination policies in the United States and many other nations emphasized that discriminatory practices had excluded women and minorities from many opportunities (e.g., Fullinwider, 2014). From this perspective, it would be an egregious violation of equal opportunity and antidiscrimination laws, for example, to exclude women musicians from symphony orchestras. Although obvious, overt discrimination of that type is no doubt less common in recent years, discrimination can still be present in relation to obtaining jobs and attaining higher wages and promotions (e.g., Addison, Ozturk, & Wang, 2014; Correll, Benard, & Paik, 2007; Gaddis, 2015; Lips, 2013; Reskin, 2000). The cumulative effects of such discrimination contribute to the underrepresentation of women and minorities on corporate boards and other decision-making groups. Eliminating discrimination would increase diversity in such settings, thus serving social justice goals. However, the faster route of compensatory affirmative action (i.e., reverse discrimination) that disfavors those who were historically advantaged continues to meet considerable public resistance in the United States (Kahlenberg, 2013; Sharp, 1999).

Beyond the matter of continuing discrimination lies an even more fundamental social justice argument. This principle is that, in a democracy, citizens should have equal access to the decision making that shapes their lives. Political scientists refer to this consideration as *substantive representation*, the idea that leaders represent the interests of certain societal groups. To the extent that women and minorities do not have *descriptive representation*—that is, numerical representation in decision making that is proportional to their numbers in the population—they are unlikely to have their interests fairly represented (Mansbridge, 1999; Wängnerud, 2009). The issue is whether the ideals of democracy are violated if decision making is dominated by the rich, the white, and the male. Then the needs of the poor, the minorities, and the female may be neglected.

Whether women and minorities truly lack substantive representation raises two questions. Do they have different attitudes and values than the white men who dominate corporate and political decision making? The answer to this question is yes. Do these differences emerge in women and minorities' advocacy and their decisions when they do gain power in organizations and governments? The answer to this question is a somewhat more tentative yes.

On the first question of attitudes and values, women tend to be more compassionate, other-oriented, and egalitarian (i.e., favoring policies supporting families, education, health care, the poor, etc.) than men, yet more supportive of traditional morality (e.g., Beutel & Marini, 1995; Clawson & Oxley, 2012; Dietz, Kalof, & Stern, 2002; Eagly, Diekman, Johannesen-Schmidt, & Koenig, 2004; Huddy & Cassese, 2013; Huddy, Cassese, & Lizotte, 2008; Miah, 2013; Schwartz & Rubel, 2005; Schwartz & Rubel-Lifschitz, 2009). Women are also more opposed than men to military spending and are generally more dovish (Eichenberg & Stoll, 2012; Huddy & Cassese, 2013). African American and Hispanic minorities show similar trends toward more compassionate and egalitarian attitudes (Clawson & Oxley, 2012; Eagly van Engen & van Knippenberg, 2004; Kinder & Kam, 2010).

On the second question of women's and minorities' advocacy as members of decision-making groups, evidence suggests that their attitudes and values do tend to guide their behavior. Specifically, as members of legislative bodies, women, minorities, and especially women of color, are more likely than their white male colleagues to advocate for socially compassionate policies that promote the interests of women, minorities, children, families, and the poor and that support public welfare in areas such as health care and education (Griffin, 2014; Karpowitz & Mendelberg, 2014; Reingold & Smith, 2012; Swers, 2013). Because political party alignments are of overriding importance, these trends in legislative behavior are weaker among Republican than Democratic legislators, especially more recently because newly elected Republicans are more conservative than those elected earlier (Osborn, 2014).

To determine how the participation of women on corporate boards may affect women's substantive representation, some studies have examined the gender diversity of corporate boards in relation to various outcomes broadly subsumed under the concept of corporate social responsibility (e.g., charitable giving, environmental sustainability). Several projects have shown positive relations between women on boards and corporate social responsibility (e.g., Boulouta, 2013; Harjoto, Laksmana, & Lee, 2014) although such studies have varied in their ability to address causal relations (see narrative review by Rao & Tilt, 2015). Relatedly, women on boards and as owners of firms increased the likelihood that firms engaged in what economists call "labor-hoarding"—that is, they were less likely to lay off workers with economic downturns (Matsa & Miller, 2013, 2014). A tentative generalization is that women directors influence corporate decisions to be less single-mindedly concerned with shareholder value and more attentive to a wider range of stakeholders—in particular, to employees and the larger community, which are priorities generally consistent with women's relatively other-oriented and compassionate attitudes and values.

In summary, social justice considerations provide consistent arguments for more equitable representation of women and minorities in corporate and political decision making (Murray, 2014; Sierstad, 2015). To the extent that members of these groups lack access to these roles because of discrimination, equality of opportunity is violated. Moreover, when they have gained opportunities to influence organizational and social policy, they have not acted as clones of white men. Existing evidence thus suggests that women and minorities may shift corporate boards toward broader perspectives that take into account the welfare of employees, communities, and the environment. In legislative bodies, female and minority legislators would tend to direct more resources toward supporting families and vulnerable groups such as children, disadvantaged minorities, and poor people. Therefore, aside from ideological debates about whether such changes would produce a better society, equitable substantive representation of women and minorities would not only serve social justice but promote more compassionate and egalitarian social policy.

Social Scientists as Honest Brokers

In diversity research, as in many other areas of social science, research literatures are often much more extensive than anticipated by most advocates, who may fix on particular studies that support their favored policy positions, with little concern for how typical, generalizable, or scientifically valid their findings are. Psychologists and other social scientists may be swept up by the excitement of seeing their findings used in advocacy and policy contexts. However, in contemporary science, researchers often have the benefit of relatively even-handed meta-analyses that aggregate and integrate findings across the available studies. Although meta-analyses are subject to various forms of bias (Matt & Cook, 2009), the generalizations they yield are typically much more valid that those based on traditional narrative reviewing and vastly more valid than those based on spotty knowledge of a few relevant studies (Cooper & Hedges, 2009).

The publication of multiple independent meta-analyses addressing the same question and producing consistent conclusions inspires trust in scientific conclusions. Such an unusually large display of consistent evidence has emerged in tests of the effects of diversity on corporate success and group performance (see prior sections *Women on Corporate Boards* and *Gender Diversity of Task Groups*). Two meta-analyses have been published concerning the business case for women on boards and six for the diversity-performance relation in workgroups. Moreover, narrative reviews reached compatible conclusions, with one pertaining to women on boards and four to workgroup performance. Given this abundance of social scientific effort, each of these topics features a high-quality scientific consensus that diversity-performance relations are mixed and produce null or very small means when aggregated across studies. Such a consensus is fully worthy of presentation to advocates and policy makers (Fiske & Borgida, 2011). However, social scientists have a long way to go before understanding the mediators and moderators of relations between diversity and outcomes, most especially the causal relations that are involved. Links to social policy cannot become strong and meaningful until scientific understanding becomes more developed (Antonakis van Engen, & van Knippenberg, 2010).

How might social scientists who are expert on diversity research approach advocates and policy makers? Any outreach should anticipate that scientists' goals of producing valid knowledge are not the same as advocates' goals of promoting their favored causes or policy makers' goals of efficiently deploying resources to attain organizational or societal goals. Despite these differing goals, advocates and policy makers generally perceive some advantage in basing their work on valid evidence and therefore may welcome social scientific expertise. From their side, scientists often welcome such collaboration because they hope that their research can be useful to others. Of course, scientists have a better chance of facilitating the flow of research into advocacy and policy if their relations with these stakeholders are cooperative and cordial. Yet, interactions may not be easy when scientific knowledge does not fit comfortably into advocates' or policy makers' agendas.

The larger issue is the role that scientists should adopt in relation to social policy (Pielke, 2007). There are several possibilities worthy of consideration by scientists who wish to promote the public interest. One role is that of scientific expert who does not reach out to engage public issues but merely stands ready to provide relevant scientific information when asked to do so by advocates or policy makers. Another role, which entails more policy engagement, is *issue advocate*, whereby a scientist (or a nonscientist) deploys supportive scientific findings to promote favored issue positions. The danger is that issue advocates may act rather like lobbyists for ideologically driven public policies. Scientists, like other advocates, may find it difficult to overcome fixing on research findings based on their compatibility with their policy preferences or political ideology (e.g., Nisbet, Cooper, & Garrett, 2015). Yet another role for scientists is the *honest broker of policy alternatives*, who considers the full range of scientific information in relation to policy options (Pettigrew, 1967; Pielke, 2007). Such scientists reach out to enlarge policy makers' thinking with input from the all relevant scientific findings. By expanding thinking, the honest broker encourages decision makers to think beyond personal values and ideologically driven preferences to consider options that may make sense from a variety of perspectives. In contrast, the issue advocate works to narrow policy makers' thinking to favor a particular policy.

Does the honest broker actually stand a chance with issues as politically volatile as the effects of diversity on groups and organizations? The role is challenging if advocates and policy makers are guided by deeply held ideologies, but it is not impossible. As my two case studies illustrate, science can produce findings that are not what advocates want to hear. Few scientists want to undercut advocacy for causes that they too may believe in. Therefore, knowledgeable social scientists may retreat from engaging policy and just silently cringe when encountering advocacy based on misleading claims about research findings. However, merely withdrawing from discussions is not a responsible way for scientists to proceed. For the two case studies featured in this article, the danger for diversity advocates is that in the longer run, the opponents of inclusive diversity goals may study the science and undercut false claims, probably with "junk science" accusations that would not be entirely misplaced.

How should social scientists move forward? Their first responsibility is to pursue research that allows more confident conclusions about the mediators and moderators of diversity's relations to important outcomes. At the same time, scientists should abandon silent cringing and speak up when they encounter misrepresentations of the existing research. Although speaking up risks backlash from advocates, scientists should have the courage to stand behind their consensus findings. They should also be attentive to the dangers of gradually slipping into issue advocacy while consulting with advocates and policy makers. Should this "stealth advocacy" (Pielke, 2007) involve selectively representing only some scientific findings or misrepresenting them altogether, evidence-based policy would lose out.

As honest brokers, social scientists seek to communicate valid scientific knowledge through multiple channels. They may reach out to engage social policy by writing articles and books designed for broader publics, giving talks for nonacademic audiences, and engaging social media. Above all, scientists should create and seek access to settings where policy makers and scientists think broadly and deeply about their society and do not merely pursue narrow political ends. For example, the Society for the Psychological Study of Social Issues (http://www.spssi.org/) features a Congressional Seminar Series in which expert social scientists present findings pertaining to key issues (e.g., psychology of prejudice and discrimination) for members of Congress and their staffs. Northwestern University's Institute for Policy Research (http://www.ipr.northwestern.edu) arranges briefings that bring together leading social science experts to present their policy-relevant research at public meetings involving outreach to journalists, advocates, and politicians. The Brookings Institution's Hamilton Project (http://www.hamiltonproject.org) seeks to introduce innovative proposals from leading economists that are guided by evidence, not ideology or doctrine. More such initiatives should be undertaken to bring thoughtful consideration of social science research into the policy arena.

To conclude, this article conveys some ways in which science, advocacy, and policy have not related easily or harmoniously. I have told two somewhat complicated stories, one pertaining to women on corporate boards and the other to workgroup diversity—two domains with extensive social scientific research relating diversity to performance outcomes. Despite the striking lack of research support for the optimistic generalizations about these outcomes that have been widely shared among advocates, policy makers, and the general public, many social scientists with relevant expertise have remained silent. It is time for more social scientists to take stock of what diversity research has produced so far and join those who are addressing the complexities of diversity's effects on group and organizational performance. It is also time for all stakeholders in diversity initiatives to focus on the violations of social justice inherent in the limited access of women and minorities to decision making in most political and corporate contexts.

References

Adams, R. B. (2015). Women on boards: The superheroes of tomorrow? *The Leadership Quarterly*. Available at http://ssrn.com/abstract=2696804 or http://dx.doi.org/10.2139/ssrn.2696804

Adams, R. B., & Ferreira, D. (2009). Women in the boardroom and their impact on governance and performance. *Journal of Financial Economics*, *94*, 291–309. http://dx.doi.org/10.1016/j.jfineco.2008.10.007.

Adams, R. B., & Kirchmaier, T. (2015). Barriers to boardrooms. *Social Science Research Network*. http://dx.doi.org/10.2139/ssrn.2192918. Accessed at December 19, 2015.

Addison, J. T., Ozturk, O. D., & Wang, S. (2014). The role of gender in promotion and pay over a career. *Journal of Human Capital*, *8*, 280–317. http://dx.doi.org/10.1086/677942

Allmendinger, J., & Hackman, J. R. (1995). The more, the better? A four-nation study of the inclusion of women in symphony orchestras. *Social Forces*, *74*, 423–460. http://dx.doi.org/10.1093/sf/74.2.423

Antonakis, J., Bendahan, S., Jacquart, P., & Lalive, R. (2010). On making causal claims: A review and recommendations. *The Leadership Quarterly*, *21*, 1086–1120. http://dx.doi.org/10.1016/j.leaqua.2010.10.010

Antonakis, J., Bendahan, S., Jacquart, P., & Lalive, R. (2014). Causality and endogeneity: Problems and solutions. In D.V. Day (Ed.), *The Oxford handbook of leadership and organizations* (pp. 93–117). New York, NY: Oxford University Press. http://dx.doi.org/10.1093/oxfordhb/9780199755615.013.007.

Ashmore, R. D., Deaux, K., & McLaughlin-Volpe, T. (2004). An organizing framework for collective identity: Articulation and significance of multidimensionality. *Psychological Bulletin*, *130*, 80–114. http://dx.doi.org/10.1037/0033-2909.130.1.80

Bell, S. T., Villado, A. J., Lukasik, M. A., Belau, L., & Briggs, A. L. (2010). Getting specific about demographic diversity variable and team performance relationships: A meta-analysis. *Journal of Management*, *37*, 709–743. http://dx.doi.org/10.1177/0149206310365001

Beutel, A. M., & Marini, M. M. (1995). Gender and values. *American Sociological Review*, *60*, 436–448. http://dx.doi.org/10.2307/2096423

Bodenhausen, G. V., Kang, S. K., & Peery, D. (2012). Social categorization and the perception of social groups. In S. T. Fiske & C. N. Macrae (Eds.), *Sage handbook of social cognition* (pp. 311–329). Los Angeles, CA: Sage. http://dx.doi.org/10.4135/9781446247631.n16

Boulouta, I. (2013). Hidden connections: The link between board gender diversity and corporate social performance. *Journal of Business Ethics*, *113*, 185–197. http://dx.doi.org/10.1007/s10551-012-1293-7

Catalyst. (2004). *The bottom line: Connecting corporate performance and gender diversity.* From http://www.catalyst.org/. Accessed at July 20, 2015.

Catalyst. (2007). *The bottom line: Corporate performance and women's representation on boards.* From http://www.catalyst.org/. Accessed at July 20, 2015.

Catalyst. (2011). *The bottom line: Corporate performance and women's representation on boards (2004-2008).* From http://www.catalyst.org/. Accessed at July 20, 2015.

Catalyst. (2015). *Women in S&P 500 companies.* From http://www.catalyst.org/knowledge/women-sp-500-companies. Accessed at July 20, 2015.

Clawson, R. A., & Oxley, Z. M. (2012). *Public opinion: Democratic ideals, democratic practice* (2nd ed.). Los Angeles, CA: Sage.

Committee for Economic Development. (2015). *Every other one: More women on corporate boards.* Washington, DC: Committee for Economic Development. From https://www.ced.org. Accessed at July 20, 2015.

Cooper, H., & Hedges, L. V. (2009). Potentials and limitations. In H. Cooper, L. V. Hedges, & J. C. Valentine (Eds.), *The handbook of research synthesis and meta-analysis* (2nd ed., pp. 561–572). New York, NY: Russell Sage Foundation.

Correll, S. J., Benard, S., & Paik, I. (2007). Getting a job: Is there a motherhood penalty? *American Journal of Sociology*, *112*, 1297–1339. http://dx.doi.org/10.1086/511799

Correll, S. J., & Ridgeway, C. L. (2006). Expectation states theory. In J. D. DeLamater & A. Ward (Eds.). (2006). *Handbook of social psychology* (pp. 29–51). New York, NY: Springer. http://dx.doi.org/10.1007/0-387-36921-x_2

Cross, S. E., & Madson, L. (1997). Models of the self: Self-construals and gender. *Psychological Bulletin, 122,* 5–37. http://dx.doi.org/10.1037/0033-2909.122.1.5

Davies, E. M. (2011). Women on boards (the "Davies Report"). *Government of the United Kingdom: Department for Business, Innovation & Skills.* From https://www.gov.uk/government/uploads/system/uploads/attachment_data/file/31480/11-745-women-on-boards.pdf. Accessed at July 20, 2015.

Dawson, J., Kersley, R., & Natella, S. (2014). The CS gender 3000: Women in senior management. Zurich, Switzerland: Credit Suisse Research Institute. From https://publications.credit-suisse.com/tasks/render/file/index.cfm?fileid=8128F3C0-99BC-22E6-838E2A5B1E4366DF. Accessed at July 20, 2015.

Definition of diverse teams. (n.d.). *Financial Times online.* From http://lexicon.ft.com/Term?term=diverse-teams. Accessed at July 20, 2015.

Desvaux, G., Devillard-Hoellinger, S., & Baumgarten, P. (2007). *Women matter: Gender diversity, a corporate performance driver.* Paris, France: McKinsey & Co. From http://www.mckinsey.com/search.aspx?q=women+matter. Accessed at July 20, 2015.

Desvaux, G., Devillard, S., & Sancier-Sultan, S. (2010). *Women matter 2010: Woman at the top of corporations: Making it happen.* Paris, France: McKinsey & Co. From http://www.mckinsey.com/search.aspx?q=women+matter. Accessed at July 20, 2015.

Dezső, C. L., & Ross, D. G. (2012). Does female representation in top management improve firm performance? A panel data investigation. *Strategic Management Journal, 33,* 1072–1089. http://dx.doi.org/10.1002/smj.1955

Dietz, T., Kalof, L., & Stern, P. C. (2002). Gender, values, and environmentalism. *Social Science Quarterly, 83,* 353–364. http://dx.doi.org/10.1111/1540-6237.00088

Dobbin, F., & Jung, J. (2011). Corporate board gender diversity and stock performance: The competence gap or institutional investor bias? *North Carolina Law Review, 89,* 809–838.

Duarte, J. L., Crawford, J. T., Stern, C., Haidt, J., Jussim, L., & Tetlock, P. E. (2015). Political diversity will improve social psychological science. *Behavioral and Brain Sciences, 38,* 1–13. http://dx.doi.org/10.1017/S0140525X14000430

Eagly, A. H., Diekman, A. B., Johannesen-Schmidt, M. C., & Koenig, A. M. (2004). Gender gaps in sociopolitical attitudes: A social psychological analysis. *Journal of Personality and Social Psychology, 87,* 796–816. http://dx.doi.org/10.1037/0022-3514.87.6.796

Eagly, A. H., Johannesen-Schmidt, M. C., & van Engen, M. L. (2003). Transformational, transactional, and laissez-faire leadership styles: A meta-analysis comparing women and men. *Psychological Bulletin, 129,* 569–591. http://dx.doi.org/10.1037/0033-2909.129.4.569

Eagly, A. H., & Johnson, B. T. (1990). Gender and leadership style: A meta-analysis. *Psychological Bulletin, 108,* 233–256. http://dx.doi.org/10.1037/0033-2909.108.2.233

Eagly, A. H., & Karau, S. J. (1991). Gender and the emergence of leaders: A meta-analysis. *Journal of Personality and Social Psychology, 60,* 685–710. http://dx.doi.org/10.1037/0022-3514.60.5.685

Eichenberg, R. C., & Stoll, R. J. (2012). Gender difference or parallel publics? The dynamics of defense spending opinions in the United States, 1965–2007. *Journal of Conflict Resolution, 56,* 331–348. http://dx.doi.org/10.1177/0022002711420983

Ernst & Young. (2014). Time for diversity: Accelerating performance in corporate boardrooms. *EYG Report AU2555.* Retrieved from http://www.ey.com/Publication/. Accessed at July 15, 2015.

European Commission. (2012). Proposal for a directive of the European Parliament and of the Council on improving the gender balance among non-executive directors of companies listed on stock exchanges and related measures. *EUR-Lex: Access to European Union Law.* From http://eur-lex.europa.eu/legal-content/EN/TXT/?uri=CELEX:52012PC0614. Accessed at July 20, 2015.

Fiske, S. T., & Borgida, E. (2011). Best practices: How to evaluate psychological science for use by organizations. *Research in Organizational Behavior, 31,* 253–275. http://dx.doi.org/10.1016/j.riob.2011.10.003

Fullinwider, R. (2014). Affirmative action. In E. N. Zalta (Ed.), *The Stanford encyclopedia of philosophy* (Winter 2014 ed.). From http://plato.stanford.edu/archives/win2014/entries/affirmative-action/.

Gabriel, S., & Gardner, W. L. (1999). Are there "his" and "hers" types of interdependence? The implications of gender differences in collective versus relational interdependence for affect, behavior, and cognition. *Journal of Personality and Social Psychology, 77*, 642–655. http://dx.doi.org/10.1037/0022-3514.77.3.642

Gaddis, S. M. (2015). Discrimination in the credential society: An audit study of race and college selectivity in the labor market. *Social Forces, 93*, 1451–1479. http://dx.doi.org/10.1093/sf/sou111

Galinsky, A. D., Todd, A. R., Homan, A. C., Phillips, K. W., Apfelbaum, E. P., Sasaki, S. J., Richeson, J. A., Olayon, J. B., & Maddux, W. W. (2015). Maximizing the gains and minimizing the pains of diversity: *A policy perspective. Perspectives on Psychological Science, 10*, 742–748. http://dx.doi.org/10.1177/1745691615598513

Goldin, C., & Rouse, C. (2000). Orchestrating impartiality: The impact of "blind" auditions on female musicians. *American Economic Review, 90*, 715–741. http://dx.doi.org/10.1257/aer.90.4.715

Griffin, J. D. (2014). When and why minority legislators matter. *Annual Review of Political Science, 17*, 327–336. http://dx.doi.org/10.1146/annurev-polisci-033011-205028

Gross, N., & Fosse, E. (2012). Why are professors liberal? *Theory and Society, 41*, 127–168. http://dx.doi.org/10.1007/s11186-012-9163-y

Grutter v. Bollinger, 539 U.S. 306 (2003).

Gurin, P., Nagda, B. R. A., & Lopez, G. E. (2004). The benefits of diversity in education for democratic citizenship. *Journal of Social Issues, 60*, 17–34. http://dx.doi.org/10.1111/j.0022-4537.2004.00097.x

Harjoto, M., Laksmana, I., & Lee, R. (2014, early view). Board diversity and corporate social responsibility. *Journal of Business Ethics*, 1–20. http://dx.doi.org/10.1007/s10551-014-2343-0. Accessed at July 20, 2015.

Harrison, D. A., & Klein, K. J. (2007). What's the difference? Diversity constructs as separation, variety, or disparity in organizations. *Academy of Management Review, 32*, 1199–1228. http://dx.doi.org/10.5465/AMR.2007.26586096

Hillman, A. J., Shropshire, C., & Cannella, A. A. (2007). Organizational predictors of women on corporate boards. *Academy of Management Journal, 50*, 941–952. http://dx.doi.org/10.5465/AMJ.2007.26279222

Hogg, M. A. (2006). Social identity theory. In P. J. Burke (Ed.), *Contemporary social psychological theories* (pp. 111–136). Redwood City, CA: Stanford University Press.

Homan, A. C., van Knippenberg, D., van Kleef, G. A., & De Dreu, C. K. (2007). Bridging faultlines by valuing diversity: Diversity beliefs, information elaboration, and performance in diverse work groups. *Journal of Applied Psychology, 92*, 1189–1199. http://dx.doi.org/10.1037/0021-9010.92.5.1189

Hong, L., & Page, S. E. (2004). Groups of diverse problem solvers can outperform groups of high-ability problem solvers. *Proceedings of the National Academy of Sciences of the United States of America, 101*(46), 16385–16389. http://dx.doi.org/10.1073/pnas.0403723101

Horwitz, S. K., & Horwitz, I. B. (2007). The effects of team diversity on team outcomes: A meta-analytic review of team demography. *Journal of Management, 33*, 987–1015. http://dx.doi.org/10.1177/0149206307308587

Howard, J. A. (2000). Social psychology of identities. *Annual Review of Sociology, 26*, 367–393. http://dx.doi.org/10.1146/annurev.soc.26.1.367

Hsu, T. (2012). Women on board: Firms with female directors do better, study says. *Los Angeles Times*. From http://articles.latimes.com/2012/aug/01/business/la-fi-mo-women-board-performance-20120801. Accessed at July 20, 2015.

Huddy, L., & Cassese, E. (2013). On the complex and varied political effects of gender. In R. Y. Shapiro & L. R. Jacobs (Eds.), *The Oxford handbook of American public opinion and the media* (pp. 471–487). Oxford, UK: Oxford University Press.

Huddy, L., Cassese, E., & Lizotte, M. K. (2008). Gender, public opinion, and political reasoning. In C. Wolbrecht, K. Beckwith, & L. Baldez (Eds.) *Political women and American democracy* (pp. 31–49). New York, NY: Cambridge University Press. http://dx.doi.org/ 10.1017/CBO9780511790621.005

Hülsheger, U. R., Anderson, N., & Salgado, J. F. (2009). Team-level predictors of innovation at work: A comprehensive meta-analysis spanning three decades of research. *Journal of Applied Psychology, 94*, 1128–1145. http://dx.doi.org/10.1037/a0015978

International Finance Corporation. (2014). Corporate governance: Women on boards. From http://www.ifc.org/. Accessed at July 20, 2015.

Joshi, A. A., & Roh, H. (2009). The role of context in work team diversity research: A meta-analytic review. *Academy of Management Journal, 52*, 599–562. http://dx.doi.org/10.5465/AMJ.2009.41331491

Kahlenberg, R. (2013). The class-based future of affirmative action. *American Prospect.* From http://prospect.org/article/class-based-future-affirmative-action. Accessed at July 20, 2015.

Karpowitz, C. F., & Mendelberg, T. (2014). *The silent sex: Gender, deliberation, and institutions.* Princeton, NJ: Princeton University Press.

Kinder, D. R., & Kam, C. D. (2010). *Us against them: Ethnocentric foundations of American opinion.* Chicago, IL: University of Chicago Press.

Kirby, K., & Burns, C. (2012). The top 10 economic facts of diversity in the workplace: A diverse workforce is integral to a strong economy. *American Progress.* From https://www. americanprogress.org/issues/labor/news/2012/07/12/11900/the-top-10-economic-facts-of-dive rsity-in-the-workplace/. Accessed at July 25, 2015.

Klein, K. J., & Harrison, D. A. (2007). On the diversity of diversity: Tidy logic, messier realities. *The Academy of Management Perspectives, 21*, 26–33. http://dx.doi.org/ 10.5465/AMP.2007.27895337

Kristoff, N. (2013). Twitter, women, and power. *The New York Times.* From http://www. nytimes.com/2013/10/24/opinion/kristof-twitter-women-power.html?_r=0. Accessed at July 30, 2015.

Kurth, B. (2015). 2020 women on boards: Gender diversity index: 2011–2014 progress of women corporate directors. *2020 Women on Boards.* From http://www.2020wob.com/ sites/default/files/2020GDI-2014Report.pdf. Accessed at July 30, 2015.

Lee, M. D. (n.d.). Business advantages of diversity in the workplace. EthnoConnect: Multicultural diversity & awareness articles. From http://www.ethnoconnect.com/ pdf/9_business_advantages_of_workplace_diversity.pdf. Accessed at July 30, 2015.

Levinson, R. B. (2011). Gender-based affirmative action and reverse gender bias: Beyond Gratz, Parents Involved, and Ricci. *Harvard Journal of Law and Gender, 34*, 1–36.

Lips, H. M. (2013). The gender pay gap: Challenging the rationalizations. *Perceived equity, discrimination, and the limits of human capital models. Sex Roles, 68*, 169–185. http://dx.doi.org/10.1007/s11199-012-0165-z

MacInnis, C. C., & Page-Gould, E. (2015). How can intergroup interaction be bad if intergroup contact is good? Exploring and reconciling an apparent paradox in the science of intergroup relations. *Perspectives on Psychological Science, 10*, 307–327. http://dx.doi.org/10.1177/1745691614568482

Mannix, E., & Neale, M. A. (2005). What differences make a difference? The promise and reality of diverse teams in organizations. *Psychological Science in the Public Interest, 6*, 31–55. http://dx.doi.org/10.1111/j.1529-1006.2005.00022.x

Mansbridge, J. (1999). Should blacks represent blacks and women represent women? A contingent 'yes'. *Journal of Politics, 61*, 628–657.

Matsa, D. A., & Miller, A. R. (2013). A female style in corporate leadership? Evidence from quotas. *American Economic Journal: Applied Economics, 5*, 136–169. http://dx. doi.org/10.1257/app.5.3.136

Matsa, D. A., & Miller, A. R. (2014). Workforce reductions at women-owned businesses in the United States. *Industrial & Labor Relations Review, 67*, 422–452. http://dx.doi.org/10.1177/001979391406700206

Matt, G. E., & Cook, T. D. (2009). Threats to the validity of generalized inferences. In H. Cooper, L. V. Hedges, & J. C. Valentine (Eds.), *The handbook of research synthesis and meta-analysis* (2nd ed., pp. 537–560). New York, NY: Russell Sage Foundation.

McGregor, J. (2014). More women at the top, higher return*s*. *Washington Post*. From http://www.washingtonpost.com/news/on-leadership/wp/2014/09/24/more-women-at-the-top-higher-returns/. Accessed at July 30, 2015.

Miah, M. S. (2013). Social insurance and public good motive: Is there a gender difference in the demand for welfare programs? *Southwestern Economic Review, 40*, 75–89.

Miller, C. C. (2014). Women on boards: Quotas have limited success. *The New York Times*. From http://www.nytimes.com/2014/06/20/upshot/women-on-the-board-quotas-have-limited-success.html?abt=0002&abg=1. Accessed at July 30, 2015.

Milliken, F. J., & Martins, L. L. (1996). Searching for common threads: Understanding the multiple effects of diversity in organizational groups. *Academy of Management Review, 21*, 402–433. http://dx.doi.org/10.2307/2647821

Murray, R. (2014). Quotas for men: Reframing gender quotas as a means of improving representation for all. *American Political Science Review, 108*, 520–532. http://dx.doi.org/10.1017/S0003055414000239

Nisbet, E. C., Cooper, K. E., & Garrett, R. K. (2015). The partisan brain: How dissonant science messages lead conservatives and liberals to (dis) trust science. *The Annals of the American Academy of Political and Social Science, 658*(1), 36–66. http://dx.doi.org/10.1177/0002716214555474

Nishii, L. H. (2013). The benefits of climate for inclusion for gender-diverse groups. *Academy of Management Journal, 56*, 1754–1774. http://dx.doi.org/10.5465/amj.2009.0823

Osborn, T. (2014). Women state legislators and representation: The role of political parties and institutions. *State and Local Government Review, 46*, 146–155. http://dx.doi.org/10.1177/0160323×14542441

Page, S. E. (2007). Making the difference: Applying a logic of diversity. *The Academy of Management Perspectives, 21*, 6–20. http://dx.doi.org/10.5465/AMP.2007.27895335

Page, S. E. (2008). *The difference: How the power of diversity creates better groups, firms, schools, and societies*. Princeton, NJ: Princeton University Press.

Pettigrew, T. F. (1967). SPSSI as honest broker. *SPSSI Newsletter, 117*.

Pettigrew, T. F., & Tropp, L. R. (2006). A meta-analytic test of intergroup contact theory. *Journal of Personality and Social Psychology, 90*, 751–783. http://dx.doi.org/10.1037/0022-3514.90.5.751

Pielke, R. A. (2007). *The honest broker: Making sense of science in policy and politics*. New York, NY: Cambridge University Press.

Pletzer, J. L., Nikolova, R., Kedzior, K. K., & Voelpel, S. C. (2015). Does gender matter? Female representation on corporate boards and firm financial performance–A meta-analysis. *PloS one, 10*(6), e0130005. http://dx.doi.org/10.1371/journal.pone.0130005

Post, C. (2015, first posting). When is female leadership an advantage? Coordination requirements, team cohesion, and team interaction norms. *Journal of Organizational Behavior, 36*, 1153–1175. http://dx.doi.org/10.1002/job.2031

Post, C., & Byron, K. (2015). Women on boards and firm financial performance: A meta-analysis. *Academy of Management Journal, 58*, 1546–1571. http://dx.doi.org/10.5465/amj.2013.0319

Rao, K., & Tilt, C. (2015). Board composition and corporate social responsibility: The role of diversity, gender, strategy and decision making. *Journal of Business Ethics*, 1–21. http://dx.doi.org/10.1007/s10551-015-2613-5

Reingold, B., & Smith, A. R. (2012). Welfare policymaking and intersections of race, ethnicity, and gender in U.S. state legislatures. *American Journal of Political Science, 56*, 131–147. http://dx.doi.org/10.1111/j.1540-5907.2011.00569.x

Reskin, B. F. (2000). The proximate causes of employment discrimination. *Contemporary Sociology, 29*, 319–328. http://dx.doi.org/10.2307/2654387

Rhode, D. L., & Packel, A. K. (2014). Diversity on corporate boards: How much difference does difference make? *Delaware Journal of Corporate Law, 39*, 377–425.

Schwartz, S. H., & Rubel, T. (2005). Sex differences in value priorities: Cross-cultural and multimethod studies. *Journal of Personality and Social Psychology, 89*, 1010–1028. http://dx.doi.org/10.1037/0022-3514.89.6.1010

Schwartz, S. H., & Rubel-Lifschitz, T. (2009). Cross-national variation in the size of sex differences in values: Effects of gender equality. *Journal of Personality and Social Psychology, 97*, 171–185. http://dx.doi.org/10.1037/a0015546

Seierstad, C. (2015). Beyond the business case: The need for both utility and justice rationales for increasing the share of women on boards. *Corporate Governance: An International Review*, DOI: 10.1111/corg.12117.

Sharp, E. B. (1999). *The sometime connection: Public opinion and social policy*. Albany, NY: SUNY Press.

Stanwick, P. A., & Stanwick, S. D. (1998). The relationship between corporate social performance, and organizational size, financial performance, and environmental performance: An empirical examination. *Journal of Business Ethics*, *17*, 195–204. http://dx.doi.org/10.1023/A:1005784421547

Swers, M. L. (2013). *Women in the club: Gender and policy making in the Senate*. Chicago, IL: University of Chicago Press.

Taylor, K. (2012). The new case for women on corporate boards: New perspectives, increased profits. Forbes. From http://www.forbes.com/sites/katetaylor/2012/06/26/the-new-case-for-women-on-corporate-boards-new-perspectives-increased-profits/. Accessed at July 30, 2015.

Toosi, N. R., Babbitt, L. G., Ambady, N., & Sommers, S. R. (2012). Dyadic interracial interactions: A meta-analysis. *Psychological Bulletin*, *138*, 1–27. http://dx.doi.org/10.1037/a0025767

Trawalter, S., Richeson, J. A., & Shelton, J. N. (2009). Predicting behavior during interracial interactions: A stress and coping approach. *Personality and Social Psychology Review*, *13*, 243–268. http://dx.doi.org/10.1177/1088868309345850

van Dijk, H., & van Engen, M. L. (2013). A status perspective on the consequences of work group diversity. *Journal of Occupational and Organizational Psychology*, *86*, 223–241. http://dx.doi.org/10.1111/joop.12014

van Dijk, H., van Engen, M., & Paauwe, J. (2012). Reframing the business case for diversity: A values and virtues perspective. *Journal of Business Ethics*, *111*, 73–84. http://dx.doi.org/10.1007/s10551-012-1434-z

van Dijk, H., van Engen, M. L., & van Knippenberg, D. (2012). Defying conventional wisdom: A meta-analytical examination of the differences between demographic and job-related diversity relationships with performance. *Organizational Behavior and Human Decision Processes*, *119*, 38–53. http://dx.doi.org/10.1016/j.obhdp.2012.06.003

van Engen, M. L., & Willemsen, T. M. (2004). Sex and leadership styles: A meta-analysis of research published in the 1990s. *Psychological Reports*, *94*, 3–18. http://dx.doi.org/10.2466/pr0.94.1.3-18

van Knippenberg, D., van Ginkel, W. P., & Homan, A. C. (2013). Diversity mindsets and the performance of diverse teams. *Organizational Behavior and Human Decision Processes*, *121*, 183–193. http://dx.doi.org/10.1016/j.obhdp.2013.03.003

Wängnerud, L. (2009). Women in parliaments: Descriptive and substantive representation. *Annual Review of Political Science*, *12*, 51–69. http://dx.doi.org/10.1016/j.obhdp.2013.03.003

Williams, K., & O'Reilly, C. (1998). The complexity of diversity: A review of forty years of research. In B. Staw & R. Sutton (Eds.), *Research in organizational behavior* (Vol. *21*, pp. 77–140). Greenwich, CT: JAI Press.

Wittenberg-Cox, A. (2014). It's time for a new discussion on "women in leadership." Harvard Business School blog. From https://hbr.org/2014/03/its-time-for-a-new-discussion-on-women-in-leadership&cm_sp=Article-_-Links-_-Top%20of%20Page%20Recirculation. Accessed at July 18, 2015.

Wood, W. (1987). Meta-analytic review of sex differences in group performance. *Psychological Bulletin*, *102*, 53–71. http://dx.doi.org/10.1037/0033-2909.102.1.53

Wood, W., Polek, D., & Aiken, C. (1985). Sex differences in group task performance. *Journal of Personality and Social Psychology*, *48*, 63–71. http://dx.doi.org/10.1037/0022-3514.48.1.63

ALICE H. EAGLY is Professor of Psychology and of Management and Organizations, James Padilla Chair of Arts and Sciences, and Faculty Fellow in the Institute for Policy Research, all at Northwestern University. She has also held faculty positions at Michigan State University, University of Massachusetts in Amherst, and Purdue University. Her research interests include the study of prejudice, gender, stereotyping, attitudes, and leadership. She is the author of several books and numerous journal articles and chapters in edited books. Awards for her research include the Distinguished Scientific Contribution Award from the American Psychological Association. She is also a member of the American Academy of Arts and Sciences.

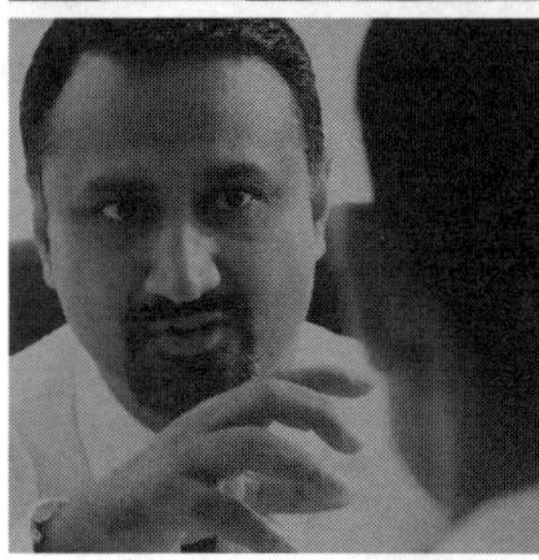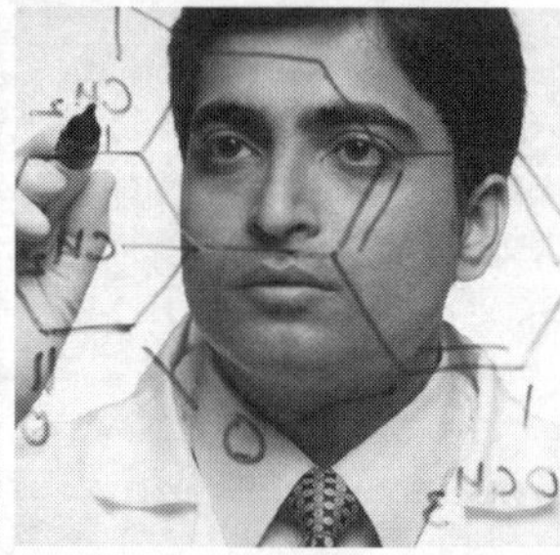

Ageism: Health and Employment Contexts

Issue Editors: Sheri R. Levy, Jamie L. Macdonald, and Todd D. Nelson